D0712101

THE
RACING
BICYCLE

A Quintessence Book

First published in the United States of America in 2013 by
UNIVERSE PUBLISHING
A Division of Rizzoli International Publications, Inc.
300 Park Avenue South
New York, NY 10010
www.rizzoliusa.com

Copyright © 2012 Quintessence Editions Ltd.

All rights reserved. No part of this publication may be reproduced, stored in a retrieval system
or transmitted in any form or by any means, electronic, mechanical, photocopying, recording,
or otherwise, without the permission of the copyright holder.

2013 2014 2015 2016 / 10 9 8 7 6 5 4 3 2 1

ISBN: 978-0-7893-2465-8

Library of Congress Control Number: 2012934938

QSS.VL22

This book was designed and produced by
Quintessence Editions Ltd.
230 City Road
London EC1V 2TT

Project Editor	Simon Ward
Editors	Becky Gee, Ben Way
Designer	Tom Howey
Production Manager	Anna Pauletti
Editorial Director	Jane Laing
Publisher	Mark Fletcher

Color reproduction by Chroma Graphics Pte Ltd., Singapore
Printed in China by 1010 Printing International Limited, China

THE
RACING
BICYCLE
DESIGN FUNCTION SPEED

FOREWORD BY
ROBERT PENN

GENERAL EDITORS
RICHARD MOORE
DANIEL BENSON

UNIVERSE

Contents

Foreword

As long as I can remember, I've had the specifications for one dream bicycle or another floating around the fringes of my imagination. Thirty years ago, my fantasy bike was a sleek, lugged racer with chrome stays, painted Malteser-orange like Eddy Merckx's bikes. Twenty years ago, my ideal machine was a rigid mountain bike: a steed strong enough to tackle everything from the byways of Hampshire to the high mountain passes of the Hindu Kush. Ten years ago, I dreamt of owning a stylish touring bike, finely finished with bespoke racks, ready to cross continents.

Rewind five years and the bicycle of my dreams morphed again. I realized that what I wanted was a "riding" bike—a machine that looked like a racing bike, but was uniquely designed to meet my cycling aspirations. I wanted a talismanic bike, a bike that reflected my devotion to the machine. I wanted craftsmanship, not technology. I wanted a bike built to last. I'll ride it around Wales where I live, and across Britain. I'll ride "centuries" with my friends and cyclosportives. I'll ride it over Col du Galibier, up Mont Ventoux, and down the Pacific Coast Highway. When I'm feeling blue, I'll ride it for a moment of grace. And when I'm seventy, I'll ride it to the pub.

This is the bike I eventually decided to build: the dream I chose to make a reality. I was lucky enough to convince a publisher to commission a book about my journey to create this bike and the BBC then decided to make a documentary based on it. The remit was simple: design my dream bike, choose the components, visit the manufacturers to see the components being made, and ride off on the finished machine into the brilliant light of a new dawn.

Curiously, when this long-held fantasy to build my dream bike finally got the green light, I was paralyzed by indecision: a bit like a little kid in a sweet shop given sixty seconds to grab anything he wants, I just didn't know where to start. I wish I'd had a copy of *The Racing Bicycle* in my hands then.

The pages of this book abound with passion for the beautiful machine. The precision of Ugo De Rosa, the creativity of Cino Cinelli, the cunning of Tullio Campagnolo, the inventiveness of Mavic, the ingenuity of SRAM, the innovation of Time, and the remarkable rise of Cervélo—all these inspiring stories have a burning fanaticism for the racing bicycle at their heart.

In the end, my indecision was lifted when I remembered that in all the imaginings of my dream bike, there had been one common theme: the frame, the diamond soul of the bicycle, would be handmade by a British frame-builder, and made from steel.

Steel has been the backbone of the bicycle for more than a century. Until the mid-1970s, it was the only real option. Even in the early 1990s, the majority of high-quality bikes had steel frames. Today, there are many alternative materials to choose from, as this book illustrates: aluminium, titanium, and carbon fibre reinforced polymers are common, but you might choose to have your frame made from moulded plastic, magnesium, beryllium (a toxic chemical element found in minerals and used in rocket nozzles), hemp, wood, or bamboo.

Over the decades, I've tried all the major frame materials. I've had an aluminium road bike with carbon forks, steel mountain bikes, aluminium mountain bikes, steel touring bikes, a titanium road bike, a full-carbon road bike, and an aluminium mountain bike with carbon seat stays. I have an opinion on all of these bikes but I know these opinions are tainted by my personal experiences. I also know my opinions are prejudiced by what the pros ride. Subconsciously, the partnerships between Lance Armstrong and Litespeed titanium frames, Mario Cipollini and aluminium Cannondales, and Eddy Merckx and steel Colnagos have all somehow affected me. These relationships are laid bare in the pages of The Racing Bicycle. Collectively, the stories reveal the intimate and symbiotic relationship between bike manufacturers and elite riders—a relationship that has existed since the infancy of the bicycle.

Objectively, I'd be pushed to say which material provides the best overall ride. I know from reading and talking to other cyclists that frame materials do have different properties, but such things are very subtle. The reality is that a good bike builder or manufacturer can make a good frame out of any of the materials mentioned, with almost any desired ride qualities: if the diameter of the tubes, the thickness of the tube walls, and the geometry of the frame are right, the bike will be right.

Most bikes are still made from steel, mainly in China and India from the cheapest, heaviest form of the alloy. High-quality, handmade steel bicycles, on the other hand, are made with senior grade, light, and tremendously strong iron alloys. There are several noted marques still producing steel bicycle tubing, including the British inventors of double-butted tubing, Reynolds—a story eloquently told in these pages.

Almost every other great innovation in the realm of the racing bike—from quick release wheel clamps to Shimano Total Integration gears, and aluminium rims to clipless pedals—is also covered in this book. The stories behind the landmark bikes— Fausto Coppi's 1952 Bianchi, Chris Boardman's Lotus, and Cavendish's Specialized Venge among others—are covered, too.

The Racing Bicycle is a eulogy to the efficiency, technological triumph, and sheer beauty of road racing bicycles. If you are wondering what your dream bicycle might look like, you will find the inspiration is here within these pages.

Introduction

by Richard Moore and Daniel Benson

The Racing Bicycle is a celebration of the bicycle, but it is a certain type of bicycle that we pay particular tribute to in these pages.

Although eagle-eyed readers will spot the odd track, cyclo-cross, or mountain bike, our main focus is on the classic road racing bicycle. There are two principal reasons for this: firstly, the diamond-framed road bike has prevailed for more than a century; and secondly, much of the sport's history and folklore has been written in the great road events, with the bikes ridden by the champions almost inseparable from their epic feats in the Alps of the Tour de France, the Dolomites of the Giro d'Italia, or pavé of Paris–Roubaix. Thus, the iconic frame-builders and component manufacturers are every bit as worthy of their place in the pantheon as legendary riders such as Fausto Coppi, Eddy Merckx, Jacques Anquetil, Bernard Hinault, Greg LeMond, and Lance Armstrong.

We have set out to tell the stories of the world's greatest manufacturers by including all aspects of their various successes: from the personal contributions of the people behind the companies to the evolution of their products and the triumphs of the great champions who have graced their bikes. After all, it is impossible to imagine certain brands having the same cachet without their association with a particular rider.

Raphaël Géminiani descends the Col du Tourmalet in the French Pyrenees during stage eighteen of the Tour de France on July 14, 1952.

In this sense, the great riders might be said to have "made" some of the great bikes—or at least endorsed them in the most effective way, on the greatest stage. For example, without the patronage of the great Italian rider of the 1950s, Fausto Coppi, would Bianchi occupy such a special place in cycling history and be so widely recognized as one of the world's iconic marques? And conversely, would Coppi have achieved all that he did had he not been riding a Bianchi? (Bianchi might say no; but of course it is impossible to know.) Undoubtedly, riders have been much more than mere pedaling advertisements for their bikes. The marriage between the top professionals and the bike companies has always been one of mutual convenience. It is a two-way street: the riders need machines that are, at the very least fit, for purpose, and ideally give them an edge; the manufacturers in turn rely on riders for

■ Coppi pictured in 1951. He enjoyed his greatest successes on a Bianchi.

■ A close-up of the Campagnolo chainset on Felice Gimondi's Bianchi bike.

feedback, garnered from the most intense testing environment, and to push product development that—ultimately—should lead to better results for everybody.

The Coppi and Bianchi pairing is, perhaps, the best example of a special marriage between rider and brand, and one that is very important to that maker. However, other champions have been closely identified with a particular bike, or bikes: the greatest of them all, Eddy Merckx, with Colnago and later with De Rosa; the King of the Classics, Roger De Vlaeminck, with Flandria; the British sprinter Reg Harris with Raleigh; Cyrille Guimard and Bernard Hinault with Gitane; Miguel Indurain with Pinarello; Italian stallion Mario Cipollini with Cannondale; seven-time Tour de France winner Lance Armstrong with Trek… the list goes on.

Furthermore, there are lower profile frame-builders, who have not—or not openly, at least   supplied bikes to great riders, but who have established a fine reputation nonetheless. Dario Pegoretti, for example, is an Italian craftsman whose name is not as well known as his countrymen Edoardo Bianchi, Ernesto Colnago, or Giovanni Pinarello. In his workshop in Caldonazzo in the Dolomites, Pegoretti handbuilds frames to order, and as contributor Rohan Dubash notes, "Only a guide to personal colour preference is required; the rest is left to Dario, his mood, and imagination. The result is a truly personal interpretation." You can wait two years for a frame (and pay a lot of money), but, judging by the paucity of second-hand Pegorettis on the market, few are disappointed.

The experience of a frame-builder like Pegoretti highlights another phenomenon—one that makes it difficult, in some cases, to know how much acclaim a particular manufacturer is due. Since 1975, Pegoretti, like his mentor Luigino Milani, has built frames for numerous champions whose bikes have subsequently been plastered in the decals of a different manufacturer. This is the clandestine world of frame-building, some knowledge of which can perhaps act as a guide to those thinking of buying a prestige frame.

Although most of the bikes featured in this book originate from the sport's European heartland, one notable recent trend is the advance of some exceptional US manufacturers, and nowadays the Tour de France is as likely to be won on a frame that has been built in the United States as one made in Italy, which has the highest proportion of craftsmen frame-builders. But while Trek, Cannondale, and Specialized have become giants of the industry, there is also space for the US equivalent of Pegoretti, Ben Serotta. As contributor Ellis Bacon writes: an "obsession with sourcing the right materials and the frame fitting its rider perfectly has established Serotta as one of the most desired, fit-like-a-glove bikes a rider could own."

Bikes can be highly personal, of course, and the contributors to *The Racing Bicycle*—all of them leading cycling journalists—have included anecdotes and tales

The artist Damien Hirst designed this iridescent butterfly Trek frame for Lance Armstrong.

of the top riders' idiosyncrasies and obsessions. Is it a coincidence that Merckx, the greatest of all, was also perhaps the most obsessed with his bike? The man known as "The Cannibal" had an obsession with his equipment that dated back to his early days as a racing cyclist, when he took his bike to pieces just so that he could count the individual components. He tinkered endlessly with his saddle height on training rides, even sometimes in races.

Some of the frame-builders and company founders are equally as driven and special as Merckx. Tullio Campagnolo was determined to reinvent the wheel—literally—and his name became synonymous with the most desirable components on a bike. Campagnolo and Shimano, who are best known for their components, Mavic, best known for its wheels, and Columbus and Reynolds, who build tubesets, are included for their huge contribution to the road racing bicycle, even if they are not primarily known as frame-builders.

As with any "special" individuals, there are stories that range from the sublime to the ridiculous, with a sprinkling of quirkiness and eccentricity, too. A favourite might be that of the Belgian company Flandria, run by a family whose feud led to the business being split down the middle—literally. A brick wall was constructed down the centre of the factory, even through machinery that was too heavy to be moved.

Finally, it is worth noting that the classic diamond-shaped road racing bike that we celebrate in *The Racing Bicycle* has prevailed for more than a century in part because radical innovations have tended to be stifled by cycling's international governing body, the UCI. Its strict guidelines on the design and weight of racing bikes are welcomed by many, because they help to preserve the classic design, and keep cycling simple and affordable, although manufacturers can feel constrained (witness Cannondale's "Legalize my Cannondale" campaign for its lightweight bikes). However, in acknowledgement of some of the companies and individuals who have attempted to push the boundaries, we celebrate some rather different machines as "Landmark Bikes," including Graeme Obree's Old Faithful. He—like all the other frame-builders, engineers, and riders who feature in this book—has contributed his own colourful chapter to the gloriously rich history of the racing bicycle.

Here's to the bike—we hope you enjoy reading *The Racing Bicycle*.

■ The handmade Pegoretti Blob is a typically idiosyncratic design from the Italian manufacturer.

Richard Moore and Daniel Benson

Atala

The heritage of Italian bicycle company Atala is interwoven with the history of the country's beloved national tour, the Giro d'Italia. Atala even won the race in 1912, when the Giro recognized teams rather than individual riders.

It is well known among cycling fans that the Giro d'Italia's *maglia rosa* (pink jersey) is the same shade of pink as the race's first sponsor, *La Gazzetta dello Sport*, but many are not aware of the role that the Italian cycling manufacturer, Atala, played in creating the race.

One of the many stories about the Giro concerns the initial rivalry between two newspapers that wanted to launch an event. Bianchi was working with the *Corriere della Sera* newspaper on its own answer to the Tour de France. That was until the smaller and newer

firm, Atala, found out about it, took the news to the *Gazzetta*, and the rest, as they say, is history.

The Atala bicycle company was started in Milan by Guido Gatti in 1908, the year before the very first Giro d'Italia was held, and it sponsored a team almost immediately. In 1910, the second year of the race, Atala won the team prize, and in 1912—when the organizers were still experimenting with the format of the race and there was no individual winner, only a team prize—Atala-Dunlop won again. This was, in part, thanks to Carlo Galetti, who had won the *maglia rosa* for the previous two years, and this time won the fifth stage. Another Atala rider, Giovanni Michelotto, started the race in fine style and went on to win stages one and eight.

With the outbreak of World War I, the Giro d'Italia was put on temporary hiatus, and when it restarted, Atala could not replicate its early success. In 1919 the company was sold to Steiner of Milan, then in 1938 it was bought by Cesare Rizzato, a bicycle-maker who had started his own firm, Ceriz, in 1921.

The Atala team never managed to provide another Giro winner, but its bikes were represented in the higher echelons of Italian racing. It sponsored riders sporadically between 1923 and 1947, although in 1947 it only sponsored a single rider—a certain Giovanni Pinarello, who went on to set up his own successful bike company—but between 1948 and 1962 the Atala team won twenty-four Giro stages. The company stepped away from team sponsorship, but returned to the sport twenty years later in 1982, and won nineteen more Giro stages over seven years, as its previous all-Italian identity was expanded to include Urs Freuler.

Freuler was a Swiss cyclist of diverse talents, and garnered most fame on the track as points race world champion eight times between 1981 and 1989, and keirin champion in 1983 and 1985. During his seventeen-year career (1980–97), he won seventy-one victories, and while he was with Atala, he won twelve of his fifteen Giro stages. Although Freuler was not the only Atala rider to win races, he was by far the most successful, and when he left the team in 1987, it could not find a replacement for him.

In 2002, the brand was sold to a consortium as Atala SpA, and became best known for children's bikes. Since 2011, like many other celebrated bicycle names, the company has been part-owned by the Accell Group. Today, the Atala brand lives on in the form of leisure and urban bikes, fitness equipment, and accessories. **sc**

■ A 1909 engraving from Italian newspaper *La Domenica del Corriere* shows cyclists passing a staging point in the Giro d'Italia.

■ This 1980s Atala features, from top to bottom, steel front forks, Shimano 105 groupset, Atala headbadge, and Campagnolo aero seatpost.

Batavus

This Dutch bicycle manufacturer is more than a century old, and its greatest successes have come courtesy of the country's leading female riders, including Monique Knol and the peerless Leontien van Moorsel.

In the run-up to the much-anticipated 1988 Olympic road race in South Korea, all eyes were on Jeannie Longo, the French cycling superstar who was coming back after an injury to her hip the month before. The course in Seoul was a flat one, and when, with 1.8 miles (3 km) to go, Inga Benedict of the United States attacked, it was Longo who chased her down. However, when it came to a bunch sprint, no one was faster than twenty-four-year-old Monique Knol, who spotted a gap and accelerated, winning the Olympic gold in style for the Netherlands.

Four years later, Knol took bronze behind Australia's Kathy Watt with Jeannie Longo in silver medal position, which gave the Netherlands another cycling medal to add to Erik Dekker's silver in the men's road race. And the bike the Dutch team was riding? Batavus.

Batavus was no stranger to Dutch cycling success. In 1975, Tineke Fopma had ridden one of its bikes to win the world road race title, a feat repeated in 1991 by Leontien van Moorsel, who, with her eight world championships and four Olympic golds on road and track, is one of the top Dutch athletes of all time and one of the best cyclists in the world. Van Moorsel had two triumphant years riding Batavus machines, including winning the Tour de France Féminin— the women's equivalent of the Tour de France and one of the biggest races of the women's calendar—in both 1991 and 1992. Undoubtedly, these are the sporting highlights for the Dutch company, which has been in the bike-making business for more than a hundred years.

The company was founded in 1904, when Andries Gaastra opened a shop selling clocks, sewing machines, and other household goods. Shortly after, he added bicycles to his range. At first he imported Presto bikes from Germany, but soon took over a factory and began to produce bicycles under the Batavus name, selling them alongside the Prestos that he stocked.

In 1932, the company branched out to make 150 cc motorbikes, and by 1936 it was selling mopeds for men and women. The outbreak of World War II halted all production, but after the conflict was over business was better than ever and demand for bikes rocketed. By the 1970s, Batavus was the leading bike manufacturer in the Netherlands, producing some 70,000 mopeds and 250,000 bikes a year.

Since the 1960s, the company has been trying to make its production as environmentally friendly as possible, and has developed its own water-based paints and emission-free acrylic coatings. Furthermore, its 64,580-square foot (6,000-m^2) factory in Heerenveen in the Netherlands has extensive solar and wind power generation, as well as its own water treatment plant. The modern range is now sold as part of the Accell Group, which owns a number of long-established European bike brands, including Koga, Redline, and Hercules. Accell produces electric, children's, and city models, focusing in particular on the leisure market, but also manufactures racing bikes used by the Vacansoleil professional road team in 2009 and 2010—most notably by Bobbie Traksel to win Kuurne–Brussel–Kuurne in 2010.

Batavus has continued its commitment to supporting Dutch women's racing, and sponsors the ten-strong Batavus Ladies Cycling Team that is managed by Paul Tobacco. Hopefully they will see a return to their gold medal–winning days before too long. *SC*

Leontien van Moorsel
won the Tour de France
Féminin twice riding
Batavus bikes.

■ The Vuelta a España, was first held in 1935 and then annually since 1955.

■ Spain's Alvaro Pino Couñago defies expectations to win the overall title at the 1986 Vuelta a España.

BH

One of the biggest names in Spanish cycling, the bicycle manufacturer BH is rooted firmly in the sport's Basque heartland. Having started out making guns, the company is now a giant and market leader not only in Spain but also in world cycling.

The history of BH Bikes closely mirrors that of Spain's other major bicycle manufacturer, Orbea. The two companies started industrial production on premises just a short distance apart in the heart of Basque Country and are still based in that cycling-obsessed region today.

Founded in 1909 by the Beistegui brothers—Beistegui Hermanos in Spanish, hence the name BH—the company did not start out in bike production. Indeed, the company had been trading for twenty years before it began to produce its first bicycles. Domingo, Juan, and Cosme Beistegui's original workshop in the Basque town of Eibar manufactured pistols and rifles.

What was a small enterprise in its early years grew rapidly as war threatened across Europe and then broke out in 1914. Prior to the war the company employed only four workers, but halfway through the conflict the BH workforce expanded tenfold as demand for armaments of all kinds soared.

The drop in demand brought about by the cessation of hostilities at the end of World War I resulted in a crisis within the armaments industry across the globe, which naturally affected

BH. Half of its workforce had to be shed as the company looked for other areas where its barrel-like tubing could be used. Like fellow manufacturer Orbea, who also started in the armaments industry, BH saw an opportunity as demand for bicycles grew. Bike frames required tubes, and BH had the skilled workforce to produce them. Using gun steel tubes for welding bicycle frames, the company turned out its first bikes in 1923.

BH combined armaments and bike manufacturing until after the Spanish Civil War. However, even before the start of this conflict in 1936, BH and Eibar were already firmly on the map of Spanish cycling. In 1935, the fourth edition of the GP de la República race covered more than 621 miles (1,000 km) between Madrid and Eibar and back again. Just weeks later, the first edition of the Vuelta a España took place, covering twice that distance and once again underlining that Basque Country was Spanish cycling's undoubted heartland.

The event pitched Basque manufacturing rivals BH and Orbea against each other. The riders taking part were split in two groups: one half

supplied by BH, the other by Orbea. However, a dispute arose when a number of talented Belgian riders were signed up to race. In the end, BH earned the contractual right to supply the Belgians, and it paid off immediately when Antoon Digneff won the opening stage and became the first rider to wear what was then the orange jersey of the Vuelta leader. Two stages later in Bilbao, Digneff's teammate Gustaaf Deloor won the stage, took the jersey, and, protected by his strong BH-backed team, went on to become Vuelta's first champion. In subsequent years, BH has recorded seven further Vuelta successes among a host of major titles.

During the 1940s, Cosme's son, Jose Beistegui, took over the running of the business, and after the post-war years, BH was one of the many bike companies that expanded its manufacturing operations into motorbikes. In 1959, this led to the company vacating its premises in Eibar and heading south 30 miles (50 km) to Vitoria in the neighbouring province of Alava. With more manufacturing space available in a modern, bigger factory, BH began to produce spokes, rims, and every other kind of componentry to the extent that bikes leaving the factory were almost entirely equipped with the self-produced parts. Better road and railway links from Vitoria also contributed to the expansion of the business over subsequent decades.

In 1975, BH moved in another direction, and introduced the first upright gym bike in Europe. The success of this exercise bike spawned the creation in 1986 of a new branch of the company called Exercycle, which has continued to flourish right up to the present day. In 1996, BH launched the first bike trainer in Europe, followed four years later by the world's first home trainer featuring a magnetic braking system.

After some years in the background on the elite road scene, BH began to make a bigger impact in the mid-1980s. The trigger for this success was Alvaro Pino Couñago's victory for

An Italian rider, in a French team, on a Spanish bike: Rinaldo Nocentini wore the *maillot jaune* for eight days during the 2009 Tour de France.

the Zor-BH team in the 1986 Vuelta a España, which marked the start of a long and successful link with *directeur sportif* Javier Mínguez. Although Pino was a talented rider, his victory came as a surprise to everyone, not least race favourite Robert Millar, who had been denied victory the previous year thanks to a ridiculous degree of collaboration between the Spanish teams. Although Pino called in some favours to keep Millar in check on the long climb to the Sierra Nevada, he finished a minute clear of the Scot when the race concluded in Jerez.

Such was the boost that BH obtained from Pino's victory that the company increased its backing in 1987. Although the Vuelta did not turn out as well as team director Mínguez had hoped, there was to be more than ample compensation at the Tour de France, where Federico Echave won the "queen" stage to Alpe d'Huez and in doing so was placed among the legendary winners on the Alpe whose names are immortalized on the twenty-one hairpins leading up to the summit.

The following year, BH returned to the Vuelta looking for victory with a powerful team that included Pino, Echave, Anselmo Fuerte, and young pretender Laudelino Cubino. Building on what was at that time a very rare victory for a Spanish squad in a team time trial, BH kept a firm grip on the leader's jersey, firstly thanks to Cubino and then to Fuerte. Sadly, though, after holding the lead for every day since the second stage, BH relinquished it in the climactic time trial on the final weekend, as Fuerte and Cubino fell back to third and fourth overall behind Ireland's Sean Kelly, who gave a formidable performance.

Since that period, BH has rarely been away from the sport's biggest events. Recently the Spanish manufacturer has supplied bikes to Liberty Seguros and Ag2r. The link with the French Ag2r team proved particularly beneficial, boosting the brand's standing largely as a result of Rinaldo Nocentini's eight-day spell in the yellow jersey at the 2009 Tour de France.

■ The ultralight monocoque carbon frame weighs less than 28 ounces (800 g).

■ The G5 seatpost creates stiffness at the point where the top tube, seat tube, and seat mast meet.

1909

BH is founded by the Beistegui brothers.

1923

After initially making pistols and rifles, BH turns to bike production after World War I as demand for weaponry declines.

1935

The opening stage of the first Vuelta a España is won by a Belgian, Antoon Digneff, riding a BH bike. His teammate Gustaaf Deloor goes on to become the first overall winner.

1975

BH anticipates the gym and fitness craze by producing Europe's first stationary exercise bike for a market in which BH continues to be in the vanguard.

On the commercial side, BH has been equally successful. Now the primary brand of an umbrella company, Bicicletas de Alava, BH is well established as one of the world's most innovative manufacturers. Its rise towards the summit of the bike world was triggered by its purchase of Cycleurope in the early 1990s. This pan-European company included French bike manufacturing giants Peugeot and the well-known Bianchi and Gitane brands.

In 1996, BH sold Cycleurope in order to focus on the Spanish and Portuguese markets. However, at the turn of the century, BH refocused on the international markets, boosting its reach in the United States and Asia.

On the back of increased sponsorship in professional road racing, mountain biking, and among elite-level triathletes, the company has reached a new generation of fans. This is particularly the case in mountain biking, via BH's backing of the BH-Suntour team, whose French star Julie Bresset won the World Cup in 2011.

Building on more than one hundred years of industrial heritage and development, BH's engineers are at the forefront of bike design and technology. As a fundamental part of this ongoing initiative, BH has developed a specific line of higher-performance bikes that are extremely light, stiff, and ergonomic, effectively creating a new line within the company known as Ultralight Bicycles. This included the development of the first monocoque carbon frame weighing less than 28 ounces (800 g). Other recent innovations include the first use of an extended seat tube, the development of a 1.5-inch (3.8-cm) tapered carbon fibre fork in conjunction with Edge Composites, and a patented cable guide system within a channel beneath the down tube that

has resulted in what BH claims is the stiffest and strongest derailleur hanger in the world.

With offices in the United States and Taiwan, BH continues to grow its international outlook. The Vitoria-based company is also finding new areas for its cutting-edge technology. In 2011, BH launched a range of electric bikes under the label BH E-motion. Built almost entirely from parts produced in Vitoria, the models in the range are equipped with the latest pedal-assist technology and are designed to provide greater independence and mobility within cities, while offering an experience that is environmentally friendly, easy to use, and maintenance free. Underlining the fact that BH's E-motion bikes mark a huge step forwards in the world of e-bikes, the NEO range won the 2011 Eurobike award for best design and functionality among hybrid bikes.

BH continues to develop and expand, while maintaining its reputation for quality at the top end of the road market. **PC**

1986	1987	2009	2012
Alvaro Pino wins the Vuelta for the Zor-BH team, aboard a BH bike. It gives the company a major boost.	The racing success continues when Federico Echave wins the biggest stage of the Tour de France, to Alpe d'Huez, on a BH.	Rinaldo Nocentini, an Italian with a French team, spends eight days in the yellow jersey of the Tour de France leader while riding a BH bike.	After more than a century, BH is firmly established as one of the biggest manufacturers in the world.

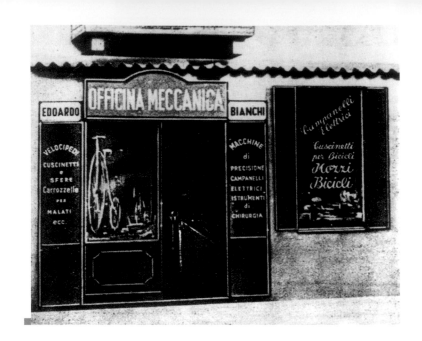

- Edoardo Bianchi opened his first workshop at No.7 Via Nirone, Milan, in 1885.

- In 1895, Bianchi was appointed Official Supplier by Appointment to the Royal Court.

- By 1907, the Bianchi plant in Viale Abruzzi, Milan, employed around 400 workers.

Bianchi

Few names evoke such passion as Bianchi, the world's oldest bicycle manufacturer. Its trademark celeste paint job and association with such legends of the sport as Fausto Coppi and Marco Pantani make it an instantly recognizable marque.

Bianchi is the most iconic of all bicycle brands, not simply because it is the oldest bicycle manufacturer still in existence, nor because of the company's long and close association with some of the sport's all-time greats, nor even because it has the most distinctive colour scheme in cycling. It is because of all these things, and more. As with so many Italian brands, it all began with a single, visionary founder: Edoardo Bianchi, an engineer who was a mere twenty-one years old when he started the company.

Born in 1865, Edoardo was orphaned at an early age, but was fortunate to be taken in by a Milanese orphanage that provided basic schooling.

He also worked, from the age of eight, in an iron works where he developed an early interest in mechanics and in making things, which he put to good use as an engineer. Later, he repaid the debt that he felt he owed the orphanage by donating a percentage of his income—a gesture he apparently continued throughout his career.

The first two-room Bianchi workshop occupied an address that became almost as legendary as Edoardo's later creations: 7 Via Nirone, in the heart of Milan (an address that later emblazoned one of the company's bikes). However, the workshop was not established with the sole intention of manufacturing bicycles. Like many entrepreneurs, Edoardo sought business security through diversification: his workshop produced an eclectic range of items, from surgical instruments and mobility scooters, to electric doorbells and hubs.

When it came to bicycles, Bianchi's creative flair and appetite for innovation prompted him to reject some of the popular designs of the day. Having initially manufactured penny farthings, he was relatively quick to embrace a design very similar to that of the modern bicycle, with metal frames (rather than wood), wheels of equal size, a chain drive, and pneumatic tyres.

As his reputation began to grow in the early 1890s, Edoardo was summoned to teach Queen Margherita how to ride a bicycle. It represented a priceless marketing opportunity. With the royal endorsement, he soon had Italian gentry knocking at his door, interested in his bicycles. There followed a royal appointment in 1895, just ten years after opening his doors for business,

which allowed him to use the coat of arms on his bikes. Ever the entrepreneur, Edoardo did not focus only on bikes. He continued to branch out, building motorcycles from 1897 and automobiles in 1900. Even World War I could not stop him. As hostilities raged across Europe and beyond, Bianchi turned his manufacturing business over to military application and developed what were perhaps the world's first full-suspension off-road bicycles—a prototype mountain bike, you could say—destined for the Bersaglieri, Italy's elite light infantry division.

Bianchi's manufacturing empire may have appeared to be a bit of a mixed bag, with Edoardo himself a jack of many trades in what was now a huge factory, rather than a two-room workshop. However, by 1907, Bianchi's plant in Viale Abruzzi was engaged in mass production and employed some 400 workers.

Almost from the start, Bianchi's approach to bicycle design development was pioneering. He

- A bike for travel and leisure, featuring two brakes, a stainless steel mudguard, and a freewheel.

- This bike, ideal for everyday use, weighed only 28 pounds (13 kg) and cost 406 lire (old Italian currency).

- This racing bike was one of Bianchi's lightest and most resilient.

- Weighing 22 pounds (10 kg), this track racing bike was the same style as one used by Giovanni Ferdinando Tomaselli in 1898–99.

was the first to recognize the benefit of testing new products in competition; he believed that this practice could refine and accelerate the process of innovation, and so the "Reparto Corse" (Racing Department) was born.

Edoardo was testing bicycles in competitions within three years of founding the company. Furthermore, the company achieved its first major international victory in 1899, in the Grand Prix of Paris, thanks to Giovanni Tommaselli. Edoardo

had singled out Tommaselli after his success at the Italian track championships, and his win in Paris had a dramatic effect on Bianchi sales.

The racing successes continued. In 1907 Lucien Mazon won the first Milan–San Remo on a Bianchi. In 1911 Carlo Galetti won the third edition of the Giro d'Italia, also on a Bianchi. The company continued to win many of the world's top races over the next decade, and in 1936 came the blue riband Hour record set by prolific

1885	1888	1899	1907
Edoardo Bianchi, a mechanic's apprentice, opens his first workshop at No.7 Via Nirone in Milan.	The Bianchi company moves to Via Bertani to concentrate on bicycle design and manufacture.	Giovanni Tommaselli rides to victory on a Bianchi in the Grand Prix of Paris. This gave the bicycle company its first major win.	The Bianchi plant in Viale Abruzzi employs 400 workers to mass-produce cars, motorbikes, and bicycles.

sprinter Giuseppe Olmo, whose name would later adorn his own frames.

Three years later there was a significant technological breakthrough, when Edoardo adopted his countryman Tullio Campagnolo's revolutionary new gear-changing system. Bianchi's bike sales were by then booming, with in excess of 70,000 bikes produced a year. The production of automobiles continued under the Autobianchi banner, working with Fiat and Pirelli before the

name eventually disappeared when the company was absorbed by Lancia. Consequently, it was the bicycle that Bianchi came to depend on. Likewise, cycling in Italy, to some extent, came to depend on Bianchi. Or cycle racing, at least, for there is no other manufacturer that is so indelibly linked to particular riders.

Think of Bianchi and inevitably Fausto Coppi springs to mind. Il Campionissimo—the "Champion of Champions"—is as much a part of

1912	1950	1965	1997
The company catalogue features a range of fourteen bicycles for "ladies, children, priests, and gentlemen." Three years later Bianchi will be producing bikes for the Italian army.	Bianchi's international reputation is established by Fausto Coppi's victory in the Paris–Roubaix.	Felice Gimondi wins the Tour de France on a Bianchi, a bike he spends most of his career riding.	The world's oldest bike manufacturer is taken over by Swedish company Cycleurope.

the company's history as the celeste paint job. Coppi was born in 1919, one of five children, and as a child he was generally in poor health. However, he loved being outside and, at the age of eight, regularly played truant to ride a bicycle that he claimed to have found. Aged thirteen, he left school to work as a messenger—a job he undertook on his bike.

Coppi's uncle nurtured his passion for cycling and, as a result, he rode and won his first race when he was just fifteen—not from a sprint but alone, having broken clear of his rivals. It was not long before Italy had a world-class rider on its hands, and, what is more, one with considerable charisma. For Coppi cycling was a sport, a pastime, and a lifestyle that thrived on romance and passion, and Italy fell in love with Coppi.

Having signed for the SS Lazio Ciclismo-Bianchi team in 1945, Coppi became synonymous with Bianchi, despite the fact that he had spent the early part of his pro career on a Legnano, on which he rode to his first Giro d'Italia win in 1940.

Images of the slight, beak-nosed figure, with his immaculately combed dark hair, aboard his Bianchi bike, now adorn the walls of bike shops the world over. They act as a reminder of another time, but one that stands as cycling's first golden era: an era represented by Coppi and the spell he cast on the *tifosi* (fans).

The reputations of both Coppi and Bianchi soon spread beyond Italy. The rider's victory in the 1950 Paris–Roubaix, on a Bianchi equipped with the Campagnolo gear system, resulted in a limited edition model being launched. It was yet

"Ride your bike, ride your bike, ride your bike."

FAUSTO COPPI when asked what it takes to become a champion

■ Fausto Coppi finishing
the seventeenth stage
of the Giro d'Italia
on June 5, 1952.

■ Coppi in 1949, four
years after he joined
the SS Lazio Ciclismo-
Bianchi team.

■ Felice Gimondi, winner of the 1965 Tour de France, spent most of his career on a Bianchi.

■ Gimondi won the world championship road race in 1973 on a Bianchi.

another example of how Bianchi saw the racing scene both as an important testing ground—and there was no greater test of a bike than the cobbles of Paris–Roubaix—and as a marketing tool.

After Coppi, who won two Tours de France and five Giri d'Italia, other greats followed. The 1965 Tour de France winner Felice Gimondi is a rider that also stirs emotions. A talented all-rounder and winner of all three Grand Tours, Gimondi would have been an even more prolific winner if a young Belgian named Eddy Merckx had not arrived on the scene around the same time. Gimondi is not alone; there are many riders who might say that Merckx, "The Cannibal," cost them more successful careers. Gimondi spent most of his life on a Bianchi bike and now works for the company at its headquarters in Bergamo, northern Italy.

Bianchi's knack for identifying and equipping Italy's great champions continued in the 1990s when Marco Pantani gave the country another Giro and Tour de France champion. Born in 1970

in Cesena, Pantani established a link with Bianchi early on, when he took up cycling with the local Fausto Coppi Cycling Club.

Pantani reputedly became one of Bianchi's most demanding clients; he was obsessed by the weight of his bikes and constantly badgered the Reparto Corse division of the company, requesting various tweaks to their specification. This quest for perfection is not an unusual trait in a climber, for whom weight is all-important, and Pantani was one of the greatest climbers the sport has ever seen.

As other materials began to challenge steel, Pantani was also one of the first Bianchi riders to enjoy success on an aluminium frame. It differed from Coppi's machine in another respect, too— in addition to celeste, it featured a splash of a different colour, with the tips of the forks and the seat tube/top tube triangle fading into yellow.

Although Pantini's career and indeed his life would eventually be destroyed by doping scandals, he was—briefly—a superb advert for Bianchi. His electrifying attacks in the mountains thrilled fans

■ This Specialissima uses Campagnolo brakes, Vittoria Corsa CX tyres, Campagnolo skewers, and unique Bianchi fork crowns.

■ A colour-coordinated Jan Ullrich wins the individual time trial of the 2003 Tour de France.

and carried him to the Giro-Tour double in 1998; he remains the last rider to achieve that feat.

However, perhaps the most memorable of his rides to win that Tour was his blistering attack on stage fifteen. While the other favourites, including defending champion Jan Ullrich, suffered in the freezing cold and wet conditions, Pantani danced away over the Galibier and up Les Deux Alpes to take an epic stage win.

After an *annus mirabilis*, Pantani's career went into freefall. He was ejected from the following year's Giro after failing a blood test, and he battled against allegations of doping for the remainder of his career before retiring, in some bitterness, in 2003. Tragically, he died just a year later, alone in a hotel room in Rimini on Valentine's Day; cocaine poisoning was the official verdict. Pantani was, in some ways, a victim of a particular era of cycling, in which the use of the blood booster EPO was rampant. Despite the question marks against his greatest successes, he left an indelible mark on cycling history.

The list of riders to have enjoyed successful careers on Bianchi bikes reads like a who's who of modern cycle racing. It includes the legendary Italian sprinter Mario Cipollini, the world road race champion Moreno Argentin, and, more recently, names such as Danilo Di Luca and Giro d'Italia winner Stefano Garzelli. Ullrich also spent a year aboard one, when, riding for the briefly reborn Bianchi team, he pushed Lance Armstrong close in the 2003 Tour de France.

Bianchi's founder, Edoardo, died in 1946, sixty-one years after setting up the company. The company was taken over by Edoardo's son, Guiseppe, and he oversaw some golden years, thanks in large part to Coppi's exploits. Throughout its history, Bianchi has continued to innovate and it has always been quick to adopt new materials and techniques, particularly when carbon and aluminium began to proliferate in the late 1980s and early 1990s. Bianchi incorporated the materials in a range of frames that has included radical new styles, such as sloping top tubes and compact sizes.

The world's oldest bike company, although no longer owned by the Bianchi family, having been taken over by Cycleurope in 1997, has always displayed a healthy willingness to embrace change. However, there is one aspect of Bianchi that has remained more or less constant throughout: the celeste paint scheme. Some have described it as celeste green; others call it duck egg blue. The shade has altered over the years, and on some models and in some light, it looks more green—or possibly more blue. Yet while there is no argument over its distinctiveness, there is a question over its origins.

The paint scheme first appeared on Bianchi frames in 1913, but it did not become ubiquitous until 1940. As for how it originated, one theory is that it was chosen to match Queen Margherita's eyes, which must have made quite an impression on Edoardo Bianchi during her riding lessons. Another viewpoint is that the colour was mixed to match the Milan sky, or that it was blended with army paint—a plausible theory given Bianchi's military connections.

Nowadays, such a hue might be rejected by a marketing department as too much of a gamble because it is the kind of shade people either love or hate, and more often hate. Arguably, however, the colour choice was a stroke of genius. While the company has adapted continually to the modern world, the celeste paint job has helped give Bianchi its unique identity for almost a century. **RD**

The Oltre features X-Tex technology:
added strength but no extra weight.

FAUSTO COPPI'S 1952 BIANCHI

By 1952 Fausto Coppi and Bianchi went together like Italian bread and olive oil. Il Campionissimo, as Coppi was known by his many admirers, first began riding Bianchi bikes in 1945, having spent his early years as a professional racer on a Legnano, and won the Giro d'Italia on one in 1940. In total, Coppi claimed another four Giro victories on a Bianchi. However, it was on the bike pictured here that he enjoyed arguably his greatest season ever. Even if it was not truly his best, it was his best remembered—if only for one performance.

Having won the Giro for a fourth time in 1952, Coppi went to the Tour de France bidding for a second victory. In the end, he won in some style, reaching Paris with a twenty-eight-minute advantage over Stan Ockers. However, it was one day in particular that would go down in history. On July 4, the 165-mile (266-km) stage started in Lausanne and took the riders to the ski station at L'Alpe d'Huez—the Tour's first ever summit finish. Coppi attacked 3.7 miles (6 km) from the top and flew up the mountain, his performance captured—for the first time—by television cameras and broadcast live. The Coppi legend was sealed, and it was virtually inseparable from his celeste green Bianchi.

The distinctive paint job first appeared on Bianchi frames in 1913, although it did not become ubiquitous until 1940. The unusual colour still features on Bianchi frames today, and forms a direct line to the most celebrated bike in the Italian company's long history: Coppi's 1952 machine.

A riveted leather saddle was de rigueur. Coppi used a model made by Selle San Marco, founded in Rossano Veneto in north-east Italy in 1935 and still going strong.

Campagnolo Gran Sport derailleur with a five-speed freewheel.

Despite his light build, Coppi liked to push big gears, hence the large chainrings. He climbed the Alpe d'Huez using a comparatively monstrous 46 x 19 gear.

Coppi's bike was fitted with a quill stem and handlebars made by Turin firm Ambrosio.

Toe-clips and straps were the only option until clipless pedals arrived in the mid-1980s.

DESIGN DETAILS

HANDLEBARS

Ambrosio, who made the handlebars and stem, was a pioneer in using aluminium for components. Founded in Turin in 1923, Ambrosio is perhaps best known for its alloy wheel rims, which were also used by Coppi.

WATER BOTTLE

Fausto Coppi's 1952 Bianchi featured a spring-loaded down tube water bottle cage. The insulated water bottle helped keep fluids hot or cold, depending on the weather and the race conditions.

Billato

Founded in 1954 by Silvio Billato, the company expanded to become one of Italy's most prominent bike manufacturers. However, Billato is best known for some of the legendary riders who rode its machines under different logos.

Watching the Tour de France for the first time on television can be a confusing business. Not only are there the different jerseys to understand, there are also the stories, the hints, and the jokes. Some of the comments that a brand new cycling fan might puzzle over are the cryptic allusions to the bikes being ridden, and how they can be marked up with one manufacturer's name, but be made by another company entirely—by Italian company Billato Linea Telai, for example.

Billato was founded in Padua in 1954 by Silvio Billato, who started designing and making steel frames to order, but not necessarily under his own name. Billato grew in different directions, expanding when Silvio's sons—Roberto, Silvio, and Stefano—joined, and made it one of Italy's biggest and most prestigious companies—for those in the know. The company is happy to boast that the greatest Classics, road, and mountain bike world championships and the Tour de France have all been won on bikes it has made, but it also likes to keep its secrets.

There are rumours about how, at the height of their rivalry, both Gino Bartali and Fausto

Coppi were riding Billato bikes in disguise, and apparently five teams at the 1999 Tour de France were also using the bikes under different names. When Billato made bike frames for Lampre's 2001 Paris–Roubaix team, Ludo Dierckxsens is said to have loved his so much that he would not give it back and took it to the Tour de France where he came second on stage four. It is possible that Gilberto Simoni won the 2001 Giro d'Italia on a Billato, and that Chris Boardman rode one when he beat the Hour record. Only the Billato family and the riders know for sure.

Publicly, Billato made frames for Marin and for Greg LeMond's range, including those ridden by the Z and GAN teams. Billato also produced the Concordes ridden by PDM-Concorde in the Sean Kelly era, when the Irishman won the green jersey in the 1989 Tour de France, as well as the World Cup and Liège–Bastogne–Liège. However, it was not until 2003 that the company started to sell bikes openly under the Billato brand. By that time it was a huge company that made bikes at all levels of the market. The following year it radically changed direction and moved back to a small, five-man team, designing and building custom frames in aluminium, titanium, steel, and carbon.

Billato continues to innovate and work in partnership with other brands. The Classics star of the late 1990s and early 2000s, Belgian Johan Museeuw—the only man to win the World Cup and world road race championship in the same year—looked to it for help with his own range of bikes, and brought Roberto Billato on board as chief designer for his innovative flax fibre range of bicycles. If the Lion of Flanders thinks someone is an expert, it is praise indeed.

The company, run by the three brothers, continues to make frames to order for road, cyclo-cross, mountain bike, and track. Billato might not be as well known as some of the bigger names in bicycle manufacturing, but with such an impressive history, it can afford to be proud. **sc**

> *"Carbon is not so difficult to use if you know how to make the fibres work for you."*
>
> ROBERTO BILLATO

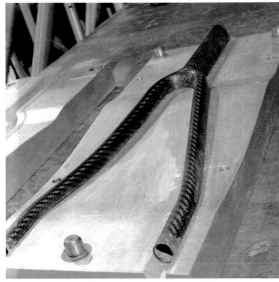

■ The Billato Epoca features carbon forks and rear end, and Campagnolo wheels.

■ To mould their High Resistance carbon fibre frames and forks, Billato designers draw the shapes they want to work with and a machinist makes a mould in two halves.

Bottecchia finds an impromptu way to cool down during the 1925 Tour de France.

Loyal fans, pictured here in the Pyrenees, followed Bottecchia the length and breadth of his Tour.

Bottecchia

Italy's first Tour de France winner died at the peak of his career and in mysterious circumstances, when his bike company was still in its infancy. Almost eighty years later, the legend of Ottavio Bottecchia lives on through the frames that bear his name.

The dramatic story of the life of Ottavio Bottecchia would surely whet the appetite of Hollywood. He was an uneducated Italian boy who worked as a bricklayer, fought in World War I, discovered cycling late in life, and went to France with only a minimal grasp of the language. Remarkably, he was crowned the first Italian winner of the Tour de France, and then became the first Italian to win it two years in a row, only to die in mysterious circumstances two years later. The unresolved nature of his death is undoubtedly compelling, but it is through his bikes that his name lives on.

With his swept-back dark hair, gaunt appearance, long, lean legs, and sharp cheekbones, Ottavio Bottecchia bore more than a passing resemblance to Fausto Coppi. In other respects, too, he could be seen as the great Coppi's predecessor. Like Coppi, he found fame in both France and Italy. He also had similarly humble origins, born in 1894 into a family of nine children in San Martino di Colle Umberto, 37 miles (60 km) north of Venice, where he attended school for a year before starting work as a bricklayer.

At the outbreak of World War I, Bottecchia joined the Bersaglieri corps of the Italian army,

> "Bottecchia—
> Italy's greatest
> champion cyclist
> and legendary hero."
>
> LEE F. BEVERIDGE
> *Bicycling* magazine

and was awarded a bronze medal for his valour. He was twenty-four when the war ended. His cycling career had not yet started, although the seeds had been sown when an Italian officer noticed his strength and speed as he cycled (possibly a Bianchi model, since it supplied the Italian army with bikes), and told him he should try competitive cycling.

Bottecchia followed the officer's advice and showed instant promise. His performances caught the eye of Teodoro Carnielli, the owner of a bicycle shop in nearby Vittoria Veneto, in north-east Italy, who recognized Bottecchia's talent and

the fact that he won races on bikes that were barely fit for purpose. By way of encouragement, he gave him one of the Ganna racing machines that he sold, named after Luigi Ganna, winner of the inaugural Giro d'Italia in 1909.

Bottecchia raced in the 1923 Giro d'Italia as an independent rider, without the backing of a team, and came fifth. This achievement prompted an invitation from Henri Pélissier to join his team, Automoto-Hutchinson. He won a stage of the Tour de France that same year, and wore the yellow jersey until it was claimed by the eventual winner, Pélissier, who predicted in Paris that

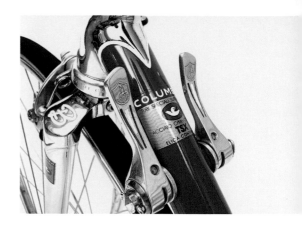

Bottecchia, twelfth in his debut Tour, would be his successor. He was right. However, Bottecchia did not only win the following year; he also took four stages and became the first man to hold the yellow jersey from start to finish of the Tour. Importantly, he was the first Italian winner, and the following year he became the first Italian rider to win two Tours in a row.

When he turned professional, Bottecchia was illiterate, but he soon learnt to read and pored over the pages of *La Gazzetta dello Sport*. He also took a great interest in anti-fascist, anti-Mussolini literature. This, it has been suggested, was the reason behind his decision, on stage nine of the 1924 Tour from Toulon to Nice, to wear his team jersey rather than the *maillot jaune* that he was entitled to wear. As the Tour passed close to Italy, it might have been an anti-Mussolini gesture. Another theory is that Bottecchia, by now tremendously popular in his native country, was worried that he would be mobbed by Italian fans—wearing his team jersey allowed him to ride incognito.

In 1925 he again won four stages. Adelin Benoit of Belgium briefly relieved him of the yellow jersey in the middle section of the race, but in the end Bottecchia's dominance was absolute: he won by almost an hour from his Automoto teammate Lucien Buysse, who acted as his *domestique* throughout (perhaps the first rider to perform such a role). These were the days of monster stages: many of them were more than 186 miles (300 km) in length. In 1924 the maximum stage length was 299 miles (482 km), which was reduced to a modest 269 miles (433 km) the following year.

Perhaps the demands of these races combined with Bottecchia's level of success took its toll because he never recaptured his 1925 form. In 1926, in atrocious weather conditions in the Pyrenees, he withdrew from the Tours in tears and left his *domestique*, Buysse, to inherit his crown—in the same way that Bottecchia had

■ Bottecchia chases Lucien Buysse through the streets of St Cloud during the final stage of the 1925 Tour de France.

■ This 1992 Bottecchia Equipe features, from top to bottom, Columbus tubing, Campagnolo Delta brakes, authentic Bottecchia emblem, and a Campagnolo Record crankset.

inherited Pélissier's. There was no doubt that Bottecchia was in a bad way: depressed and suffering from a persistent bronchial cough. In other respects, things looked good for Bottecchia. He was married with three children, and in 1926 he entered into business with his old mentor Teodore Carnielli, who suggested producing bikes under his name.

On June 3, 1927, as Bottecchia prepared for the Tour—by now fully recovered and optimistic that he could win a third title—he set off for a training ride. He had woken at dawn in his home in Peonis, not far from the border with Slovenia. He asked his wife to prepare a hot bath for him to enjoy on his return, which he estimated to be in three hours. After leaving the house, he called in on his friend and training partner, Alfonso Piccini, who declined to join him; then he tried to recruit Riccardo Zille, although he too was unable to accompany Bottechia. And so he set off alone.

He never returned. A couple of hours later, Bottecchia was discovered lying by the roadside, close to his home village. He had a cracked skull and other broken bones. His bike lay on the curb, surprisingly unmarked: there was nothing to suggest that he had been hit by a car, or even that he had crashed. He was carried to a bar and given the last rites by a priest, then taken by cart to a hospital where he died—reports as to how long he survived in hospital range from several hours to twelve days. However, the circumstances of his death are shrouded in an even more perplexing mystery.

It was suggested that he had suffered from sunstroke and collapsed. The undamaged bike and the fact that it lay a few feet away from Bottecchia make this theory unlikely. Some people—including the priest in the bar—

speculated that he had been killed, most likely by fascists, angry that he had aligned himself with the left. Further intrigue followed when the local police commander, a fascist, called off the investigation into the death. Bottecchia's family received a generous life insurance payout, which led to speculation regarding the apparent cover-up.

The mystery deepened years later when an Italian man in New York, who lay dying after being stabbed, owned up to Bottecchia's murder. He claimed that he had been hired as a hit man by a local godfather. However, there was another deathbed confession, even later: a farmer said that he had caught Bottecchia eating grapes in his vineyard and thrown a rock that hit his head. Neither of the confessions adds up: the godfather named by the dying man in New York appeared not to exist; the farmer's vineyard was 34 miles (55 km) from the spot where the cyclist was found dying.

However he died, Bottecchia was not the last great Italian cyclist to meet a premature end: his successors as Tour de France winners—Coppi and Marco Pantani—also suffered tragic fates. In Bottecchia's case it is sad that not only were his life and career cut short, but also that he did not live to see his bike business flourish, as it did—and indeed still does.

Carnielli continued to produce bikes in Bottecchia's name—his workshop employed one hundred people in the 1930s—and to protect his legacy. Indeed, a touching story was told in a 1970 edition of *Bicycling* magazine, in which a Bottecchia owner, unsure about the story behind his machine, told of writing to the company to request new decals. He also asked about Bottecchia. It responded with a set of

1920	1923	1923	1924
Bottecchia wins the Giro del Piave, the Coppa della Vittoria, and the Duca D'Aosta.	Leading French racing cyclist Henri Pélissier asks Bottecchia to join his professional team, Automoto-Hutchinson.	Bottecchia wins a stage of the Tour de France and wears the yellow jersey until it is claimed by the eventual winner and teammate, Pélissier.	He wins the first stage of the Tour and keeps his lead to the end to become the first Italian to win the race and wear the yellow jersey from start to finish.

■ Salvador Dalí, circa 1964, with his Bottecchia Graziella, a folding bike that could be stowed in a car trunk.

■ Gianni Motta leads through a mountain pass astride his Bottecchia, on his way to winning the 1966 Giro d'Italia.

1925

Riding for Automoto, Bottecchia becomes the first Italian to win back to back Tours.

1927

He is found dead by the roadside while training on June 3. The mysterious circumstances surrounding his death are never resolved.

1989

American Greg LeMond wins the closest ever Tour de France on a Bottecchia bike.

2006

Nearly eighty years after his death, the company that Bottecchia founded sells more than 50,000 bikes in Europe, including racing bikes and mountain bikes. It is still based in Italy.

replacement lettering for the frame, together with a cover letter outlining what happened to the late cyclist. But that was not the end of it. Days later came another delivery: an illustrated booklet from Teodoro Carnielli's private library telling the story in more detail.

The booklet contained an account of Bottecchia's death, relating that he had been riding at speed when one of his toe-clips caught the road. Bottecchia looked down, lost control, crashed, and fractured his skull. How the author could have known so definitively what happened, when Bottecchia was alone, is unclear. According to this account he lingered for twelve days in hospital before dying on June 15, 1927. He was buried in a cemetery in San Martino.

Bottecchia remains a formidable name in Italian bicycle manufacturing, if not quite in the elite division occupied by the likes of Bianchi, Pinarello, and Colnago. After World War II, the bikes began to infiltrate the professional peloton, with Gianni Motta winning the 1966 Giro on one, and Rudi Altig winning the world road race title

on a Bottecchia the same year. Giuseppe Saronni was another Bottecchia-riding Giro winner, although the most notable success came in 1989, when Greg LeMond won the closest ever Tour de France on a Bottecchia. Oddly for a company named after the first Italian Tour winner, that remains its only Tour win.

Bottecchia has innovated, too, although less in racing than in other areas. In 1951 Teodoro's son, Guido, invented the first stationary exercise bike: the Cyclette. And in 1964 the company claimed to have made the first folding bike designed to be transported in the trunk of a car: the Graziella (Salvador Dalí had one). By the late 1960s Teodoro's sons, Guido and Mario, had taken over the company and it remained in the Carnielli family until the mid-1990s, when the company moved from its long-time home in Vittorio Veneto to Cavarzere, in the Province of Venice. There, Bottecchia continues to produce around 50,000 bikes a year, including the state-of-the-art carbon racing machines used by the Acqua & Sapone team. *RM*

- The Emme 2 frame was used by the UCI Professional Continental Cycling Team.

- LeMond had an average speed of 34.52 mph (54.55 km/h) during the final stage of the 1989 Tour de France.

CARBONIO CREATIVO

DT SWISS

FATTA A M

94°

DURA-AC

The Acqua & Sapone team rode the Emme 2s
in the 2011 Giro d'Italia.

■ The young Tullio
Campagnolo began his
amateur racing career
in 1921.

■ Tullio Campagnolo
poses beside a bicycle
equipped with the
renowned Cambio
Corsa derailleur.

Campagnolo

More than seventy-five years after Tullio Campagnolo first took component innovation into his own hands, Campagnolo has become one of the most respected and most coveted of cycling's brands, the name synonymous with quality, craftsmanship, and style.

No name is so closely associated with, or so integrally involved in, cycling success as Campagnolo. Whereas there are numerous master frame-builders—Colnago, Pinarello, Bianchi—when it comes to similarly revered component makers, there have always been rivals, but Campagnolo has been way out in front for much of the last century. It is no surprise, therefore, that bikes equipped with Campagnolo have won everything: every Classic, every Grand Tour, and every smaller stage race. There are no blanks, no "ones that got away." Campagnolo's success is complete.

The name is sometimes shortened—Campag and Campy are some variations—but in all its abbreviated forms Campagnolo came to stand for the very highest standard in terms of design, function, and finish; the elegant, scrolled, and italicized "Campagnolo" signature is as redolent of uncompromising quality as Ferrari's prancing horse. And, for many an amateur cyclist, just as aspirational—that is, expensive. However, there is a striking contrast between the quality and luxury that Campagnolo came to represent and the story of the humble son of a hardware store owner, Getullio "Tullio" Campagnolo, whose horrendous experience on a bike—on an obscure Italian mountain, the Croce d'Aune—led to one of the most successful premium brands. Indeed, it is an unlikely source of inspiration for such

"This rear wheel thing needs changing!"

TULLIO CAMPAGNOLO

an iconic brand. The Croce d'Aune appears unremarkable. It is overshadowed by many higher and more magnificent Dolomite peaks, submerged in woodland and, it seems, anonymity. The slopes are not particularly steep, the vistas are unspectacular, and the town of Pedavena, where the road to the summit begins, is hardly on the tourist trail. It has a brewery, but little else worthy of mention.

Yet, 5.2 miles (8.5 km) and 2,300 vertical feet (700 m) away, at the summit of the Croce d'Aune, there stands a statue that is well known throughout the cycling world because it commemorates a moment that is as important as any in the evolution of the racing bicycle. Its inscription bears a date: November 11, 1927, and a name: Tullio Campagnolo.

Tullio, from Vicenza, in north-east Italy, was a gifted engineer who built a three-wheeled cart for his father and who then turned his hand to building bikes after World War I. He was also a moderately gifted cyclist, not that races at the time were necessarily a pure test of athletic ability. Campagnolo's experience as he climbed

the Croce d'Aune, during the Gran Premio della Vittoria, illustrates the point. Tullio might easily have been romping towards victory—or at least lurching over the summit faster than his opponents—but he was barely able to detach his frozen fingers from the handlebars.

This meant trouble: changing gears in those days involved unscrewing the rear wheel by hand, flipping it through 180 degrees, and using the single sprocket on the other side of the central hub. With numb hands, what was usually little more than a time-consuming inconvenience became an impossibility. "Bisogno cambiá qualcossa de drio!" ("This rear wheel thing needs changing!") cursed Tullio in his nasally Vicentino dialect as he wrestled furiously with the nuts holding the wheel in place. Meanwhile, rivals sped by, and Tullio's chances of victory disappeared with them.

However, there was so much more at stake that day than local bragging rights and a cheap piece of silverware. Three years later, inspired by his misadventure on the Croce d'Aune and after endless experimentation and tinkering, Tullio

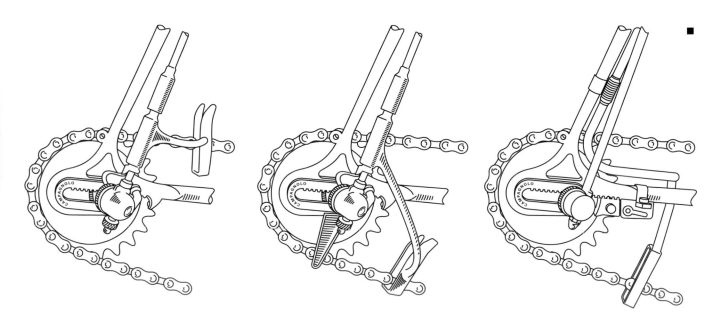

■ Variations of
Campagnolo's
revolutionary
dual-rod changer.

■ The cyclist had to
pedal backwards to
operate the lever and
make the gear change.

perfected the quick-release wheel mechanism that remains de rigueur on all but the cheapest of mass-produced bicycles today. As with all great innovations, its genius lay in its simplicity: a skewer slotted through the hollow axle of the wheel, a cone nut at one end, a cam assembly at the other, and cycling had its equivalent of the corkscrew or the can opener.

As the popularity of the new quick-release mechanism spread, so too did Tullio Campagnolo's reputation as an engineering visionary. It was destined to grow yet further; having registered his company in Vicenza's Corso Padova in 1933, Campagnolo set his sights on the next frontier of component design: gearing.

Although not the first system to dispense with the old wheel-flipping rigmarole, Campagnolo's "dual-rod" solution was viewed as the gold standard by amateurs and professionals alike for much of the 1940s. Its successor, the Gran Sport launched in 1950, was considered to represent the last quantum leap in gear technology prior to the advent of indexed gearing in more recent years. It was also the first system to employ a rear derailleur of similar form and functionality still widely used post-2000.

Andy Schleck's skipping chain (not made by Campagnolo, incidentally) on the seventeenth stage of the 2010 Tour de France cost him the lead, though few riders or manufacturers would claim that the choice of componentry is often the decisive factor in cycling's major races. But it was not always so. In the years immediately before and after World War II, as Fausto Coppi and Gino Bartali fascinated and divided Italy with their rivalry, the legend of Campagnolo soared not least because this was the age in which component manufacturers could be kingmakers. In the same way that the infamous episode on the Croce d'Aune had cost Tullio Campagnolo a win in the Gran Premio della Vittoria, so the Giri d'Italia and Tours de France were won and lost—in Campagnolo and Coppi's case, usually won—by the consistency or capriciousness of the gear system the rider had chosen and his adeptness at using it.

Culturally, too, Campagnolo had begun to establish itself as an Italian national treasure. Vittorio Di Sica's 1948 neorealist film *Ladri di bicicletta* (*Bicycle Thieves*) featured bikes that were equipped with Campagnolo Corsa components. More than forty years later, Tullio, who died aged eighty-one in 1983, may or may not have been turning in his grave when his now iconic signature appeared on caps and clothing in the cult US basketball movie *White Men Can't Jump* (1992). Either way, it was eloquent confirmation of how far his legacy had reached and how loudly it resonated.

Julio Marquevich, president of Campagnolo USA, once said of meeting the company's founder, "I felt like a gnat in the presence of an elephant." Tullio's son, Valentino, must have felt similarly daunted when he stepped out of that elephant's shadow in 1983. In his first

> ## *"I felt like a gnat in the presence of an elephant."*
>
> JULIO MARQUEVICH on meeting Tullio Campagnolo

■ Cyclists display their trophies outside the Campagnolo factory in Vicenza.

■ Gino Bartali puts the Cambio Corsa to good use on the Galibier pass in the 1948 Tour de France.

■ Campagnolo components, from top to bottom: a Campagnolo Record rear mech, wheel, front brake and gear shifters, and crankset and pedal.

■ The bicycle of Francesco Moser. Using a bike fitted with Campagnolo components, Moser broke the Hour record.

■ The Croce D'Aune *gruppo* featured the Pentadrive braking system, designed to provide greater stopping power at the rim's surface.

1927	1933	1943	1950
Tullio Campagnolo's frozen hands cause an epiphany that will change cycling forever.	After fabricating parts in the back room of his father's hardware store, Tullio founds Campagnolo S.R.L.	The first official Campagnolo logo appears: the winged wheel highlighting the quick release.	A prototype of the Gran Sport cable-actuated parallelogram rear derailleur is shown in Milan.

decade at the helm, under growing threat from Japanese rival Shimano and the rise in popularity of mountain biking, the good ship Campagnolo teetered, but stayed afloat, thanks largely to continued success in the pro road racing elite (one statistic attests to its continued dominance here: in 1980, thirty-eight of the top forty professional teams were Campag-equipped.) However, Shimano was emerging fast, although it is astonishing to note that the Japanese company took until 1999 to break the Italian firm's stranglehold on overall victory at the Tour de France.

Between 1973 and 1987, most of the important victories were achieved on bikes that were equipped with Campagnolo's flagship groupset, the Super Record. Campagnolo was a pioneer here, too, as the first manufacturer of the groupset—or *gruppo*—concept. Since the late 1950s, it had been producing the full range of bicycle components under the "Record" marque: crankset, derailleurs, brakes, seatpost, headset, and pedals. Previously, bicycle manufacturers had tended to adopt a pick 'n' mix approach to componentry. Campagnolo's groupset offered synchronicity in style and, most importantly, function. The different parts were designed not only to satisfy a very Italian craving for aesthetics, but also to work together more efficiently. Other groupsets followed: Chorus, Athena, Centaur, and Veloce are enduring names, whereas others have come and gone including, in the late 1980s, a familiar one: the Croce d'Aune, a stylish but short-lived *gruppo* that offered a cheaper alternative to the top of the range Super Record.

1953	1973	1992	2008
Fausto Coppi wins the Lugano world championship road race using Gran Sport derailleurs.	Campagnolo launches its Super Record *gruppo*.	Ergopower levers are introduced for the first time.	Campagnolo revolutionizes the world of cycling yet again with the eleven-speed drivetrain.

However, it was the Super Record that became the groupset of choice in the professional peloton in the 1970s and 1980s, until it went into hiatus in 1987 (the name was revived in 2009). The Super Record groupset marked the final stage of an evolution that began with the Gran Sport rear derailleur in 1950 and continued with the Record version in 1962 and the Nuovo Record model, launched three years later and used by Eddy Merckx in his first four Tour de France victories. The Super Record came along just in time for his fifth and final win in 1974.

The Super Record groupset was refined over the next decade, consolidating its status as the market leader. However, Shimano's equivalent, Dura-Ace, began to exert serious pressure throughout the 1980s.

Campagnolo responded in a number of ways, renaming the Super Record the C-Record, and, more radically, introducing the Delta brake, which came with the C-Record and Croce d'Aune groupsets. These devices were large, cheese-shaped wedges of polished silver—marvels of craftsmanship and design—and they appeared to represent a radical improvement in aerodynamics, even if they were slightly heavier than the old side-pull calipers. Delta brakes certainly looked as though they would be a great success. However, in a sign that Campagnolo had perhaps lost the Midas touch, this was not the case. Problems emerged in the first year when the Delta brakes proved difficult to set up; neither did they work very well. Although the functional issues were resolved, these early problems sounded the death knell for the Delta brakes. These days, they survive only as prized collector's items.

While Campagnolo persevered with the doomed Deltas, Shimano, instead of working on futuristic new brake designs, was developing an integrated gearing and braking mechanism. When Shimano Total Integration appeared, Campagnolo rapidly found itself playing catch-up. It fought back with Ergopower, its own integrated

DERAILLEUR EVOLUTION

GRAN SPORT

Tullio Campagnolo's first parallelogram derailleur was developed in the late 1940s and released as the Gran Sport in 1953.

NUOVO RECORD

One of the first to be made from aluminium, the Nuovo Record was light, strong, and very expensive. It dominated pro road racing for sixteen years.

SUPER RECORD

The Super Record derailleur featured a new logo, black anodizing, titanium bolts, and a different cage geometry with twenty-eight-tooth capacity.

gearing-braking system. The early models were stylish, and, unlike Shimano, they had concealed gear cables as well as brake cables; however, they were clunkier and, when it came to shifting gear, stiffer and not as user-friendly as Shimano's Total Integration version.

Continuing Tullio's legacy, there were other novel innovations: the Shamal deep-section wheels introduced in 1992 and used by the all conquering Gewiss team in 1994, for example. Then, in the late 1990s, Campagnolo fully embraced carbon fibre and titanium, and used these materials in most of its components and wheels. In 1998 a composites department was established; today it accounts for a third of the workforce. It has allowed Campagnolo to restore its reputation for cutting-edge equipment, and, perhaps, to overcome the popular perception that although it beats its Japanese rivals for style, it lags behind in innovation and reliability. When it introduced the first ten-speed *gruppo* in 2000, Campagnolo stole a march on its great Japanese

rivals; nine years later, it upped the ante again with an eleven-speed drivetrain released under the old Super Record name.

It is unlikely, though, that Campagnolo will ever return to the pre-eminence, bordering on utter domination, that lasted more or less from the 1950s through to the 1980s. The fact that Shimano did not win its first Tour until 1999, when Lance Armstrong claimed the first of his seven consecutive titles, seems extraordinary. So too is another statistic: since 1999, Campagnolo has only won one Tour, and that was by default when Oscar Pereiro inherited Floyd Landis's 2006 victory, after Landis failed a drug control test in September 2007.

Despite this, Campagnolo remains arguably the most feted of cycling brands, and the choice of many purists; the mystique of the great Italian component manufacturer prevails, with its origins, of course, nestled among the peaks to the north of Vicenza, on the Croce d'Aune. As for the mountain where it all began, even

■ A poster from the 1950s displays derailleurs alongside top cyclists of the day.

C-RECORD

Released in the 1980s just after Tullio Campagnolo's death. It was big and heavy at 7.4 ounces (221 g), but went on to feature on many Tour-winning bikes.

RECORD EPS

Twenty years in the making, the Record Electronic Power Shift (EPS) features tactile and audible shift feedback.

SUPER RECORD EPS

The Super Record rear derailleur uses materials including ceramic, aluminium, and titanium.

if the groupset named in its honour did not last, Campagnolo has nourished the legend of the climb by making it the centrepiece of its prestigious mass participation ride, the Granfondo Campagnolo. Renamed the GP Sportful in 2009, the event and its thousands of entrants continue to visit the Croce d'Aune, Veneto, in the Dolomites-Alps, every year to sweat and suffer up its slopes—although not as much as Tullio Campagnolo suffered back in 1927. At the top, riders can stop and pay homage to the company founder, whose son, Valentino, and grandchildren, Francesca and Davide, remain at the helm.

The Giro d'Italia is an occasional visitor to the mountain on whose slopes Campagnolo was "born," although it is a stage of the 1964 race that is most memorable. Appropriately, it was not the climb that posed problems for the riders but the

demands that it placed on their equipment. The best climber in the race and pre-stage favourite, Italy's Vito Taccone, punctured seven times on the gravel surface of the descent into Pedevena, losing all hope of victory in the process. The *Corriere delle Alpi* later reported that Taccone had finished the stage possessed by a "legendary rage" and that the Croce d'Aune had cost the peloton "something like 300 punctures—definitely a record."

For its centenary the Giro returned to the Croce d'Aune in 2009. The road had been tarmacked so the ascent from Pedevena did not produce the same level of drama, mechanically induced or otherwise. Croce d'Aune is an obscure, almost forgotten mountain. Yet, to cognoscenti of cycling's great brands, there is no more iconic destination. **RM**

FAMOUS CAMPAGNOLO RIDERS

BERNARD HINAULT

The charismatic Frenchman was a good fit for Campagnolo's marketing people, and he featured in their advertisements: "Hinault chooses Campagnolo. Is it coincidence?"

FELICE GIMONDI

Racing for Bianchi-Campagnolo, Felice Gimondi competes in the 1975 Tour de France, in which he won one stage and was fifth in the mountains classification.

MIGUEL INDURAIN

Miguel Indurain had a stunning winning streak racing with Campagnolo, and became the first person to win five consecutive Tour de France titles between 1991 and 1995.

MARCO PANTANI

Marco Pantani gave Campagnolo its most recent outright Tour de France win in 1998, but competition from other manufacturers has seen the brand lose its cachet in recent years.

A quartet of Italian team time triallists on their Campagnolo-equipped machines.

Campagnolo

Gimondi won the world cycling championships
in 1973 using Campagnolo components.

The Athena crankset comes with matching silver aluminium chainrings.

Athena's stylish aluminium rear mech.

The front derailleur is compatible with a standard or compact crankset.

The Ergopower levers come in black, silver, or with a carbon finish and use Campagnolo's Power Shift technology; this allows for multiple gear changes in a single shift.

The classic single-pivot rear brake.

ATHENA

In the age of sleek carbon fibre groupsets, there is something to be admired in Campagnolo's Athena alloy range. Combining performance, style, and value, this mid-range groupset is the perfect partner for a winter training bike or an update to a vintage frame.

The rear derailleur incorporates carbon fibre parallelogram knuckles and titanium hardware.

Optional titanium axle and reverse thread titanium fixing bolt on the Super Record 11.

The Super Record front derailleur with mounted motor.

The rechargeable Li-ion battery (top) and LED indicator—the latter can be mounted to the stem or the brake housing.

The Super Record D-Skeleton braking system.

The Super Record EPS Ergopower shifters are lighter than their Record counterparts and have additional sculpting throughout their design.

SUPER RECORD EPS

A similar concept to Shimano's Di2 range of electronic gear shifting, Campagnolo's EPS (Electronic Power Shift) goes one step further providing slightly better gear transmission and a close feel to its much-loved Ergopower levers.

■ Cannondale founder
Joe Montgomery used
to pilot his private jet to
company meetings.

■ The 1983 ST500
touring bike featured
Shimano components
and retailed at US $550.

Cannondale

These US bikes were a radical departure from thin-tubed, steel-framed machines when
they appeared in the late 1980s. A pioneer in aluminium frame production, Cannondale
paved the way for oversized, lightweight frames that would become ubiquitous.

When Cannondales first began to appear on
roads in the late 1980s and early 1990s, the
considered opinion of the cognoscenti was
predictable—that is, largely unfavourable. The
majority of the road cycling fraternity thought
that Cannondales, with their bulbous tubes, were
ugly—the down tube, in particular, fattening all
the way to the bottom bracket. Over the years
road cyclists have tended to be traditionalists,
with fairly rigid and conservative ideas about
how a road racing bike should look: thin tubes in
the classic diamond shape, preferably adorned,
discreetly and tastefully, with an Italian name. Fat-
tubed Cannondale road bikes looked too much
like mountain bikes. And the last thing a road bike
should resemble was a mountain bike.

Gradually the opinions of many road cyclists
began to change, prompted not by the look of
the Cannondale but by the feel of the bike. Apart
from being ridiculously light, the aluminium-
framed bikes were incredibly responsive. They
could be lifted with one finger and, when riders
got out of the saddle to accelerate, it felt as
though they were about to take off. A short
ride was enough to convince most people:
Cannondales felt fast.

In fact, Cannondale was not quite the upstart
that many had assumed when its road bikes
began to garner attention in the early 1990s. The
company had started building road bikes before
it built mountain bikes; perhaps not surprisingly,
however, the mountain biking community was
quicker to embrace the fat-tubed alloy frames.

The company, founded by Joe Montgomery,
Jim Catrambone, and Ron Davis, has been around
since 1971, when it started out, as legend has
it, "in a crowded loft above a pickle factory." But
it was not a bike company. It was twelve years
before Cannondale produced its first bicycle. The
company concentrated initially on backpacks,
cycling trailers, clothing, and accessories. Although
it gained a reputation for a child trailer known
as the Bugger—not a name that endeared it to
the UK market—it was in 1983 that the first
Cannondale bike rolled out of the company's
factory in Bedford, Pennsylvania, more than
300 miles (483 km) from its headquarters.

As for the Cannondale name, it has its
roots in the location of the headquarters in
Bethel, Connecticut. The unlikely inspiration
for a company with a global reputation for
innovation and cutting-edge technology is the

tiny Cannondale Metro-North railroad station in Wilton, Connecticut. The station has a decidedly rustic look and feel, although it is only an eighty-four-minute journey to New York's Grand Central. Bethel, where Cannondale has its head office, is nearby (battery-making giant Duracell is based in the same small town.) As well as adopting the name, the Cannondale Bicycle Corporation originally used the station's logo, too.

Cannondale's first bike was a road model, but, surprisingly for a company that later cultivated a reputation for featherlight racing bikes, it was aimed at the touring market. While the forks were steel, the main triangle of the frame was aluminium, as were the oval-shaped seatstays and chainstays. The down tube was oversized and there were no lugs, another Cannondale trademark. The tubes were simply welded together—the joints were imperfect, although far from ugly. The overall finish was a lustrous red and white, as though the bike had been treated to hundreds of coats of glossy paint.

Red was the colour of Cannondale in the early years. A year after the tourer, a road racing

bike and a mountain bike were launched. The small Reynolds and Columbus stickers still identified the true racers, but, slowly, rivals were beginning to hove into view, threatening the duopoly. Furthermore, although initially it was carbon fibre that seemed to pose the greatest threat—especially when a TVT-carbon-tubed frame was ridden by Greg LeMond to victory in the 1986 Tour de France, and then in later Tours by Pedro Delgado, LeMond again, and Miguel Indurain—there was a good argument to be made for CAAD (Cannondale Advanced Aluminium Design) as the company branded its frames. Aluminium was, after all, lighter and more affordable (not that Cannondale frames have ever been cheap) than carbon, and unlike steel, it is rust-proof.

Given the resistance of the purists to the original fat boys—and their preference for classic Italian-built frames—it was ironic that Cannondale, when it did make a splash in continental road racing, it did so with an Italian team, Saeco, and an Italian rider. In the late 1990s Mario Cipollini was to Italian cycling what, later, Silvio Berlusconi

In matching bike and jersey, Mario Cipollini competes in the 1997 Tour de France.

The darker carbon components of the Six13 frame can be seen surrounded by aluminium.

*"The best bike—
Cannondale.
The best bike."*

MARIO CIPOLLINI

1971	1983	1997	1999
The company is founded by Joe Montgomery, Jim Catrambone, and Ron Davis above a pickle factory in Connecticut.	The first road frames are produced. Made from aluminium, they are finished with steel forks and come in either white or red.	Ivan Gotti wins his and Cannondale's first Giro d'Italia as part of the Saeco team. The Italian climber outperforms Pavel Tonkov and Giuseppe Guerini.	Mario Cipollini wins four stages in a row at the Tour de France.

was to the country's politics: unmistakably, flamboyantly, and at times outrageously, Italian.

Yet Cannondale and Cipollini were the perfect match. Cipollini was the über-showman; he could hardly go training without creating a fuss. He was, in short, a marketeer's dream. When Super Mario, the self-styled "Lion King," rode the 1997 Tour de France on his Cannondale, he sprinted to two stage wins and enjoyed three days in the yellow jersey, at which point he swapped his red Cannondale for a yellow one. Indeed, Cipollini, with his yellow shorts and yellow glasses, was the first rider to customize his kit according to what jersey he happened to be wearing, although his fondness for costume changes moved to another level in 1999 when he and his Saeco teammates appeared dressed as Romans—with Super Mario, inevitably, as Julius Caesar—during a Tour in which he won four consecutive stages.

Each such stunt incurred a fine, but the attendant publicity made it money well spent. Moreover, you could almost sense the invisible hand of the US bike company gently pushing Cipollini to make ever-more outrageous gestures. Every time he was noticed, so was his bike. During the 1997 Tour, as the television motorcycle rode alongside the yellow-clad Cipollini, he turned to the camera and said, "The best bike—Cannondale. The best bike." A US commentator noted: "I tell ya, this guy is marketing magic."

In 2004, when Cipollini had moved on to another team and Specialized, Saeco, and Cannondale were still deploying the same attention-seeking tactics, the Saeco team raced a stage of the Tour wearing jailbird-style, striped kit emblazoned with one of the best ever marketing slogans: "Legalize my Cannondale."

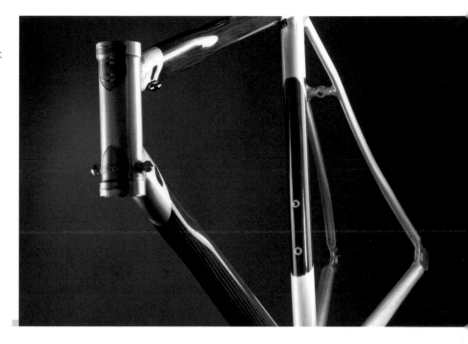

This was a mock protest over the Union Cycliste Internationale's (UCI) weight restrictions on bikes, which—according to Cannondale—rendered their Six13 prototype bikes illegal.

It was clever marketing in more ways than one. In fact, only the very smallest of the Six13 bikes was lighter than the UCI-permitted 15 pounds (6.8 kg); and most of Cannondale's competitors' frames weighed more or less the same as the Six13s. The frames were composite carbon/alloy, with carbon main frames and aluminium stays, and they were launched to the market in 2004 with considerable hype, thanks to the "Legalize my Cannondale" campaign and associated merchandise. In the minds of many, the perception had been established that Cannondales were the lightest bikes on the market.

2000	2004	2005	2012
Cadel Evans is seventh in the men's mountain bike race at the Sydney Olympics. He later transfers to the road with the Saeco team, remaining on a Cannondale for a further year.	The "Legalize my Cannondale" advertising campaign begins with Saeco team leaders posing behind prison bars.	The brand launches its first fully carbon road bike, the Synapse.	Twenty-three-year-old Italian sprinter Elia Viviani wins five races in the first two months of the season.

The Italian connection continued, with Cannondale winning the Giro d'Italia five times thanks to Ivan Gotti, Gilberto Simoni, Damiano Cunego, Danilo Di Luca, and Ivan Basso. In 2010, the year of Basso's Giro success, his Liquigas teammate, Vincenzo Nibali, won the Vuelta a España, giving Cannondale two out of three Grand Tours (overall victory in the Tour de France has so far been elusive).

This success has helped to establish Cannondale as a world leader in road bikes, even as the company itself has undergone radical change. The company overstretched in the late 1990s when it moved into motorsports, and produced off-road motorbikes and all-terrain vehicles. Even while bike sales were booming, this decision proved disastrous, and, in 2003, the company was declared bankrupt. Its assets were purchased at auction by a private equity firm and five years later, with motorsports abandoned and the bike business stable and flourishing, the Cannondale Bicycle Corporation was sold for US $200 million to Dorel Industries, a Canadian conglomerate that sells mass production bikes badged with such long-established and respected names as Schwinn, Mongoose, and GT.

Production shifted from the Bedford, Pennsylvania, factory to Taiwan and Vietnam, and then, at the end of 2010, to a new plant in Taichung, Taiwan, where hourly labour costs are much less expensive than in the United States. Hourly rates make a big difference when a carbon fibre frame takes forty-five hours to manufacture. Whether this move has had a material effect on the quality of the bikes is debatable. Cannondales were always mass-produced; all that has changed is the location where they are put together. The company still has its headquarters in Connecticut. The bikes feature both carbon and alloy. However, with their fat tubes and their lightness and stiffness, they remain unmistakably Cannondale. **RM**

■ Ivan Basso arrives in the Verona arena just after crossing the finish line and winning the ninety-third Giro.

MARIO CIPOLLINI'S 1997 CANNONDALE CAD3

It was the flamboyant Italian Mario Cipollini who brought Cannondale to the attention of the cognoscenti in the European heartland of professional road racing. They were a perfect match: Cipollini, the self-styled "Lion King," challenged the sport's conservative traditions, as did Cannondale's fat-tubed aluminium bad boys (as the US company later named one of its urban bikes).

Cipollini, the most dominant sprinter of the 1990s and early 2000s, notched up some of his biggest victories on a Cannondale, including many of his record forty-two stage wins in the Giro d'Italia, and, in 1999, four consecutive stages of the Tour de France.

Indeed, Cipollini commanded so much attention as a rider that you would almost be forgiven for failing to notice his bike. But in case you did, Cipollini pointed at his machine while in the yellow jersey at the 1997 Tour, saying: "Cannondale—the best bike!" It is this bike, the CAD3, that is featured here; it is similar to the one ridden by Cipollini in the 1997 Tour—apart from during his four days in the yellow jersey, when he switched to an all-yellow Cannondale to match his all-yellow kit. He incurred a fine, but the publicity he attracted made it worth paying.

The "CAD" initials on this bike refer to "Computer-Assisted Design." In 1996, by which time computers had lost their novelty value, the acronym changed to CAAD (Cannondale Advanced Aluminium Design) although, strangely, the "CAD" initials survived on the frames until 1999.

Although Cannondale replaced CAD with CAAD in 1996, the original acronym (Computer-Assisted Design) remained on the frames until 1999.

Spinergy wheels: their bladelike carbon spokes made them light and aerodynamic, but they were deemed dangerous by cycling's governing body, the UCI, and banned for mass-start road races.

Shimano Dura-Ace chainset with thirty-nine- and fifty-three-tooth chainrings.

Saeco is an Italian espresso machine manufacturer that sponsored Mario Cipollini's team. The team began riding Cannondales in 1997.

The CAD3 matched carbon fibre forks with the aluminium frameset.

DESIGN DETAILS

FRAME

The lustrous finish is a feature of Cannondale's oversized aluminium frames. They are all smooth lines, boasting luxurious paint jobs and without the lugs often used to join steel or carbon tubes.

COMPONENTS

Not only did Cipollini, who came from the home of handbuilt frames and Campagnolo components, ride a US-built alloy frame, he would also later use the flagship Shimano Dura-Ace groupset, made in Japan.

■ French artist Jacques Charlier styled Gilbert's "Balls and Glory" frame, which was later auctioned for charity.

■ The Canyon Ultimate CF SLX—the name stands for stiffness, lightness, and comfort.

Canyon

Still run by its original founder, the German manufacturer Canyon bypasses bike shops by selling direct through the internet. Its frames have been proven at the highest level by Philippe Gilbert and Cadel Evans.

Most bike companies distribute their bikes through high-street stores, but Canyon is different—and groundbreaking. Based in Koblenz, Germany, and run by founder Roman Arnold, it sells its own brand bikes direct via the internet. With more than 200 employees, it is the largest such bike company in the world.

The story of Canyon's rise to fame starts with a bike-mad teenager. Roman Arnold was fifteen years old and besotted with cycling when he turned up at a cycling bar in Italy while on a family holiday. He was looking for local enthusiasts to ride with, but they would not let him join them unless he had his hair cut and got some white socks, which he promptly did. "I just wanted to

be in on the action… and I would have done anything for that," he said, many years later. After that experience, he was seriously bitten by the cycling bug, got his first custom-built frame, a Somec, and began racing.

Like so many young bike racers, Roman was supported and chauffeured by his father, Toni, a salesman for a chemical company. In order to occupy his time waiting at the roadside while Roman raced, Toni began selling high-quality bike equipment sourced during the family's frequent trips to Italy. "People knew they could get the best stuff from us," said Roman.

From his father's trailer full of bike parts, the business that would become Canyon—then called Radsport Arnold—grew to occupy a garage and then a shop. Understanding how close the Arnold family was to the German cycling scene, brand managers would pick their brains about specs for forthcoming bikes. "At some point I finally realized that we could do that ourselves," said Roman, and in 1990 Radsport Arnold began making Quintana Roo triathlon bikes under licence in Germany. Soon after, the company began sourcing bikes from the booming hub of world bike production, Taiwan.

Sourcing bikes directly from Taiwan and elsewhere allowed Radsport Arnold to offer better value for money than brands that passed

through an importer. Canyon has carried on with that business model to this day and adopted its current name in 1996. Two years later came a crucial development. Rather than just badging off-the-peg bikes, Canyon began selling its first bike designed in-house—a full-suspension mountain bike. However, Roman Arnold had ambitions beyond just selling value-for-money bicycles. "We wanted bikes that were unique," he said. Having read an article in *Bike* magazine about German bike-makers, Roman contacted the designer and aluminium specialist Lutz Scheffer, who had worked for Porsche. "That was the start of a long and fruitful partnership," acknowledged Roman.

"We wanted bikes that were unique."

ROMAN ARNOLD

Then disaster struck. The bike world raced to make ever lighter frames from the new wonder material, carbon fibre, and in 2002 Canyon proudly launched the Photon carbon fibre mountain bike. The bottom bracket shell broke during a magazine test. It was every bike-maker's worst nightmare. Today, Roman Arnold is philosophical. "You only really grow through your set-backs," he said.

After recalling the Photon frames, Canyon built its own test laboratory, so that it could have even closer control over the quality of the frames it sold, and worked with a brilliant young composites engineer, Michael Kaiser. The result in 2005 was the F10 road racing frame, which became, at the time, the holder of the record for the best stiffness to weight ratio in tests by *Tour* magazine. It was "the best racing frame in the world," said Arnold.

With a carefully selected group of components, many handmade for the task, Canyon was able to build an 8-pound 2-ounce (3.7 kg) bike around the F10, further increasing the company's prestige among weight-obsessed German cyclists. However, it is not enough to make superstiff and superlightweight bikes. In order to really prove that your machines have what it takes, they have to race—and win—at the highest level possible. Canyon had always been involved with racing, with programmes such as the Young Heroes scheme, which supplies fifteen talented young riders with top-grade equipment and mentoring from legendary German sprinter Erik Zabel.

In 2009, Canyon took the ultimate plunge and sponsored a top pro team, Silence-Lotto. The gamble paid off when the formidable Belgian Philippe Gilbert took numerous wins over the year, and the team's Australian star, Cadel Evans, rescued a season dogged with problems by winning the world road race championship. "I was there myself… and it was simply out of this world," said Roman Arnold. **JS**

■ Team Silence-Lotto, during the team time trial at the 2009 Tour de France.

"The F10… the best racing frame in the world."

ROMAN ARNOLD

*"Right from the start
we didn't have a clue
what we were doing."*

GERARD VROOMEN

Cervélo

The Cervélo story is a cycling fairy tale: two students at university in Canada came up with a design for a frame, managed to sell it, then saw their bikes win some of the world's biggest races—culminating with the Tour de France in 2008.

"Right from the start we didn't have a clue what we were doing," commented Cervélo's co-founder, Dutchman Gerard Vroomen. He met Phil White, his Canadian business partner, when they were both engineering students at McGill University in Montreal in the 1990s. For their university project they devised a bike frame with an aerodynamic design, based around fluid dynamics and hours of wind tunnel testing, but they did not know the bike industry. All they had, in fact, was a design that they believed in— and persistence.

"We put our own money, a couple of thousand dollars, into the prototype," said Vroomen. "We thought the best way to make that money back was to set up a patent, sell it to

people, and then go into the real world and find jobs." In the early 1990s that plan proved difficult. However, in 1994, in a desperate attempt to launch their fledgling business, Vroomen decided to write to the double world road race champion Gianni Bugno. He pointed out to the racer that although he had a strong position on his Coppi road bike, he lacked aerodynamics when in time trial mode. The trouble was that Vroomen did not have Bugno's address. All he knew was that the rider lived in Italy. The envelope therefore read "Gianni Bugno, Italy."

"I thought someone in the post office would know which city he lived in," said Vroomen, "and that it would end up in the right hands." That assumption was hopeful, to put it mildly.

Gerard Vroomen and Phil White making the one-off Baracchi frame in the 1990s.

The Cervélo P3's aerodynamic styling reduces drag resistance. It is the most copied bike in time trial history.

However, a week later the telephone rang, and it was Bugno on the other end. He sounded interested but his existing bike supplier had a different reaction. "We took some bikes to his sponsor and they went ballistic," said Vroomen. "We even offered them the bikes with their logo on, but they weren't having any of it."

Vroomen and White persisted, and set up Cervélo in 1995, the company name a portmanteau of *cervello*, the Italian word for brain, and *vélo*. The first mini breakthrough came at the Sydney Olympics in 2000. White knew the Canadian team mechanic, who introduced him to the rider Eric Wohlberg. Wohlberg had not been confirmed for the Olympics at that time and his sponsor, GT, had not given him a bike. When he was called up to the Canadian team a week before the Games began, it was Vroomen and White who came to the rescue, and supplied him with a bike. Wohlberg went on to win the national title—and the next six titles—on a Cervélo. These victories helped to establish the Cervélo name in Canada. Or, as Vroomen acknowledged: "That helped jump-start some notoriety. We started to build some bikes and sell them in Canada."

Triathlon initially proved a receptive market, but road racing was a harder nut to crack. Yet, oddly, a significant point in Cervélo's favour was the Union Cycliste Internationale's (UCI) 2000 ruling on bike dimensions, which rendered illegal some of the more cutting-edge designs and configurations of the time. Fortunately for Vroomen and White, their bikes conformed to traditional measurements. In addition they had tested them in the wind tunnel, with excellent results. After the ruling, many other manufacturers almost gave up on innovation— or, in Vroomen's words, "dumbed down their designs to fit the rules," but Vroomen and White studied the regulations, then tried to rise to the challenge of producing bikes that were more aerodynamic, but also legal.

■ Used by Fabian
Cancellara, Stuart
O'Grady, and Johan
Vansummeren, the
R3 has been on the
Paris–Roubaix podium
every year from 2006
to 2011.

Carlos Sastre in time
trial action on his way
to winning the 2008
Tour de France.

An early example was the P3 time trial bike, with its curved seat tube. It proved popular with triathletes, which did not necessarily curry favour with the highly traditional road community. However, one of the giants of the US market, Trek, began to take triathlon seriously and Vroomen believes that this decision legitimized a market that Cervélo had pioneered.

In the years following Wohlberg's endorsement of Cervélo bikes—and thanks to the expanding triathlon market—the company enjoyed a period of huge growth. It developed a new and influential triathlon bike, the Eyre, with an aero down tube. Other manufacturers copied it, which, like Trek's decision to take them on in the triathlon market, only increased Cervélo's credibility.

Next came the leap from triathlon to road, completing a circle that had begun with Vroomen's letter to Bugno. Again, it saw the company reaching out to the European peloton, but this time to a team. In the autumn of 2002, as Cervélo toyed with the idea of supplying a

pro Tour team for the first time, it heard that Bjarne Riis's CSC squad was on the lookout for a sponsor. Litespeed, the North American brand that pioneered the use of titanium, was also in the running, but Riis's desire to push technological and aerodynamic boundaries saw him team up with Cervélo. "We'd won events in time trialling but the effort it takes to sponsor a top-level team isn't something you can afford as a small company," explained Vroomen. "Riis was really interested in new technology and using aero frames on the road. He really made us a great deal, but that didn't change the fact that we had to deliver close to 200 frames to a team and offer them support."

The honeymoon period turned out to be brief. It became clear that providing bikes for a consumer market was poor preparation for supplying a pro team. Bikes were written off one after another at the start of 2003; the majority of the issues stemmed from a problem with the seat tube. "We thought they were going to cancel the contract with us," said Vroomen.

"So we scheduled a trip to Lucca to meet Riis. We were worried, because we'd lose so much face if we lost the contract after just four months. But he was calm and gave us more time."

Although Vroomen admits that Cervélo and Riis's other equipment suppliers—Speedplay and Zipp—"were all equally clueless about being in the pro peloton," he gives credit to Riis for sticking with them "when a lot of people were screaming at him." In fact, the partnership between CSC and Cervélo went on to blossom in a way that no one could have imagined. The team became the best in the world, with back to back wins in the Paris–Roubaix Classic courtesy of Fabian Cancellara and Stuart O'Grady, victory in the 2006 Giro d'Italia with Ivan Basso, and then, in 2008, the big one: the Tour de France, won by Carlos Sastre.

Vroomen picks out Sastre's Tour win as a highlight of the collaboration, although, perhaps surprisingly, not the ultimate highlight. "Paris–Roubaix with Cancellara and then O'Grady were the best. For equipment, that really is the race of truth. It's not that hard to make a frame for a 128-pound (58-kg) climber going up a hill, but to have a 187-pound (85-kg) guy going over the cobbles is a real test of material." "Cancellara's win was only two or three weeks after we introduced his bike, the R3, which had been designed specifically for the race." A year later O'Grady won as well. Speaking in 2011, Vroomen added: "And we've not been off the podium in that race since."

When the relationship with CSC ended in 2008, Cervélo took an even bolder step: it launched the Cervélo Test Team. Like its frames, it was a new concept. Tired of the constraints of working with another team, and also the doping scandals that overshadowed some of CSC's successes, the Cervélo Test Team decided to set up its own pro squad.

Initially the plan was to start small and grow. As the name suggests, the intention was also to

*"Riis was calm
and gave us more
time... when a lot
of people were
screaming at him."*

GERARD VROOMEN

- Cervélo Test Team riders compete in the fourth stage of the 2009 Tour de France.

- Thor Hushovd starts stage two of the 2011 Tour of California, from Nevada City, riding for Garmin Cervélo.

1994	2003	2006	2008
Gerard Vroomen writes a letter to Italian legend Gianni Bugno in which he suggests ways that the rider can improve his position on his bike.	Bjarne Riis's CSC team becomes the first European professional squad to use Cervélo bikes.	Ivan Basso annihilates the field at the Giro d'Italia, winning by more than nine minutes. His reputation plummets months later when he is embroiled in a doping scandal.	Carlos Sastre, a reliable but unspectacular climber, stuns the cycling world by winning the Tour de France. It is Cervélo's first Tour de France win.

use the team to gain quality feedback in order to develop new products. With a modest budget, the team began assembling the necessary partners and infrastructure. But days after the 2008 Tour, Vroomen met Sastre prior to a criterium in Belgium. Vroomen informed the Spaniard that the company would be parting with Riis at the end of the season and thanked Sastre for providing a Tour win as a send-off. Sastre's ears pricked up. His contract with Riis was up at the end of the season and he told Vroomen that he wanted to join his new team. Taken aback—but delighted— Vroomen and White discussed the possibility. It meant significantly upping the ambitions of the team, and the budget, but it was far too good an opportunity to pass up: with the addition of Sastre, the Cervélo Test Team would be playing with the big boys.

Thor Hushovd was the other major signing, and the team opened its debut season in 2009 with a bang, winning multiple races. Heinrich Haussler had a breakthrough spring, whereas Sastre won two stages and finished in the top ten of the Giro. Hushovd won the green points jersey at the Tour, where Haussler won a stage.

In contrast, the second year proved a relative disappointment, but the biggest challenge was financial. The team was always on the lookout for a title sponsor, but it could not have been searching at a worse time because the world recession sent companies running for the hills when asked for the millions of euros required to back a team. Vroomen and White were forced to pull the plug during the 2010 Vuelta; even a scintillating world road race win by Hushovd could not save them. "The team grew too quickly," admitted Vroomen. "The results we achieved in the first few months were based on

the riders, who gelled really well together. It still wasn't a big team, and we had a relatively modest budget, but expectations really rose quickly."

Sastre moved to Geox, but he never truly rediscovered the form that had carried him up Alpe d'Heuz and towards the Tour de France title. Haussler, Hushovd, and a clutch of other Cervélo Test Team riders departed to Garmin for the 2011 season, where Cervélo became the co-sponsor and bike provider.

As for Gerard Vroomen, he departed the company in May 2011, leaving White to steer the ship. "The future is still very bright," said Vroomen. "The same thing that happened in triathlon ten years ago is happening on the road now with aero bikes. You see everyone flooding that market. And all these companies are benching themselves against Cervélo." **DB**

2009

Cervélo Test Team's first season sees it win twenty-five races, including three stages at the Giro d'Italia. The team also launches a women's squad.

2010

Thor Hushovd wins the world road race in Australia on a Cervélo. Emma Pooley wins the women's world time trial, also on a Cervélo.

2010

The Cervélo Test Team folds due to financial pressures, but the company continues to work in the sport, supplying Garmin with bikes for the next season.

2011

A new time trial bike—the P5—is launched at a press event in Spain. The most obvious change compared to its predecessor, the P4, is a much more aggressively styled frame.

The Cervélo S3S3 was ridden by Thor Hushovd during the 2011 season.

"A bike must turn into a bike which didn't exist yet."

CINELLI MANIFESTO

Cinelli bars. With saddles, he collaborated with Tommaso Nieddu, of Vittoria fame, to produce a plastic version, the Unicanitor. With pedals, he started out with a high-quality toe-strap before introducing a clipless system, the M71, in 1971—more than a decade before Look came along and consigned the toe-strap to history.

In 1978, having turned sixty-two, Cinelli sold the business to the Colombo family, and it eventually became part of the Gruppo combine, alongside the Columbus and 3T brands. When Angelo Luigi Colombo founded the Columbus tubing company in 1919, he said that he wanted to do business in iron and steel, and make a fair and honest profit. This was an ethic with which Cinelli could identify, and the Colombo family seemed the right kind of people to carry on the Cinelli name. After the company sale, Cinelli turned his back on cycling altogether and retired to a villa in the Tuscan countryside where he tried his hand at cultivating olives.

In 1978 Antonio Colombo, son of Angelo Luigi, took on the running of the Cinelli business. Cinelli's own son, Andrea, worked on the company's marketing side and later ventured into making bikes under the Cinetica name. (Andrea Cinelli's Cinetica Giotto was a failure, albeit a beautiful one.) Colombo has been nothing but faithful to Cino Cinelli's principles; however, he has also sought to push the business forward. In 1979, Colombo showed off a prototype of the Cinelli Laser. It had a futuristic-looking frame with tapered tubing and aerodynamic fairing gussets. Those who examined it assumed that it was carbon-moulded, but the Laser was all steel, with the gussets seamlessly filed by hand. The Laser was not available to be raced until 1983, but it quickly became a success. But how futuristic was it? Futuristic enough to be brought back to Eurobike 2011 and not look out of place among its modern competitors.

A decade before Colombo introduced the Laser, Cinelli himself had built a bike for Ole

■ The M71 pedal. To release the shoe, the rider had to reach down and operate a lever.

■ Gintautas Umaras rides a Cinelli Laser, representing the Soviet Union in the 1988 Olympic Games.

■ A 1967 world championship Mod B features, from top to bottom, a Cinelli engraved emblem on the head tube, a flat fork crown, Cinelli logo, and Campagnolo shifters.

■ The Spinaci handlebars were banned because they were deemed to be dangerous.

■ Gilberto Simoni during the 2003 Giro d'Italia. The bike featured Cinelli Ram combination stem and handlebars.

Ritter's 1974 attempt to reclaim the Hour record from Eddy Merckx. Although Ritter beat his own record, he failed to match Merckx's mark. Asked in the 1970s about the Hour record by *Bicycling* magazine, Cinelli outlined all the things that he would do to build a modern record-beating machine. Small wheels and longer cranks were his priorities; he believed that smaller wheels meant higher cadence, while longer cranks offered more leverage. His ideal Hour bike would also be low profile, although Cinelli figured that no one would be interested in setting a record on such a bike because it would detract from their personal achievement. His judgement was spot-on and, before the Union Cycliste Internationale (UCI) finally outlawed the bike in 2000, five different riders had set new records, only to see their bikes attract much of the glory.

The UCI's inability to make up its mind on technological issues had serious implications for Antonio Colombo in the 1990s. In the years after Greg LeMond's 1989 Tour victory—when, using a tri-bar equipped bike, he snatched the *maillot jaune* from Laurent Fignon on the race's last day—more and more manufacturers turned their attention to handlebars, and worked on ways to improve their aerodynamic efficiency and also to offer riders more riding positions. Cinelli's contribution was the Spinaci, introduced in 1993. Shorter than traditional tri-bars, Spinacis bolted on to an ordinary handlebar and offered advantages when climbing and also when riding on the flat. The UCI approved Spinacis in 1994.

Spinacis sold well, and Cinelli was obliged to open a new 4-square-mile (7,000-sq-m) manufacturing plant to keep up with demand.

1948	1963	1970	1974
Cino Cinelli founds the Cinelli company four years after his racing career ends. The headquarters are in Milan, where they remain to this day.	Somewhat later than many other manufacturers, the company begins to produce alloy stems and handlebars.	Cinelli engineers the M71, the first quick-release pedal, specifically for racing. Americans refer to them as "death pedals." Four generations of the pedal are later produced.	Using a Cinelli-designed.aerodynamic bike, Ole Ritter breaks his own Hour record but not the world record.

Then, in the 1997, Tour de France race director Jean-Marie Leblanc blamed both Spinacis and carbon-spoked wheels for an unusually high number of crashes in the opening stages of the race. When the UCI weighed in, it might have considered whether enhanced methods of doping were driving the peloton along, but it did not—the UCI banned the handlebars. Cinelli's newly opened factory no longer rang to the sounds of 500,000 Spinacis being manufactured per year.

Urban cycling helped to save the company. In 2000, Cinelli introduced the Bootleg, an on-trend bicycle for non-professional cyclists. Available only in black, the Bootleg is as much about attitude as it is a means of transport. But the most profitable venture for Cinelli in recent years was another innovation in handlebars: the Ram handlebar. A moulded carbon composite bar with an integrated stem, the Ram bar is more ergonomic than traditional bars, and has flat surfaces for the palm of the hand and the thumb, which offers a greater variety of comfortable riding positions. The Ram also looks as gorgeous as anything in Cinelli's history.

Although Cinelli's products have been used by, and associated with, many of the greatest riders over the decades, the company's biggest brand ambassador has always been Cino Cinelli's unblemished reputation for quality. Time has passed; it is now more than thirty years since Alberto Colombo took over the company, and more than a decade since Cino Cinelli died. However, people who are looking for quality still turn to the Cinelli name, which suggests that Colombo is doing something right. This is not surprising given that Cinelli hand-picked his successor and most certainly knew quality when he saw it. **FMK**

1978	1980	1985	2001
After thirty years under Cino Cinelli, the company is sold to Colombo: one of Italy's leading steel-tubing manufacturers.	The Laser pursuit and time trial model pioneers the use of tungsten inert gas welding in frames.	The Cinelli company introduces the first mountain bikes to Italy. Named the Rampichino or "little climber," the bike leaves other Italian manufacturers trailing behind.	Cino Cinelli, the Cinelli company founder, dies at the age of eighty-five.

The Cinelli Laser, with disc wheels
painted by artist Keith Haring.

■ Ernesto Colnago's first success as a cyclist came at the Coppa Gabellini in 1949.

■ The 1960 Italian gold medal team during the Olympic pursuit race in the Velodromo Olimpico.

Colnago

One of the prestige names in world cycling, Colnago encapsulates Italian style, craftsmanship, and innovation. The company's success began with the man who is still at the head of the business, Ernesto Colnago.

"We've got our own particular style," said Ernesto Colnago in 2011 as he outlined his philosophy. "The heart of this company is passion."

Set up in 1952, and celebrating its sixtieth anniversary in 2012 as Colnago himself marks his eightieth birthday, this well-known Italian brand—instantly recognizable by its ace of clubs motif—is one of the most prestigious marques in the sport. It mixes design innovation, excellence, and beauty with success in most of the great races.

Ernesto Colnago has travelled a long way with cycling: he has acted as mechanic to some of the sport's biggest names, including Eddy Merckx and Fiorenzo Magni, and produced a long line of groundbreaking bikes. However, Colnago has stayed close to his roots. Born in 1932 in

Cambiago, he still lives in this small dormitory town to the east of Milan. In fact, Colnago's home is directly across the road from the factory that carries his name. It is located in the Viale Brianza, and sixty-five years ago, the street was an unpaved track frequented by chickens. It also provided the setting for Colnago's first victory as a competitive cyclist at the age of fifteen. A photograph of the teenage Colnago holding aloft his prize hangs opposite his desk on the wall of his office, which is within yards of where the picture was taken many years ago.

By the age of fifteen, Colnago had already been working for two years at the nearby Gloria bike factory. After four years, Colnago had progressed to head of department at Gloria, but was focused on making a career in racing. This changed when he broke his leg during a race. While laid up at home, Colnago was able to build wheels for Gloria on a piece rate, and he realized that he could make five times more money working this way than earning a regular wage at the factory. Also, as news of Colnago's wheel-building skills spread, he began to get commissions from local racers, which further boosted his earnings and reputation.

Before long, Colnago handed in his notice at Gloria. In 1952, with financial backing from his father, he set himself up in a small workshop in Cambiago. Despite his youth, Colnago quickly won commissions from some of the biggest names of the day, including Giorgio Albani and the legendary Fausto Coppi. Colnago's big breakthrough came when he was introduced to Fiorenzo Magni, already a two-time winner of the Giro d'Italia and the only rider in racing history

"We've got our own particular style. The heart of this company is passion."

ERNESTO COLNAGO

to have won the Tour of Flanders on three consecutive occasions.

Towards the end of his racing career, Magni had been troubled by a knee problem that Colnago realized was caused by his cranks not being perpendicular. The champion left his bike with the mechanic, who stripped it down and replaced the crank. Two days later, Magni turned up at the Cambiago workshop to declare that his knee problem had gone and to ask Colnago if he would become his mechanic on the Nivea team.

In June 1955, just weeks into his first season as a professional team mechanic, Colnago celebrated alongside Magni as the veteran Italian won his third Giro title, edging out Coppi by a mere eleven seconds. In third place was young Gastone Nencini. Two years later, Colnago was Nencini's mechanic when he won his first Giro and told journalists on the way to that victory: "If I manage to win this jersey, the credit must go to Ernesto Colnago, a young mechanic from Lombardy who has built me an unbeatable bicycle. It's true to say that before he came to our team we had some problems with our bikes. But with Colnago my problems have been solved."

That was in 1957, by which time Colnago had been building his own bikes for three years. Initially only local amateurs raced on them, but as Colnago's fame increased, so too did demand for his bikes. The first major success on a Colnago bike came, aptly, at the Rome Olympics in 1960, when Italian team pursuit member Luigi Arienti rode one to the gold medal. Throughout the 1960s, as Colnago worked for riders such as Gianni Motta and the Italian national team, more successes followed: Motta took the Giro and a host of other titles on bikes built by his mechanic.

In the early 1970s, Colnago's reputation, both as a mechanic and frame-builder, really took off. This phase began in 1970 at Milan–San Remo, when Michele Dancelli ended a seventeen-year drought for Italy in the country's biggest one-day race. Riding one of Colnago's bikes, which was branded with the name of team sponsor Molteni, Dancelli was acclaimed as a hero who had lifted a curse from the Italians in their most cherished Classic. Photographs that were taken as Dancelli crossed the finish line on San Remo's Via Roma show Colnago standing in the team car, with Dancelli's spare Colnago bike slung over his shoulder. That same evening, Colnago met *La Gazzetta dello Sport* reporter Bruno Raschi in a restaurant in nearby Laigueglia. Raschi had written that Dancelli had won San Remo on a bike that was "in bloom." "Why don't you make a motif from that image?" Raschi asked Colnago. Hoping to become an "ace" in the bike manufacturing world, Colnago put the two ideas together; the result was the ace of clubs symbol that has adorned his bikes ever since.

By that time, Colnago had already been working with the Belgian phenomenon Eddy Merckx, and had been producing wheels for him. In 1971, the link between the two men became official when Merckx joined Molteni and began racing—and winning—on bikes designed and built by Colnago. The Italian master frame-builder later calculated that he had built more than a hundred bikes for "The Cannibal," more than twenty of them in just one season alone. "He was one of the most demanding, if not *the* most demanding rider of all. Eddy Merckx studied his bikes in minute detail. More than once he visited my workshop in Cambiago to follow the various phases of construction," Colnago later recalled.

1939	1949	1952	1966
Young Ernesto Colnago receives his first bike, a black third-hand model. He gives it the name "Perla."	Colnago achieves his first major victory at the Coppa Gabellini race. He would follow this with a further twelve wins.	The first Colnago workshop opens at No. 10 Via Garibaldi, Cambiago. The shop's sole workbench is made from a mulberry tree given to Colnago by his father.	Having left Magni to join Gianni Motta's Molteni team in 1962, Colnago's four years of hard work pay off when Motta is victorious at the Giro d'Italia.

■ Eddy Merckx wins the 1971 world professional 168-mile (270-km) road championship race on a Colnago.

"Eddy Merckx visited my workshop in Cambiago to follow the various phases of construction."

ERNESTO COLNAGO

1985

Just as his career appears to be in its twilight, Joop Zoetemelk rides a Colnago bike to victory at the world championship in Montello.

1996

Johan Museeuw wins the first of his three Paris–Roubaix titles. He ends the year by taking the world cycling championship in Lugano, Switzerland.

2002

Cadel Evans, riding a Colnago, makes history by becoming the first Australian to wear the *maglia rosa* at the Giro d'Italia.

2012

Anthony Charteau claims the prestigious polka-dot jersey of the King of the Mountains after winning the Tour de France on a Colnago C59 Italia.

- Colnago and Ferrari met in 1986. Their first bike, "the Concept" was made with hand-wrapped carbon fibre.

- The Master Pista Inseguimento track bike with a pink finish and disk wheels.

- An early carbon fibre monocoque track bike with full-disk wheels and tri-bars.

- A mid-1990s track version of the C42. Pavel Tonkov used the C42 during the Giro.

The pair's most renowned collaboration concerned Merckx's attempt on the world Hour record in 1972. Colnago knew that Merckx's bike would need to be as light as possible to give him the best chance of beating Ole Ritter's existing mark of 30.23 miles (48.65 km). Every part that could be was shaved or drilled. Special alloys were developed in the United States because the technology was not then available in Europe. The result was a supersleek set-up that tipped the scales at 12.67 pounds (5.75 kg). Riding this extremely cutting-edge machine in the rarified air of Mexico City, Merckx obliterated the record, adding 826 yards (755 m) to it.

After one more season with Molteni, Colnago took on a new challenge in 1974, and moved to

the Scic team led by Gianbattista Baronchelli. He provided the team with Colnago bikes, which made that year the first in which the ace of clubs logo appeared on a pro team's machines. Baronchelli came within twelve seconds of beating Merckx at the 1974 Giro, which initiated a run of almost unparalleled success for the frame-builder that has continued up to the present day.

During the late 1970s and throughout the 1980s, Colnago worked with many of Italy's great names, including Franco Bitossi, Giovanni Battaglin, and Giuseppe "Beppe" Saronni. Spotted by Colnago as a junior, Saronni spent most of his career racing on Colnago bikes and took the 1982 world title at Goodwood on one. The teams riding Colnago bikes during that period are almost

■ A classic Colnago steel bike with gear shifting on the down tube, and straight steel forks.

■ The Colnago used by Giuseppe Saronni to win the 1983 edition of Milan–San Remo.

■ The Colnago Ferrari road bike, equipped with Campagnolo components.

■ This innovative off-road bike is made from carbon fibre and built without a seat tube.

as renowned: Del Tongo, Inoxpran, Kwantum, Ariostea, and, later, Lampre. Colnago victories ran into the hundreds and included more major titles. Freddy Maertens and Joop Zoetemelk won the world title riding the ace of clubs marque in 1981 and 1985, respectively. Saronni won the Giro in 1979 and 1983. Yet Colnago's greatest collaboration was still to come.

In September 1993, Saronni organized a meeting in Milan between Colnago and Giorgio Squinzi, the president of Italian plastics manufacturer Mapei. Squinzi had taken over the failed Eldor team in May and wanted to expand the team into a world-leading outfit. The meeting went well, and Colnago went off to the Cologne bike show. Working as technical consultant to

the Spanish Clas team, led by Swiss rider Tony Rominger, he met up with Rominger and Clas team manager Juan Fernández at the show. There were problems with Clas, they told Colnago, who barely hesitated before calling Squinzi to say that Rominger and eight other riders were available to join Mapei, with Clas happy to be the secondary sponsor. The deal was done, and what was to become the world's most successful team of all time was established for the 1994 season.

That first year there were fifty-eight victories from a line-up that included Rominger, Franco Ballerini, Mauro Gianetti, Andrea Tafi, Gianluca Bortolami, and Abraham Olano. The highlight was Rominger breaking the world Hour record not once but twice, each time on a bike designed and

ERNESTO COLNAGO ON HIS RIDERS

"I've been involved in cycling for over fifty years and I've always tried to help young riders as much as I could, perhaps because my own career was cut short by a broken leg. I started as a team mechanic in the mid-fifties and so will always remember Italian riders like Fiorenzo Magni, Gastone Nencini, Michele Dancelli, and Gianni Motta. I worked closely with the Molteni team and so Eddy Merckx rode my bikes even though my name wasn't on the frame. I built the bike he used to break the Hour record in 1972; it weighed just 5.750 kg (12.67 lbs). I first sponsored a team in the seventies and discovered Beppe Saronni when he was a talented but very young amateur. Beppe was a huge talent, and his late attack to win the world title in Goodwood in 1982 still makes me smile and feel very proud.

In the eighties I helped Russian and Chinese riders. I saw Pavel Tonkov win the junior world title and signed him straight away. He went on to win the Giro d'Italia on a Colnago in 1996. The Mapei team was a special team for me because first Tony Rominger set a new Hour record on a special bike I built for him and then Mapei dominated Paris–Roubaix with my C40 carbon fibre bikes. Taking first, second, and third in 1996 was incredible, but I'll never forget when Franco Ballerini won in 1998. He was the last great Italian rider able to dominate the pavé."

EDDY MERCKX

Thought by many to be the greatest cyclist who has ever lived, Merckx won the 1971 Milan–San Remo on a custom-made Colnago. He won the Tour de France five times.

GIUSEPPE SARONNI

In a career lasting from 1977 to 1989, Saronni won 193 races. His partnership with Colnago reached its zenith when he won the 1982 world road title.

JOOP ZOETEMELK

The Dutchman spent the last years of his career on a Colnago; here, aged thirty-nine, he wears the rainbow jersey of world champion after becoming the oldest winner of the title in 1985.

FRANCO BALLERINI

Italian cyclist Franco Ballerini in action on his way to winning the ninety-sixth edition of the Paris–Roubaix cycling race, northern France, on April 12, 1998.

built by Colnago. He opted for steel because he believed that it would make the bike more stable and therefore more suitable for a track novice such as Rominger. Weight was saved by drilling out the chain, the specially produced sixty-tooth chainring—CNC-machined by a local artisan because Campagnolo lacked the equipment in its range—and the handlebars, and also by using titanium spokes fitted with aluminium nipples. Riding in Bordeaux, Rominger set two astonishing marks: he beat Miguel Indurain's Hour record by 874 yards (799 m), and later broke it again by 2,462 yards (2,251 m) when he completed 34.356 miles (55.291 km).

A lesser known but ultimately more influential bike was the carbon fibre C40 on which Mapei's riders won hundreds of victories, including five in Paris–Roubaix. Many people, even within the Mapei team, initially questioned Colnago's insistence that a carbon fibre frame, with its straight Precisa forks, could stand up to the rigours of Roubaix. However, Colnago was proved correct from the start, because Ballerini finished third and admitted that the C40 gave him a better ride than bikes that were fitted with suspension forks, which were in vogue at the time for the sport's toughest one-day race. "Ferrari's engineers had shown us that a straight-bladed fork absorbed shock better," Colnago said later. "Despite innumerable criticisms, everyone soon copied it and all the Roubaixs won by Mapei featured the Precisa fork." The big breakthrough came in 1995, when Ballerini took the first of his two Roubaix titles. A year later, three Mapei riders finished alone in the Roubaix velodrome, with Johan Museeuw taking victory after a spectacular team performance.

Mapei bowed out of the sport after scoring ninety-four victories in 2002, but Colnago has continued to work with some of the sport's leading teams and riders, among them Belgian cyclo-cross star Sven Nys, with whom he developed the beautiful and effective Cross

■ A 1779 Mexico Oro. A gold-plated version was presented to Pope John Paul II. It features, from top to bottom, gold rear forks, Ernesto Colnago–engraved pedal, gold-plated front forks and gear shifters, and Colnago brakes.

"We've been the first company to experiment and then everyone else has copied us."

ERNESTO COLNAGO

Prestige, and, more recently, the Europcar team. At the 2011 Tour, Thomas Voeckler rode Colnago's latest range-topping model, the C59 Italia, into the yellow jersey and almost to the most improbable of Tour victories, thus underlining Colnago's ongoing ability to provide bikes that can compete with the very best.

"For me, the whole thing revolves around my love for bicycles," said Colnago. "I don't like it when people start off with marketing and colours and then think about the technology. That's the wrong way round. You can follow the market or you can follow fashion, but elegance is still elegance no matter what your driving philosophy. There's a base of classic elegance in all of the frames that we do. We've got our own particular style. The heart of this company is passion."

That passion has produced a vast amount of innovation, including successful experiments in the 1950s with cold-forging to manufacture more responsive and less rigid forks, and a rethinking of fork design with Precisa in the 1990s. "Colnago has been the innovator of so much technology in the bike industry," the company's founder reflected. "You can see so many things that we've developed and that other companies have picked up and then mass-produced. That's one of the features of this company, that we're focused on innovation, on doing what we can to push bike technology forwards. That's often the way it has been at Colnago. We've been the first company to experiment and then everyone else has copied us." The evidence of this is everywhere. **PC**

■ Tony Rominger set his Hour record in October 1994 on a Colnago.

■ Belgium's Johan Museeuw and Team Mapei win the 1996 Paris–Roubaix.

FRANCO BALLERINI'S COLNAGO C40

Franco Ballerini's Colnago C40 did not set any world records. Nor did it demonstrate an abundance of technological advances in bike design. But as a snapshot, as a single moment in the history of the sport, it helped to produce one of the most memorable and iconic displays cycling has ever seen.

In 1998 Ballerini, having won the race three years previously, was one of the favourites going into Paris–Roubaix, but few expected him to do what he did. Breaking away on one particularly treacherous section of cobbles, the Mons-en-Pévèle, with more than 43 miles (70 km) remaining, he rode alone to hold off the entire field, and won by four minutes, fourteen seconds: the biggest margin of victory since Eddy Merckx in 1971. His rival, Magnus Backstedt, realized that the Italian was about to make his move and tried to give chase. However, with just a few bike lengths between the pair, Ballerini looked back and accelerated again. Backstedt and the chasing pack fell away; they would not see Ballerini again until the podium celebrations in Roubaix.

Ballerini's ride that day was a pure demonstration of the unadulterated synergy between man and machine. His powerful physique was ideal for the tough terrain and, while other riders bashed their way through the race, Ballerini appeared to glide over the pavé.

Ballerini died after crashing during a car rally in 2010. Poignantly, the C40 he rode to victory in the 1998 Paris–Roubaix sits in Ernesto Colnago's factory in Cambiago, the mud and grit still caked to it.

Ballerini rode to Roubaix glory on a San Marco Regal saddle. This model came with a full-sized shell, and fairly generous padding, essential for the cobbles that make Roubaix such a demanding and prestigious race.

Ambrosio supplied wheels for the Mapei team. At Roubaix they used low-profile aluminium rims.

Ernesto Colnago was a huge fan of Franco Ballerini and still keeps the Classics star's bike in his factory.

LA REDOUT
12

Rival teams and manufacturers toyed with mountain bike technology for races such as Paris–Roubaix, but Colnago stayed true to his principles in design.

DESIGN DETAILS

FULL CARBON STRAIGHT FORKS

Colnago's C40 is one of the legends of the peloton. The company was one of the first to move to straight forks, and Ballerini's bike was a full carbon set-up. Ballerini's bike was designed with standard Colnago tube and lug carbon construction.

CUSTOM GEOMETRY

This bike was structured with custom geometry with a longer rear end and additional tyre clearance for the mud kicked up along the Paris–Roubaix course. Vittoria tubular tyres were fitted, with Shimano Dura-Ace nine-speed components.

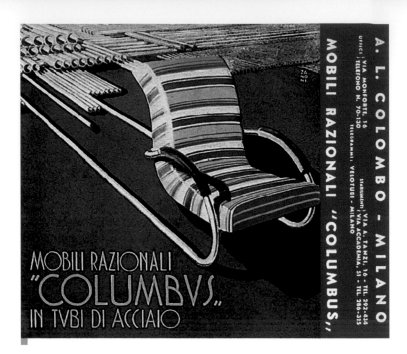

MOBILI RAZIONALI "COLUMBVS" IN TVBI DI ACCIAIO

A. L. COLOMBO - MILANO
MOBILI RAZIONALI "COLUMBUS"

Columbus

Steel was the frame-builder's material of choice for most of the 20th century, and it was Columbus who provided the lightweight tubesets to many of the best-known manufacturers. As steel makes a welcome return, the Italian firm remains a big player.

■ In the 1930s Columbus developed a reputation for quality home and office furniture, using lightweight tubes that would later be adopted to make bike frames.

■ Eddy Merckx (left) and Angelo Colombo (left centre) show off a frame bearing the great racer's name in 1973.

There has only ever been one glamorous name in the world of tubing manufacture—Columbus. This is not surprising: if anyone can make the manufacture of metal tubes anything but stultifying, the Italians can. Moreover, in the history of the country's cycle industry, there have been many respected makers of tubes, but none has had the same hold on the imagination of the bespoke bicycle enthusiast as Columbus.

The great Milanese firm's history stretches back over more than nine decades to the period immediately after World War I, when the young Angelo Luigi Colombo founded the parent company, AL Colombo. Manufacturing steel tubing suitable for seatposts, handlebars,

and pedals as well as bike frames, Colombo soon found himself supplying major cycle manufacturers such as Bianchi and Atala, and, in 1931, installed the equipment needed to draw the seamless tubes that were vital to the construction of lightweight cycles and motorcycles. The company also contributed to the construction of aircraft: in the same way that the rival British firm of Reynolds supplied steel tubes for aircraft engine mountings, so too did Colombo.

Nonetheless much of the firm's growing reputation during the 1930s was built on the making of home and office furniture— seating, in particular—based on frames of chromed tubular steel. Examples of this so-called "rational" furniture, made in collaboration with avant-garde designers and architects of the age, are stored in a vast warehouse on the Columbus premises outside Milan, where their fading, sagging fabrics contrast sharply with the still-shapely tubes from which they hang. At the same time, Colombo introduced branded steel tubesets conceived especially for cycle manufacture. While Aelle, rolled and seam-welded in a chrome-manganese steel, was to live on for more than half a century as a low-cost tubeset intended for cycles suited to touring and everyday riding, the Columbus brand was immediately differentiated by its use of advanced technologies such as the cold-drawing of seamless chrome-molybdenum steel and conical internal butting.

In 1977, Antonio Colombo—youngest son of Angelo—left his position as chairman of AL Colombo, separated the Columbus brand from the parent company, and set about turning the new Columbus Srl. into a specialist cycle tube manufacturer. However, there was a small problem: Reynolds, manufacturer of the fabled and venerable 531 tubeset, was widely considered to be the leader in the field. Its 531, cold-drawn from manganese-molybdenum steel, had been around since 1934, so could not be considered cutting edge.

Columbus began what became something of a tradition of innovation by introducing a new steel alloy called Cyclex. In essence it was the chrome-molybdenum steel that previously had been favoured by Columbus, and Cyclex became the basis for the most comprehensive line-up of tubeset designations ever offered: SLX, SL, SP, PL, Record, KL, GT, and OR.

"I want to do business in iron and steel and make a fair and honest profit."

ANGELO LUIGI COLOMBO

■ The Columbus lab is fully equipped for the production of custom tubes.

▪ The lab carries an enormous range of steel, aluminium, and carbon fibre tubing in every size.

Each was intended for a specific usage indicated by the label; SL, for example, was the correct tubeset for universal use on *strada leggera*, or well-surfaced roads, whereas the heavier (10.5 ounces/300 g per tubeset) SP was the designated tubeset for *strada pesante*, demanding surfaces such as Paris–Roubaix.

Most of these tubesets featured the internal butting that is used in lightweight steel cycle tubing; PL and Record, prescribed for individual pursuiting and track record attempts respectively, did without. With their walls drawn to a paper-thin 0.019 inches (0.5 mm) along their entire length, the plain-gauge tubes and stays of the Record set, used by Eddy Merckx for his 1972 world Hour record ride, weighed only 56.7 ounces (1,610 g) complete with fork blades and steerer tube.

Double-butting the top and down tubes, thereby adding 0.007 inches (0.2 mm) to the tube wall thickness at the ends, added 2.1 ounces (60 g) to the weight of the KL set, chosen for individual efforts on smooth roads against the clock. Fragile as they were, these tubesets were favoured by British time triallists looking not only for some imperceptible performance edge, but also for a touch of the exotic that only the gold-tinted Columbus frame decal could provide.

In addition to their Cyclex steel and decal, the tubesets shared a steerer tube with helical rib reinforcement. For a time this was perhaps the defining feature of the Columbus brand; in order to stiffen the highly stressed lower end of the steerer tube where it entered the fork crown, without adding any more weight than necessary, the cold-drawing process formed a series of ribs spiralling upwards. The same helical reinforcements featured, in addition to butting, at the bottom bracket end of several tubes in the SLX set, which was called "super-butted." Intended for use by professionals, SLX was clearly the "top" Columbus tubeset of the time. Somehow, however, it lacked for many the appeal of the plain SL (lighter by 1.05 ounces/30 g) or of the legendary SP, which with its 0.03-inch (1-mm) wall thickness seat and chain stays was not only suitable for rough road surfaces but also for the power and imposing physique of great *rouleurs* such as Francesco Moser.

SP was, however, heavy. At 81.13 ounces (2,300 g) for the set, it built into a frame that was practically indestructible thanks to the tube wall thickness. A better tubeset was called MAX,

and it arrived in 1987. It aroused immediate interest because of its use of an alloy steel called Nivacrom that had been developed for cycles by Columbus and its unmistakable ovalized tubes. Formed with "oriented ellipses and differentiated sections," MAX was not the first tubeset to employ the concept of the non-circular tube, but it was the first to be shaped in pursuit of improved mechanical performance. The main tubes were squashed into ellipses, which in turn

were aligned in order to maximize strength and stiffness in the desired planes. Allied to the use of significantly oversized tube diameters, this gave MAX greater performance characteristics than SP at a weight that was 14.1 ounces (400 g) lighter.

Although MAX represented a breakthrough in the development of steel tubing for lightweight cycles, it was not the answer to many problems. A slimmed-down (by 1/8 inch/3.175 mm) version called MiniMAX saved a little weight and offered a fraction more ride comfort, but the next step was a reversion to round section tubing, which, with "differential shape butting," was called Genius. Drawn from the same Nivacrom alloy steel, Genius was an attempt to address the problem of matching material to load by modifying the shape of the butts inside the ends of the tube.

The first steel cycle tubeset designed specifically for tungsten inert gas welding, Genius was a great success for Columbus. It spawned an off-road version and led to the development in Nivacrom steel of a succession of tubing models with variations on the differential shape butting process, each now named rather than given a letter code as had been the tubesets of the 1980s. The finest was Nemo, which was developed using an early version of a technique that was later adopted for the refinement of superlight frames by leading cycle manufacturers such as Cannondale. Columbus engineers attached strain gauges to areas of high stress on the frame tubes, measured the strain or amount of deflection, and used the information to reduce tube wall thickness in areas of low stress and add to it where stresses were greatest.

The result was called "zone butted concept" and reaffirmed the company's status just as competition in the world of steel cycle tubing

1919	1931	1950	1977
Angelo Luigi Colombo establishes AL Colombo in Via Stradella, Milan, to make tubing for bicycle manufacturers.	Colombo produces components for motorbikes, cars, and aircraft, and develops a reputation for fine office and home furniture.	Colombo's son, Gilberto, joins the company as plant manager and begins designing car chassis. Clients would eventually include Maserati, Ferrari, and Lancia.	Antonio, Colombo's youngest son, takes over the business and concentrates on the production of innovative tubing for top of the range frames.

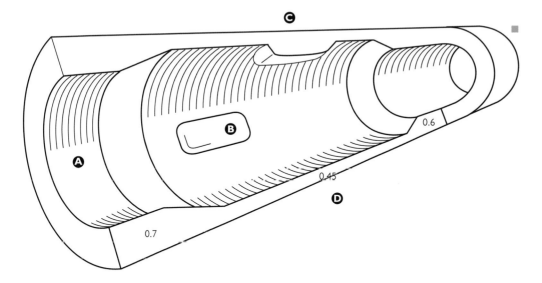

Pedro Delgado won the 1988 Tour de France on a Pinarello made with Columbus tubing.

In 1996 Columbus introduced ZBC technology (zone butted concept). This identifies areas of stress and strength where a frame can be reinforced or lightened. **A** short butted zone, asymmetric butting **B** butted zone for front derailleur **C** butted zone for bottle cage **D** numbers denote differing wall thicknesses.

began to heat up. The fledgling Dedacciai firm, established in 1993 near Cremona by brothers Luca and Stefano Locatelli, was making inroads with the impressive 18MCDV6HT alloy steel; at the same time, the traditional material for racing cycle frame construction was about to fall from favour as, first, aluminium and then titanium gained ground only to be dismissed at the summit of the sport by the wonders of carbon fibre.

Nevertheless, this was a fertile period for Columbus; tubesets with evocative names such as Metax and Neuron issued forth with bewildering frequency even as the company ventured into aluminium and produced technologically advanced tubesets such as Altec and Altec II, Starship, Zonal, and XLR8R. Using advanced 6000- and 7000-series alloys, these tubesets featured exotic profiles either inspired by the example of MAX or demanded by customers wanting a large surface area for their company logo. Titanium, too, made an appearance, and the Hyperion tubeset proved popular with many Italian artisanal builders.

Steel was not dead, however; in 1999 Thermacrom, the most advanced alloy steel yet developed for frame construction, arrived only to be supplanted within five years by Spirit, which used niobium as an alloying element to bring the state of the metallurgist's art to the point where a complete Spirit tubeset for a size 21.25-inch (54-cm) frame weighs a mere 37.39 ounces (1,060 g).

The previous year's Columbus innovation, XLR8R Carbon, was a tubeset in carbon fibre designed for the small-scale fabricators; Dedacciai developed a similar concept. The future of composites for cycle frame manufacture lay, however, in large-scale manufacture and near-monocoque construction techniques.

Contrastingly, the future of steel—or at least the highest quality, lightest, strongest steel tubes—lay with the burgeoning bespoke frame-building scene, and Columbus had one more ace to play. XCR is a stainless steel of immense strength that can be polished to a mirror finish. A road frame in Columbus XCR is as glamorous as it gets. *RH*

1991	2003	2004	2009
The Genius tubing, made of Nivacrom alloy steel, is an unprecedented success. It is followed by the Megatube in 1994, Nemo in 1996, Thermacrom in 1999, and Starship in 2000.	Columbus introduces XLR8R Carbon, a range of carbon tubes made for road racing competitions.	Steel tubing makes a comeback in the Spirit design, which uses niobium as an alloying element to create ultralight frames.	For its XCR seamless stainless steel tubes, Columbus is a winner at the International Forum Design awards.

Concorde

The much-idolized Concorde brand enjoyed a rapid rise to fame in the 1980s, and supplied many of the stars of the professional peloton with its bikes. However, the brand faded just as quickly and these days survives as a collector's item.

■ A 1981 Concorde, as seen in the company catalogue.

■ Pedro Delgado and Stephen Roche endured a tense battle during the 1987 Tour de France, with Roche the ultimate victor.

The history of Concorde is unusual. Like a manufactured pop band, it is a manufactured brand, and its bikes are made by the quality Italian frame-builder Ciöcc.

Concorde was founded in the 1980s when the huge bike importers Veltec, based in Belgium, and Weltmeister of Holland came together to create their own brand. The frames were supplied to them by Ciöcc, with Campagnolo components, Columbus tubing, and Cinelli lugs, and were painted in the Netherlands, The company celebrated the Italian connection in its advertising and in the names of the bikes—Squadra, Aquila, Astore—but on the road, it became part of

Dutch cycling history by living up to its strapline, "It's like flying!"

Concorde had supplied bikes to small Dutch and Belgium teams in the early 1980s, and to a Concorde team in 1983 and 1984, but the company really took off in 1986 with PDM-Concorde, which was well known for both its home-grown Dutch success and the huge names brought in from other countries. Racing for six years, PDM-Concorde became one of cycling's "superteams," and its successes included numerous stage wins in the Tour de France. Although the team never claimed the overall victory, it won the team prize in 1988 and 1989, and supplied the runner-up in 1987 and 1988 thanks to Pedro Delgado and Steven Rooks. In 1990, Erik Breukink took an incredible third place for Concorde, despite being hampered by mechanical problems on the Col du Tourmalet and needing three bike changes.

Sean Kelly rode for PDM-Concorde for two years, and won the inaugural World Cup and his second Liège–Bastogne–Liège in 1989. Concorde did not limit its success to the road, either—with Adrie van der Poel and Hennie Stamsnijder, it backed some of the big names in cyclo-cross.

It was all going well for Concorde until 1991. The year started on a high, with Jean-Paul van Poppel winning four stages of the Vuelta a España, and Uwe Raab taking another stage and the points jersey; then came the Tour de France, and the team suddenly withdrew en masse. Food poisoning was blamed at the time, and although the team doctor later blamed a badly stored nutritional supplement, doping was suspected. Years afterwards, Manfred Krikke, one of the team managers, said: "We were not the most ethical team in the peloton. We were just on the edge. But the directions from the PDM company was that there were to be no 'doping affairs' not that there was to be 'no drugs'." The affair hastened the end of PDM-Concorde. The team had one final season—in which Jean-Paul van Poppel again won stages in the Tour and the Vuelta—before it was disbanded at the end of the cycling year.

Concorde continued to sponsor teams and riders—including cyclo-cross rider Richard Groenendaal, who came second in the 1994 world championships—but it never recaptured its earlier glory. These days, its Squadra and Aquila bikes from the PDM days—with the distinctive white and black frames—have plenty of fans, but Concorde really was the original manufactured brand—the Bay City Rollers or the Monkees of the bicycle world—and Veltec has since moved on to other brands. *sc*

Daccordi

The family frame-builders from Tuscany began producing bikes in 1937 and developed a reputation for exquisite craftsmanship and attention to the smallest and most hidden-away parts of a racing machine, including lugs and bottom brackets.

Giuseppe Daccordi founded his frame-building business in 1937 in an era when many of the craftsmen of Italy were setting up their now iconic brands. He started from humble beginnings with an unnamed business partner, but, as with many manufacturing operations, their output was curtailed by World War II, and Daccordi disappeared for six years. When production resumed in 1945 the business grew rapidly, with Daccordi's frames establishing a good reputation in one of the most competitive markets in the world. As with so many of the Italian manufacturers, it remained a family affair, and Giuseppe's son, Luigi, came on board in the 1960s.

Something else that the Italian companies had in common was their loyalty to Columbus tubesets. Daccordi was no different. The

challenge for any frame-builder, however, was to assemble steel tubes, lugs, bottom bracket shells, and fork crowns in such a way that the end product bore its own, distinctive and attractive identity. As with other master craftsmen, Daccordi has always been committed to handbuilding its frames with skill and flair in its factory in San Miniato Bassano, about 25 miles (40 km) west of Florence.

Luigi, the heir to the family business, deserves much of the credit for Daccordi's burgeoning reputation for quality in the 1960s. As an example, he used microfusion cast junctions to ensure that his frames were as rigid as they could be. However, it is a seldom-studied part of the frame that demonstrates Daccordi's superb attention to detail. The finish of the inside of a bottom bracket shell reveals much about the skill and patience of a frame-builder. You cannot hide poor workmanship here, because this is where all the mitred sections of tube meet; bad preparation or poor brazing will be visible to those who look. However, it is also the bike equivalent of the back of a sofa; on the basis that no one (or few) will see it, it can be left a little messy. A neatly finished bottom bracket shell is not purely cosmetic, however, because it is one of the most stressed parts of a bike. Daccordi frames became well known for the quality of the workmanship in this area, and were probably sturdier as a result.

Daccordi proved it was willing to innovate when it became one of the first manufacturers to use tubing from Oria, who attempted to break the Columbus stranglehold on the Italian market in the mid-1980s. Based in—and named after—the town of Oriago, in the Venice province, Oria used new extrusion techniques with its steel tubesets, before adopting new materials and methods, including aluminium tubes and composite technology.

From around the late 1980s and early 1990s, Daccordi frames came to be renowned for their immaculate finish. Some considered that they had no equal because many of their frames were nickel-plated, which was a process that added weight but also ensured a beautiful finish and excellent durability.

Daccordi also supplied teams, both professional and amateur, for the usual reasons: marketing and product development. Among its highest profile riders was the Italian sprinter Adriano Baffi, who rode to many victories, as did the Dutchman Johan van der Velde. Van der Velde earned his place in the history books in Italy thanks to his epic ride through the snow when he was first to reach the summit of the monster Passo Gavia during the 1988 Giro d'Italia. It was one of the most inspiring days in the history of the Giro and one on which Van der Velde and his snow-covered Daccordi left their mark. **RD**

■ The fiftieth anniversary model had Columbus SLX tubing and a Campagnolo *gruppo*.

■ Giuseppe Daccordi, pictured here in the 1950s, established his bicycle company in 1937.

■ The Daccordi Divo range features, from top to bottom, massive fork blades to improve steering, carbon seat stays, internal routing for cables, and a threaded bottom bracket shell.

■ In the company's early days, Ugo De Rosa supervised every aspect of construction.

■ Throughout the 1970s and 1980s, De Rosa made around 3,000 frames each year.

De Rosa

Even among the rich assortment of great Italian frame-builders, De Rosa stands out, renowned for the quality of the bikes that bear the name and for the long-standing patronage of the greatest cyclist of all time, Eddy Merckx.

Few bicycles engender as much fanatical pride among the cognoscenti as those bearing the surname of Italian craftsman Ugo De Rosa. The marque carries a unique set of associations: superb workmanship; a link to the later career of the great Eddy Merckx, and to his post-racing efforts as a bicycle manufacturer; unique detailing; and the ineffable panache that characterizes the great Italian bicycle brands.

The story of a great marque is often said to begin when its founder sells his first bikes. However, in the case of De Rosa, its founder

Ugo De Rosa, dedicated his teenage years to preparing for a career as a bicycle-maker well before he sold his first bikes from his Milan shop in April or May 1953. Like many of his contemporaries—Ernesto Colnago, Faliero Masi, Giovanni Pinarello—the young De Rosa was a bicycle racer. But while others riders fell into bicycle manufacture because of setbacks in their racing careers, De Rosa seemed to know from a very early age what he really wanted to be: a great bicycle frame-builder. "I was thirteen years old and crazy about bikes," he said.

While studying engineering at technical school, De Rosa assembled and repaired bikes in the workshop of his uncle, Filippo Fasci. De Rosa rapidly developed a deep understanding of the technical aspects of the bicycle. After five or six years of this combination of practical and academic study, it was only natural that he would open his own shop on Via Lanfranco della Pila in Milan. He founded De Rosa Cycles at just eighteen years of age.

The 1950s were difficult times. Italy was still reeling from World War II, and a racing bike was an expensive luxury that many people simply could not afford. However, bike racing had been an Italian passion before the war, and riders such as Fausto Coppi and Gino Bartali had resumed their careers—and rivalry—after the conflict ended. Ugo De Rosa could see the potential of the post-war heroic era of cycle racing as it unfolded before him.

De Rosa's big break came in 1958. His reputation had spread beyond Milan, and when the great French cyclist Raphaël Géminiani met De Rosa at a race at the Vigorelli velodrome in Milan, he asked De Rosa to build him a bike for the Giro d'Italia. Géminiani would go on to ride that bike to eighth place in the Giro and third place in the Tour de France. For De Rosa it was the beginning of a long association with professional cycling. Over the decades that followed, De Rosa would supply bikes to teams whose names and star rides still resonate through the years.

The best known of these names is Eddy Merckx, the rider whom they called "The Cannibal" for his voracious appetite for victories. Arguably the greatest bike racer who ever lived—although Merckx himself denies the claim, saying that it is impossible to compare riders between eras—Merckx had a close association during his early career with another well-known Italian bike-maker, Ernesto Colnago. A noted perfectionist who would adjust his saddle height

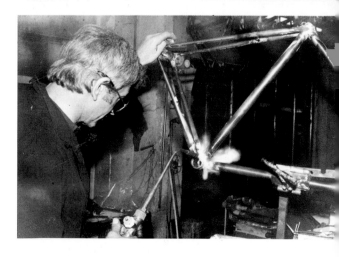

■ Raphaël Géminiani, seen here in 1953, would go on to ride De Rosa to race success.

■ This bicycle dates from 1953, around the same time the company was established by De Rosa.

1934	1953	1958	1973
Ugo De Rosa is born in Milan and develops an interest in bicycles and cycle racing in his teens.	De Rosa sells his first bikes from his shop in Milan having founded De Rosa Cycles the previous year, aged just eighteen.	The great French cyclist Raphaël Géminiani asks De Rosa to build him a bike for the Giro d'Italia. Géminiani finishes eighth in the Giro and third in the Tour on his De Rosa.	Having developed a name for building bikes for some of the world's top riders, De Rosa begins supplying the greatest of all, Eddy Merckx.

mid-race in search of the perfect setting, Merckx asked De Rosa to build him some frames as early as 1969. Merckx and Colnago parted company acrimoniously after Merckx set the Hour record in Mexico aboard a bike labelled "Windsor" (a Mexican bike company), which had been built by Colnago. Depending on which account you believe, Merckx was either trying to thank his Mexican hosts or was paid around US $10,000 to label his bike in this manner. Colnago was furious. De Rosa stepped in as Merckx's bike builder, later describing Merckx as "a champion par excellence, on the cycle and in life. Eddy was so scrupulous that sometimes he might seem capricious. How many sleepless nights, for Eddy... but how many satisfactions!"

Merckx rode De Rosa bikes until his retirement from racing in 1978, and added two more Giri d'Italia, a final Tour de France, and

a world championship to his tally on the way. Ugo De Rosa cites Merckx's 1974 season as his personal favourite. Merckx won the Giro, the Tour, the Worlds, and the Tour of Switzerland. "I built Merckx fifty bikes that year, including six in a week for the Giro. I slept in the workshop to keep on top of things," he said.

When Merckx decided to start his own bicycle company in 1978, after retirement as a professional racer, De Rosa helped him to set it up and may even have built some early bikes that were sold under Merckx's marque. Cycling historian Hilary Stone owns a Merckx frame with several De Rosa features, including slots in the bottom bracket shell and De Rosa's trademark heart-shaped cut-out in the down tube tang. Merckx may have simply bought frame components from De Rosa, but it is nonetheless a measure of the strong relationship between the

"In our half century, our history has taught us that nothing can be left to chance."

UGO DE ROSA

1974	1978	1994	1996
Merckx, who will ride De Rosa's bikes until he retires in 1978, enjoys one of his best seasons. It is his first official season aboard a De Rosa, winning the Giro, Tour, and world championships.	Merckx retires and sets up his own bike company, turning to Ugo De Rosa for advice. De Rosa helps him as a technical consultant to Eddy Merckx Cycles.	De Rosa is back in the racing spotlight and supplies the all-conquering Gewiss team. It wins more than forty races, including the Giro d'Italia, on the new titanium frames.	Aluminium frames are added to the range, with carbon fibre used for the new King frame, introduced in 2000. Steel remains a popular material, and features in the 2005 Corum frame.

Eddy Merckx was in fine form during the time trial stage in the 1974 Tour de France.

two that Ugo De Rosa was prepared to help his friend set up, in effect, a rival business.

It is possible to identify this frame's De Rosa links because of the technical artistry that gave De Rosa his reputation. "In our half century, our history has taught us that nothing can be left to chance," Ugo De Rosa once said. A detail improvement, such as the slotted bottom bracket shell, is a great example of this dedication to achieving perfection. As the frame component that carries the cranks, the bottom bracket shell has to resist all the rider's effort. In the 1970s, it was typically a stiff, heavy steel casting, but De Rosa realized that it could be safely lightened by cutting away some metal and leaving holes that also allowed water to drain out if the bike was ridden in wet conditions.

Although Merckx was the greatest rider to win aboard a De Rosa, he was by no means the only top racer to achieve victory on De Rosa's bikes. Francesco Moser, Moreno Argentin, Romans Vainsteins, and Franco Pellizotti are among the champions also associated with De Rosa. It was no surprise that Merckx retained his old friend to help get Eddy Merckx Cycles off the ground. Ugo De Rosa's technical expertise in bicycle frame manufacture had become legendary, highly sought-after, and rare. Although informed estimates put the production of some well-known steel frame-makers of the 1970s and 1980s as high as 20,000 frames per year, it is unlikely that De Rosa ever made more than 3,000, all under its founder's training and supervision.

With his passion for improving the bicycle frame, Ugo De Rosa was among the first European frame-builders to notice the challenge coming from the United States. In the late 1980s, US bicycle companies began to experiment with materials other than the steel that had been the mainstay of bike manufacturing for a century. Aluminium and titanium were the buzz metals, and it was the potential of titanium that excited Ugo De Rosa. Corrosion resistant and lighter

than steel, but still with the characteristic "spring" that produces a lively, exciting ride, titanium had the potential to be the ultimate frame material.

Following his personal maxim of "leave nothing to chance," De Rosa studied the available titanium alloys and the manufacturing techniques that were needed to work with this tough, hard to weld material. The result, in 1991, was the Titanio, perhaps the most successful titanium frame ever raced. In 1994 the Gewiss team, aboard De Rosa Titanio frames, won more than forty major races, including Milan–San Remo, Liège–Bastogne–Liège, Flèche Wallonne, and the Giro d'Italia. So dominant was Gewiss that it attracted widespread suspicion, not least when the team managed a one-two-three finish at Flèche Wallonne, and the team doctor, Michele Ferrari, was quoted as saying that EPO—the wonder drug popular in the peloton—was "not dangerous, it's the abuse that is. It's also dangerous to drink ten litres of orange juice." Although Dr Ferrari was fired—he would go on to work with Lance Armstrong—the suspicion around the Gewiss team remained. Despite this, there was no questioning the effectiveness and desirability of the De Rosa machines that the team used that year. De Rosa still makes two models of titanium frame today, although almost every other frame-builder who experimented with titanium in the 1990s eventually left the material to the specialists.

With the introduction of aluminium frames in 1996, De Rosa was late to adopt the metal compared to some bike manufacturers, which indicates that Ugo De Rosa was never very keen on the material and introduced it only when the tide could no longer be resisted. "Sometimes," the company's official history says, aluminium was used "without due consideration, too superficially." That is not the De Rosa way, and when he did eventually bring aluminium frames to the range, Ugo De Rosa—by now being helped to run the company by his sons—looked for ways

"I built Merckx fifty bikes that year [1974] including six in a week for the Giro. I slept in the workshop to keep on top of things."

UGO DE ROSA

to improve it. The result was the Merak frame in 2003, which was the first to use aluminium shaped by the "hydroforming" process that allows wildly experimental shapes and wall thicknesses.

While other manufacturers were hesitating to experiment with composite materials, De Rosa saw the potential of carbon fibre relatively early, and brought it to the range in 2000 in the shape of the King frame. The Italian supercar and Formula One industry had already built expertise in carbon fibre throughout the 1970s. By the time carbon fibre became affordable for bicycle frames, Italian sub-contractors were ready and available to advise on its application. By modern standards the King was heavy at more than 49.3 ounces (1,400 g) for a frame. De Rosa was quick to realize that carbon frames could be much lighter and pushed the development of later versions of the frame into the 35.2-ounce (1,000-g) range, with the latest King RS tipping the scales at 33.5 ounces (950 g).

Engineering and testing have been central to De Rosa's approach to new materials. Before a frame comes to market, it is subjected to a wide range of tests in De Rosa's own facilities, in the laboratories of local universities, and on the road under experienced professional riders.

Today, De Rosa is almost certainly the only bicycle manufacturer of scale still making bicycle frames in all four materials. While others have specialized—usually in carbon fibre—De Rosa understands that the different ride characteristics offered by carbon, steel, aluminium, and titanium mean that they each appeal to different types of rider, all of whom deserve to ride a De Rosa.

More typically for an Italian bike manufacturer, De Rosa remains a family operation. With Ugo De Rosa now well into his seventies, the company is run by his three sons, Danilo, Doriano, and Cristiano. Cristiano is the public face of De Rosa, greeting dealers at trade shows, charming the press, and radiating constant boundless

■ A 1986 De Rosa SLX, features, from top to bottom, Super Prestige Pernod decal to celebrate the races Eddy Merckx won in 1973, 1974, and 1975, a restored 3TTT stem and handlebar set-up, restored Cobalto caliper brakes, and a Campagnolo Record rear mech that has had its anodizing removed.

■ The Titanio was introduced in 1991, and is possibly the most successful titanium frame ever to be raced.

enthusiasm for the family's bikes. Danilo and Doriano have followed in their father's craftsman footsteps more closely. Danilo still welds titanium frames, whereas Doriano is responsible for drawing up frame designs—including the specific layouts for custom bikes. The De Rosa brothers have fond memories of growing up around bikes. "We used to come here every day after school to help out our dad," Cristiano said in 2005. "We did all the various things in the shop: filing, cleaning up, packing… then our dad taught us how to build bikes."

Ugo De Rosa once said: "First you have to know how to make bicycles, and then know how to sell them." When he started in 1953 he had to do every aspect of the job himself, and to know how to do it efficiently and to the best of his ability. Nowadays, his company builds around

7,000 frames per year, a level of production that would be impossible to maintain without the skilled team headed by his three sons.

It is often easy to romanticize a marque's history and past achievements, but Ugo De Rosa himself has always firmly eschewed nostalgia. "By force of habit, I never look back and count the years I have spent making frames," he says on his company's website. "I prefer to look ahead because, after working for half a century, I am still convinced that the bicycle has room for improvement. And just as I have done up till now, in the future too I want to contribute to the evolution of this fascinating vehicle, which is at the same time so simple and so complicated."

It seems likely that the family of the craftsman from Milan will carry on evolving the racing bicycle for another fifty years or more. **JS**

> *"I am still convinced that the bicycle has room for improvement."*
>
> UGO DE ROSA

The elegant King RS Gold frame
weighs only 2 pounds (950 g).

Merckx in his workshop
during the mid-1970s.
His attention to detail is
legendary.

The EMX-7 bicycle
features a tapered
carbon aerofork, carbon
CL frame, and a 1.4-inch
(38-mm) Eddy Merckx
wheelset.

Eddy Merckx

Known as "The Cannibal" on account of his voracious appetite for winning, Eddy Merckx is widely recognized as the greatest cyclist of all time and applies the same obsessive quest for perfection to the bicycles that carry the Eddy Merckx name.

For many, Eddy Merckx is number one in cycling. He is the man who won everything there was to win and embodied the competitive spirit that is the essence of the sport. His fearsome nickname left little to the imagination: Merckx was "The Cannibal." Furthermore, he consumed titles. His approach to bikes and the equipment he used was as exhaustive as his will to win was pure—no detail was too small not to warrant his attention. Ever since he took his first steps into the sport, he was a bike obsessive, and his career in cycling is nothing less than a lifelong romance.

For most of his professional career between 1965 and 1978, Merckx rode bikes with his name on the tubes, but they were the work of established frame-builders such as the Italian makers Faliero Masi and Ugo De Rosa. De Rosa has recalled that the Belgian rider's attention to detail also meant stress for those who built his bikes: "Eddy was so scrupulous that sometimes he might seem capricious. How many sleepless nights for Eddy… but how many satisfactions!"

"Merckx was obsessed with equipment," says Daniel Friebe, author of *Eddy Merckx: The Cannibal*. "One of the stories, which Merckx

himself has confirmed, is that he disassembled a bike as a young pro just so he could count the individual components. I'm not sure any other cyclist has ever regularly taken over a dozen bikes to Grand Tours, as Merckx did. And he often took a drill to frames to remove excess material and reduce weight."

His obsession remained throughout his career. As The Cannibal he devoured most of the big races on the calendar. Guests who visited the champion at home marvelled at the 500 tubular tyres maturing in his cellar, and the 150 wheel-sets and the thirty-five bikes lined up just so. Not his wife Claudine, though. In the same way that De Rosa recalled his constant adjustments, she became accustomed to her husband's obsession and recounted nights when he would rise from bed in the middle of the night to remeasure angles and heights. Night-time sorties to his workshop were often not enough, either. In the film *A Sunday in Hell*—the documentary film of the 1976 Paris–Roubaix—Merckx is seen stopping to adjust his saddle height with an allen key that he habitually stowed in his back pocket. To any other rider it would be unthinkable to stop mid-

race to fiddle with the bike and then chase back on. This was not the case for the redoubtable Merckx and his limitless sources of energy. Saddle position had become a constant niggle after a crash at a Derny event in Blois in 1969.

Even in his early career, his quest for the best equipment was endless. In 1967, when Merckx rode for Peugeot-Michelin-BP, he disliked the standard Peugeot PX-10 frame, so asked Falerio Masi to build him a custom bike that was decked out in team livery. The only giveaway was a tiny Masi badge on the seatpost.

Despite his unparalleled success on the bike, Merckx was no extrovert champion and he eschewed the histrionics that were favoured by some to get a psychological edge over rivals. Instead he was driven by his implacable belief

that if he was racing, he must win. After all, as he was fond of saying, people had come to see him win, and he could not disappoint them. Even away from the peloton he was demure and kept his own counsel. But one thing would consistently draw him: bikes. There are tales that if he was out training and came across an amateur labouring over a poorly set-up bike, he would break from his routine and take the time to put the bike right before resuming his ride.

Perhaps his best-known bike was the one built by his friend Ernesto Colnago for his attempt on the Hour record in Mexico in 1972. The final bike was preceded by several prototypes as Merckx, who had spent his career largely on the road, tinkered with the geometry. The end result was an orange frame that was more upright, and with

> *"He is a pedaller of violence, but the violence is carefully directed, balanced, transformed into efficient energy."*
>
> JEAN-PAUL OLLIVIER

the saddle moved further forwards than many people expected.

The geometry that Merckx had settled on was put to the test on the road in an Italian race, the Giro del Piemonte, just before he flew to Mexico City. Around 31 miles (50 km) from the line, he attacked alone and time trialled to the finish, beating his nearest challenger Felice Gimondi by more than a minute. It tested the bike and his superlative form, and he knew that he was ready for his one and only attempt on the Hour.

The bike made for the record attempt was a work of mechanical artistry. The handlebars had been drilled out in an elegant curving pattern that looked more like a decorative touch than an engineering solution to reduce weight. The

1953	1964	1969	1972
A young Merckx receives his first racing bike, a second-hand model, at the age of eight.	Merckx competes in the road race at the Olympics and finishes twelfth. The same year he becomes world amateur champion at Sallanches, France.	He wins his first Tour de France. It is the only Tour in which a single cyclist wins the general classification, points classification, and the mountains classification.	On October 25, Merckx sets the Hour record, with 30.714 miles (49.431 km) at high altitude in Mexico City. It is not broken until 1984.

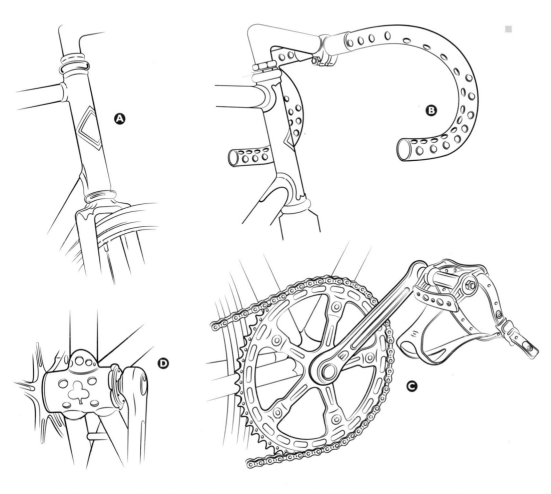

■ Merckx in 1972. He was asked to miss the 1973 Tour de France to give other riders a chance.

■ The designs for Merckx's 1972 Hour record bike. From top left:
Ⓐ the head tube, filed to a minimum, and with titanium headset cups
Ⓑ drop handlebars
Ⓒ milled chainring, lightened cranks, drilled chain, and steel toeclips
Ⓓ bottom bracket shell, complete with Colnago clover symbol.

seatpost, below where it clamps into the frame, had also been drilled, and there was liberal use of lightweight but extremely expensive titanium in the components. The bike weighed only 12 pounds 2 ounces (5.5 kg).

In typical fashion, Merckx beat the record, setting a distance of 30.714 miles (49.431 km). However, he confirmed afterwards that he would never make another attempt, such was the suffering he endured. The successful ride immortalized the bike, and today it is often displayed at bike shows around the world. As a postscript, after successful attempts on the record with improved equipment and positions led by the serial innovator Graeme Obree in the 1990s, the Union Cycliste Internationale (UCI) imposed limitations on bike design. The benchmark it chose was Merckx's orange Colnago.

Merckx retired in 1978 after a thirteen-year career at the top. He had achieved everything in

1974	1978	1980	2012
Merckx wins his fifth and final Tour de France, wearing the yellow jersey for a record ninety-six days during his entire career.	The Waasland at Kemzeke on March 19 marks his last race, where he finishes twelfth. He withdraws from competitive cycling the same year to develop his business ideas.	Eddy Merckx Cycles quickly finds favour with professional racers. In 1982, Dutch rider Peter Winnen is the first to ride a Merckx frame to a Tour de France stage victory.	The company moves to larger premises close to Brussels city centre to meet demand—Merckx bikes are now available in twenty-one countries.

■ Merckx's 1970s machine features, from top to bottom, hollowed-out brake leavers to reduce weight, the frame-builder's logo beneath the bottom bracket, Campagnolo gear shifters, and beautifully sleek seat stays.

■ Fascinated by frame geometry and ride comfort, Merckx had a reputation for leaping out of bed in the middle of the night to tinker with his bikes.

cycling. He had won virtually every race worth winning and had delighted fans on the road and in velodromes all year round. However, predictably for such a driven character, he found himself in a void when he retired. There was nothing to occupy and engage him. He drifted for a while, but on the advice of his close friend, Belgian footballer Paul Van Himst, he set his sights on building bikes for the next generation of riders. It was precisely the fillip he needed, and he threw himself into the project. He contacted De Rosa and asked if he could shadow him around the frame-builder's factory in order to fully understand the frame materials' properties and learn the builder's art. In 1980, with De Rosa kept on as a technical consultant, Merckx opened his own bike factory in his home city of Meise.

The bikes' main appeal was that they were made to Merckx's own exacting standards and they soon found favour with the professionals. He was no longer riding, but Eddy Merckx—at least, bikes bearing his name—returned to the peloton in 1982 when he secured his first professional contract with Capri Sonne. Later that year, the Dutch rider Peter Winnen was the first to ride a Merckx-designed and built frame to a Tour de France stage victory. And what a stage to claim this landmark win—a 156-mile (251-km) marathon from Bourg d'Oisans at the foot of Alpe d'Huez to Morzine. Winnen's ride was almost worthy of the great man himself.

Since then, Eddy Merckx bikes have had an almost unbroken presence in the professional peloton. Some of the best teams in the 1980s and 1990s rode them. As well as winning many of the Classics, in 1987 Robert Millar, aboard a Merckx, finished second in the Giro d'Italia. The pioneering US team, 7-Eleven, also spent its last two years aboard Merckx bikes until it morphed into the Motorola team. Motorola riders also used Merckx bikes, including the young Lance Armstrong, who forged a close friendship with Merckx over the course of his career.

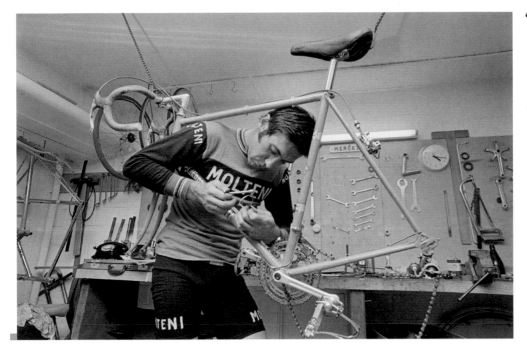

"Eddy was so scrupulous that sometimes he might seem capricious. How many sleepless nights for Eddy... but how many satisfactions!"

UGO DE ROSA

Only in the mid-2000s did Merckx's bikes enter the relative wilderness. Part of the reason it managed such a long stint at the very highest level of the sport was the company's adoption of new materials and processes. Merckx may have been a traditionalist at heart when it came to bikes—he was adamant that forks should have a degree of rake long after other manufacturers had committed to straight versions—but the company has largely moved with the times, adopting new materials and designs as they emerge.

At the end of 2009, Eddy Merckx Cycles announced a return to the pro peloton when it signed a contract to supply Tom Boonen's Quick Step squad with equipment. For many of Belgium's *wielervolk*—the diehard Flemish cycling fans—a firm line can be drawn between Merckx and Boonen, especially in the years between 2005 and 2008 when "Tommeke" dominated the beloved Classics in a way that had not been seen for a generation or more. Following a period when Belgium had been lacking a star, Boonen was heaven sent. Although the two riders were eager to play down any comparison with one another, they played up for the media, often appearing in interviews together, with Merckx offering advice on crank length to the 2005 and 2012 winner of the Tour of Flanders/Paris–Roubaix double. Boonen also once joked about going into frame-building once his career was over. "Why not?" replied Merckx. "But first he will have to learn the craft like I did more than thirty years ago." It is an observation that seems to encapsulate Merckx's view: to him, the bike has always been more than a mere tool.

Merckx sold most of his shares in the company in 2008, but remains heavily involved. Indeed, there is something comforting about knowing that, even in a world of carbon nanotubes and computer-aided design, The Cannibal—the living representative of cycling's golden age—sometimes throws a leg over a frame in the factory he founded, just to check that the geometry is still absolutely perfect. **SD**

Using this Colnago model Eddy Merckx
broke the Hour record in 1972.

Flandria

The name "Flandria" evokes one of cycling's great heartlands, and the bike company's history is inextricably linked to the story of Flanders cycling. Flandria has also survived a family feud so bitter that the workshop was cut in half by a brick wall.

■ A Flandria vehicle featured in the documentary *A Sunday in Hell* (1976).

■ This 1970s Flandria features classic Cinelli deep drop handlebars and the distinctive Flandria colours.

Flandria is a brand steeped in cycling's rich tapestry of rivalry, controversy, innovation, and success: the bitter feud between Eddy Merckx and Freddy Maertens—stemming from the 1973 world championship—and Marc Demeyer's 1976 Paris–Roubaix win, immortalized in the documentary *A Sunday in Hell*, spring to mind. Faema-Flandria's invention of the revolutionary sprint train in 1962 and Michel Pollentier's disqualification from the 1978 Tour after he was discovered with a condom full of someone else's urine at the post-stage drugs test are memorable tales, too, but the story behind the company's bikes is equally interesting.

It all started in 1896, when Louis Claeys made his first, self-designed *vélomobiel* in the family forge in Zedelgem, near the coast of West Flanders. The forge was a flourishing business that had passed into the Claeys family after Louis's father had gone to work for the blacksmith and ended up marrying his daughter. The bicycle side of the business started slowly, and four of Louis's sons—Alidor, Jeremoe, Aimé, and Remi—developed it into a company. Initially it was known as De West-Vlaamsche Leeuw (The West-Flemish Lion), but changed its name in 1924 to Werkhuizen Gebroeders Claeys (The Claeys Brothers Limited). It sold more than

25,000 bicycles in the first three years and was soon producing 35,000 bikes a year. The brothers embraced new technologies, with Aimé in particular leading the transformation from horse-powered forge to gleaming modern factories, which in 1933 started producing motorbikes alongside bicycles. Even World War II and the Claeys's refusal to produce anything for the Nazis could not stop the company's growth, and in 1940 the business was renamed Flandria.

Flandria produced everything bicycle-related, from tricycles to folding bikes, to the first exercise bikes Belgium had seen. By 1952 the company was selling 250,00 bicycles, and had factories in France, the Netherlands, Portugal, Spain, and Morocco. But behind the scenes, the brothers were not happy. Alidor left to set up his own company, and in 1956 a family feud split the remaining three brothers: Jerome retired, and Remi and Aimé divided the business—literally. A brick wall was built to separate the workshop in half—and where the machinery was too heavy to be moved, the wall split that in half, too.

Aimé took the name Flandria, and Remi claimed Superia, which just happened to be the name of Flandria's best-selling moped. The family feud lasted beyond the death of the brothers, with employees of each business prohibited from speaking to anyone who worked for the other side—on pain of dismissal.

During the new era of Aimé Claeys's Flandria, the next twist in the tale took place. According to biking legend, in 1959, Claeys, who had continued to expand and develop his business, was in a cafe in Belgium when he met Belgian sprinter Leon Vandaele by chance, and they struck up a conversation. Vandaele had been fired by his team, Faema-Guerra, after he had disobeyed his team leader, Rik van Looy, by riding for himself and winning the Paris–Roubaix and the Kampioenschap van Vlaanderen; he needed a new team. With typical Claeys speed and innovation, the Dr Mann-Flandria team was formed around Vandaele, with "Iron Briek" Schotte as captain and manager. They won forty-four races in that first 1959 season.

■ Sean Kelly was signed to Flandria in 1977 by team manager Jean de Gribaldy.

1896

Louis Claeys makes a *vélomobiel* in the family forge in West Flanders, the precursor to the formation of a bicycle company, named The West-Flemish Lion.

1924

The company name is changed to Werkhuizen Gebroeders Claeys (The Claeys Brothers Limited) as production increases from 8,000 to 35,000 a year.

1940

The Claeys Brothers is renamed Flandria Cycles, producing all manner of bikes from tricycles to folders and exercise machines.

1956

A family feud sees the company split in two, with a brick wall constructed to divide the factory. On one side was Flandria Cycles, on the other Superia, named after its motorbike.

Throughout the 1960s the Flandria team moved through various incarnations, but always with a reputation for innovation and for developing young riders. Practically every major Belgian rider of the era rode for them at some point—except for Eddy Merckx—and the team was admired for its depth of talent. In 1962, world champion Rik van Looy, the man who had been accidentally responsible for the team's creation in the first place, joined for a year. During that season, Faema-Flandria's "Red Guard" is said to have introduced the concept of the lead-out train to professional cycling.

From 1963, Flandria took over as title sponsor and the team's management moved from Italy to Belgium, as it continued to develop into a classic Belgian model: tough as nails, never giving in. Walter Godefroot, "De Vlaamse Bulldog," signed for the team in 1967. Two years later, "Monsieur Paris–Roubaix," Roger De Vlaeminck, turned professional with the team, and began his career in style by winning Omloop Het Volk, his first race with the team. By 1970, Flandria had become the team to beat in the Classics.

The 1970s was a decade of extraordinary highs and lows for Flandria, starting with new signing Jean-Pierre Monseré winning the road world championships in 1970 at just twenty-one years of age, and then tragically dying the following year while riding the Grote Jaarmarktprijs, when a car drove on to the course, and killed him instantly. Monseré's death inspired the team to greater heights in his memory, and it became well known for targeting every kind of race—and winning every major one-day or stage race except for the Tour de France, although both Jozef Plankaert and Joop Zoetemelk came second in the general classification for Flandria. With

supersprinter Freddy Maertens joining the team in 1972, it kept moving onwards and upwards.

As should be expected from a team sponsored by a bike manufacturer, the Flandria bicycles kept up with the latest technologies, and, in 1973, it became the first pro team to use components made by a Japanese firm, which brought Shimano into the European professional peloton for the first time. Flandria the company was huge by now, and while on the road its bikes were embracing Japanese technology, its moped and motorcycle business was having to adapt quickly to beat the challenges of imports from the Far East.

In 1972, the company was dealt a blow when Aimé Claeys died. Thousands of people attended his funeral, and when his son, Paul, took over the business, the company that at its peak had been producing 350,000 bicycles a year started to struggle. As cars became more affordable, the market for mopeds was collapsing.

While the parent company faltered, the team seemed to go from strength to strength. In 1976 Freddy Maertens won an astonishing fifty-four races, equalling Merckx's record, the highlight of which was the first of his world championships. The following year the team brought in talent scout supreme Jean de Gribaldy, who importantly signed up young Irishman Sean Kelly.

Flandria went on to have a fantastic year in 1977 with 103 victories. Maertens won fifty-three races in the rainbow jersey—including thirteen stages, the general classification, and points jersey in that year's Vuelta, which he followed with six stages of the Giro d'Italia. A huge crash on stage eight b took him out of the race with injuries that included a broken wrist. Apparently the team voted to withdraw from the race, but

1959	1963	1973	1981
Flandria enters professional racing, building the Italy-based Dr Mann-Flandria team around the Belgian sprinter Leon Vandaele. It wins forty-four races in its first season.	Flandria takes over as title sponsor, and six years later Roger De Vlaeminck, one of the greatest Classics riders, turns professional with them.	With another Belgian superstar, Freddy Maertens, on board, Flandria becomes the first European professional team to use Japan-made Shimano components.	Despite having dominated the Classics throughout the 1970s, a struggling Flandria is declared bankrupt. Superia buys the name, but Flandria bikes only last another five years.

Maertens convinced them to stay—and his teammate, Michel Pollentier, went on to win the overall competition in Maerten's place.

Maertens was soon back on his bike, and in 1978 it looked as though it could be the year for that elusive Tour de France win. He won stages five and seven, Kelly won stage six, and then Pollentier won on the Alpe d'Huez, pulling on the yellow jersey… before getting caught out in a fateful drugs test. The story goes that another rider had accidentally revealed his own contraption of pipes and a urine reservoir, causing the doctor to insist that other riders lift their shirts—Pollentier was caught trying to cheat the test and was disqualified.

Despite the fact that Marc Demeyer won stage nineteen, and Maertens won the points jersey, the team never really recovered from this blow. Pollentier left to set up his own team, Splendor, in 1979, and took riders including Sean Kelly. Maertens stayed, but was suffering from back problems caused by complications from the crash in 1977. Although three Flandria riders won stages in the Tour de France, and Joaquim

Agostinho came third overall, the results for the year were disappointing. It was the final season the team would ride; with the Flandria company suffering, there was no budget for the team and it closed at the end of the season.

In 1981, A. Claeys-Flandria was no longer selling bicycles, and the company went bankrupt. Remi Claeys's Superia bought the business, and, in an end to the family feud, the wall that divided the factory was pulled down. Even this could not save the brand: in 1986, the very last Superia-Flandria bikes were made. It truly was the end of an era, but although the company was gone it was not forgotten, and in 2002 the name was bought by Englishman Adam Longworth. In 2004 bicycle production began again under the Flandria name, aimed at the sportive and race market. Paul Claeys, the former boss, was pleased to see the name back on bicycles, and also that the new paint job paid tribute to the celebrated bikes of his past. Today, more than one hundred years after the first *vélomobiel* was produced, it is good to see that red and white Flandria frames are still taking on the cobbles of Belgium. *sc*

- Released in 2011, the carbon fibre Competition features nanotube technology.

- The Competition's nostalgic "Flandria Red" frame weighs in at 34.5 ounces (980 g).

Focus

A relative newcomer to the professional peloton, this German company builds bikes that have won plaudits for eye-catching designs and a commitment to innovative product development, and uses pro riders to test the latest Focus frames.

A part of giant German bike-maker Derby Cycle, Focus was born of racing and racing remains the area on which the marque concentrates, although it has grown in the last two decades to make everything from Tour de France bikes to battery-powered models to fuel Germany's electric bike boom. The last couple of years have seen Focus come to the fore as its riders have achieved success at the highest levels of road racing. In the 2011 Vuelta a España, Roberto Moreno and

Joaquim Rodríguez of the Katusha team brought Focus its first Grand Tour stage wins.

Focus brand manager Jörg Arenz has a fourteen-year association with the company, from winning the German cyclo-cross championship in 1998 to heading the design team for Focus since 2003. Arenz says that the Focus philosophy is "from professionals for professionals"—pro and former pro riders like Arenz himself drive the development of their bikes. "We are always

in touch with our teams, to get feedback on what we can do better or if we need to change something to make the frames stiffer or more comfortable," says Arenz.

Furthermore, team riders do not only suggest changes to current bikes. "The teams also test our new prototypes, which is very important for us in the development phase. Here we get direct feedback about what happens under race stress." It has been that way since Focus's inception. The mountain bike was booming all over Europe and 1992 cyclo-cross world champion Mike Kluge had been racing fat tyres, too, with considerable success: in 1990 Kluge won the mountain bike World Cup series. Kluge had an idea for a bike company that would focus on developing the best bikes for racing.

Success came quickly. In 1993 Kluge rode Focus bikes to victory in the German cyclo-cross national championships and to second place in the world championship. The first Focus range went on sale the following year and was an overnight success. With Kluge at the helm, Focus sponsored Germany's first professional mountain bike team

in 1995, and Kluge rode a Focus when mountain biking made its debut at the Olympics in 1996.

Focus was relaunched in 2004 after Arenz became product manager and introduced road bikes. Legendary German cyclo-cross rider Hanka Kupfernagel won the 'cross world championships aboard a Focus in 2005, and went on to take the world time trial title in 2006.

Focus's new effort in road bikes necessitated the exploration of new materials, and the company produced its first carbon fibre road bike—the Cayo—in 2006. Arenz says that being part of a much larger company gives Focus the resources to expand and innovate. Indeed, as Germany's biggest bike company, and one of the three largest in Europe, the "umbrella" offered by Derby allows Focus to devote much time and resources to research and development, although it can take longer for new projects to get started.

Nevertheless, Arenz heads a team of which he is clearly proud. Each member, he says, is "always involved in the creation of a new range." In his opinion, this makes Focus "the Formula One of cycling sport." *JS*

"We are always in touch with our teams, to get feedback on what we can do better."

JÖRG ARENZ

Gazelle

There is no country in the world that is as bicycle friendly as Holland, and the country's premier bike manufacturer, Gazelle, has been at the forefront of the Dutch obsession with bikes for more than half a century.

Royal Dutch Gazelle is one of the world's biggest bike producers. Its factory is located in Dieren in Holland, and has made more than thirteen million bikes for customers all over the world. Gazelles are also popular in the Dutch capital, and most people would agree that they are robust, reliable commuter bikes, because Amsterdam literally goes to work on Gazelles.

The company's involvement in the professional peloton has dwindled to nothing nowadays, but for a thirty-year spell, starting in the mid-1960s, Gazelle furnished consecutive generations of the top riders with a solid, trustworthy race frame that has come to be

a true classic: the Champion Mondial. It was the creation of Bertus Slesker, a Dutch master frame-builder, recruited in the late 1960s to Gazelle in order to help the company break into professional cycling and add some racing exoticism to what had become a staid, functional brand. The plan worked, and although the brand reserved its sponsorship almost exclusively for Dutch squads, Gazelle's Champion Mondial achieved formidable results all over the continent.

Peter Post, Rik Van Looy, René Pijnen, and Jan Raas all rode the Champion Mondial at points in their career. They enjoyed some of their most successful seasons aboard their Gazelles.

However, of all the great Classics men who rode Gazelles, Roger De Vlaeminck was probably the most prominent, after spending a couple of seasons late on in his career with the DAF Trucks squad in 1981 to 1982.

Another rider who almost made it into this hallowed group and whose name was synonymous with the Gazelle brand was the handsome Dutchman Hennie Kuiper. His face smiles beatifically out of the 1976 Gazelle brochure, aboard his Champion Mondial and resplendent in the rainbow jersey that he won in Yvoir, Belgium, the previous year. In 1977 he finished second behind Bernard Thévenet at the Tour de France by the excruciating margin of forty-eight seconds. The disappointment was compounded further when Thévenet later admitted to using cortisone in order to win the race. In 1980, Kuiper finished second again, but this time he was soundly beaten by Hendrik "Joop" Zoetemelk. However, Kuiper's career went from strength to strength, and it was in 1981, as a member of the DAF-Cote d'Or-Gazelle squad, alongside De Vlaeminck, that he had his most prolific season and won both the Tour of Flanders and the late season Giro di Lombardia.

Through both success and disappointment in the later part of his career, Kuiper kept his own counsel—he preferred to let his performances do the talking. The Dutchman knew that he was no match for the sprinters, so his trademark was to launch a break, sometimes more than a dozen kilometres out, and catch his opponents by surprise. Just as the gazelle uses surprise and quick wits to dart away from its predators, so too did Kuiper, the stealthy winner.

Although Gazelles have vanished from the pro peloton with equal stealth, ending with the TVM team in 1998, the company still produces 300,000 bikes a year from its factory in Dieren. In 2010 it was even voted the most trusted bicycle brand in the *Reader's Digest* annual Europe-wide poll. **SD**

■ Riding for DAF-Cote d'Or-Gazelle, De Vlaeminck was second in the 1981 Paris–Roubaix.

■ This 1981 Gazelle Champion Mondial uses a 4.5-pound (2-kg) A frame and is fitted with Reynolds 531 fork blades.

Giant

The Taiwanese company lives up to its name as the world's biggest manufacturer, and produces five million bicycles a year: from cheap runarounds to state-of-the-art racing machines graced by stars including Laurent Jalabert, Mark Cavendish, and Marianne Vos.

Giant founder King Liu (right) pictured with CEO Tony Lo in 1972.

Mark Cavendish (left) battles Robbie McEwen to the finish of the 2007 Scheldeprijs semi-classic.

The Scheldeprijs is a race for sprinters, and in 2007 it celebrated its centenary year. Giant provided bikes for the T-Mobile team, who went on to win the race. However, it was no ordinary win, because the victor was wild card Mark Cavendish, who was still a month shy of his twenty-first birthday, and it was his first pro race win in his neo-pro season at T-Mobile.

That April afternoon in Belgium, the pro peloton took the long way from Antwerp to Schoten, pushing the ride out to almost 124 miles (200 km). A few cobbles, no climbs. In the pack, the T-Mobile riders worked for their German sprinter André Greipel, and shared the load to hold breakaways to a manageable limit and not reel them in too soon. Inside the final 9.3 miles (15 km), their *directeur sportif*, Allan Peiper, played a wild card, cut one rider loose, and told him to

ride his own race. Everyone else was to carry Greipel to the kilometre-to-go kite and guide him through the finale, their well-drilled sprint train launching the German to the finish line with a couple of hundred metres to go.

With just 1.2 miles (2 km) left, Lotto and Milram were driving the pace and setting things up for Robbie McEwen and Erik Zabel. Past the kite, Zabel made a surprise early move. McEwen was quickly on his wheel and past him. Quick Step's Wouter Weylandt rode out of his skin and dragged Gert Steegmans in pursuit of McEwen's wheel. There was no sign of Greipel and his lead-out train. However, Peiper's wild card had zeroed in on Steegmans, and it became all about picking and choosing the right wheel to follow.

McEwen was surging for the line when Weylandt peeled away to give Steegmans clean air. And off Steegmans's wheel and past him came Peiper's wild card. McEwen was still surging for the line but began to fight his bike, trying to find that last burst of speed. Off to his right, Peiper's wild card had his whole body low, eyes fixed on the prize; his biceps bulged as he rocketed for the line. McEwen tried, but at the line it was Peiper's wild card, Mark Cavendish, who punched the air in victory.

As wins go, that 2007 Scheldeprijs victory did not rate high in the palmarès of Cavendish's bike provider—Giant—that season. This was its tenth year of providing bikes for the pros in the peloton, first to Manolo Saíz's ONCE squad and for the previous four years to T-Mobile. With ONCE and T-Mobile, Giant's bikes had already won a couple of Monuments (Liège–Bastogne–Liège and the Tour of Flanders), some true Classics (Ghent–Wevelgem and Paris–Tours), and assorted other victories. As far as Giant was concerned Scheldeprijs was just another day, another bike race—one more notch on the bed post. For Cavendish, of course, it was just the beginning.

Giant itself is, relatively speaking, one of the new kids on the block. It has "only" been operating for forty years, which is no time at

■ ONCE rider Laurent
Jalabert during the stage
one time trial of the
2000 Tour de France.

in cycling. Furthermore, the company hails from Taiwan, which has no roots in cycling's traditional heartlands. And, to add insult to injury, Giant produces bikes on an industrial scale.

Founded in Taiwan in 1972 by King Liu with the sole purpose of building and badging bikes for other people, the Giant Manufacturing Company produced almost 4,000 bikes in its first year on a start-up budget of about US $100,000. By 2007, when Cavendish won his first pro race on one of its bikes, Giant's output had grown to five million bikes a year and the company was worth a billion dollars. Turning US $100,000 into US $1 billion is an extraordinary achievement, but it might not have happened: Giant could happily have gone on being best known for the bikes it built and badged for other people, rather than bikes bearing its own name. Over the years it had built bikes for the likes of Trek, Specialized, and Colnago. However, the actions of another customer altered the course of Giant's history, and that customer was Schwinn.

In the 1970s, Schwinn was the biggest bike company in the United States, with a history dating back to the days when Major Taylor was the hottest sprinter on the planet. In the 1970s, most Americans would have said "Schwinn" when you said bicycle, in the same way that British people might have responded with "Raleigh." As the 1970s drew to a close, a new generation of Schwinns took over the family business. They immediately began to struggle, and drove the once venerable company to the brink of bankruptcy. Teetering on the edge of survival, Schwinn began to farm out production to Asia—specifically, to Giant. Thanks to the high quality and low cost of the bikes that Giant made, Schwinn was soon back in business.

Schwinn decided to diversify its supply chain and switched some of its production to China. The company decided to take a US $2 million stake in its new supplier—the China Bicycle Company—much to the annoyance of the people at Giant. They retaliated by hiring a former Schwinn marketing executive, Bill Austin, and putting him in charge of the company.

This happened in 1986 and for the previous five years or so Giant had been producing a small number of bikes under its own name, primarily for the local market. Austin decided that it was time for Giant to go global. If Giant faced one major obstacle, it was the "Made in Taiwan" tag, which too often was associated with poor quality. Convincing retailers of the quality of its bikes was easy enough: all Giant had to do was point out that it had been selling bicycles for years anyway, only they had been bearing the badges of other brands. Proving its excellence to consumers took a lot more work.

In the 1990s Giant started sponsoring pro teams in order to prove the quality of its wares. It started with mountain bikes, then became involved with the Australian Institute of Sport before moving on to the pro peloton with ONCE. Johan Bruyneel, Laurent Jalabert, and Carlos Sastre were some of the first riders to get to play with Giant's new toy, the compact road frame.

Compact road frame is just a concise way of saying a sloping top tube and a tighter rear triangle. It is another contribution to cycling's "size zero" obsession: every ounce counts and a smaller frame means less weight. A smaller frame also produces a more rigid ride and some better handling characteristics. The aesthetic cost—that superlong seatpost—riders either love or loathe. The same is true of the sloping top tube.

When Giant first took on Europe, it set up shop in the Netherlands. In the late 1990s, it opened a new manufacturing plant there. Since 2009, the Dutch Rabobank squad has been the biggest brand ambassadors for Giant's bikes, with Denis Menchov winning the 2009 Giro d'Italia and Oscar Freire adding Milan–San Remo a year later. Giant is a long way from being able to call itself a Dutch company, but it is certainly putting down roots in the Netherlands.

TCR AND RABOBANK FRAMES

OMNIUM FF
The stiff, aerodynamic ALUXX SL-grade aluminium frame features composite forks.

RABOBANK ROAD
This entirely handmade frame is constructed of strategically layered uni-directional carbon.

RABOBANK TT
Designed for speed, the TT frame moved the front brake behind the fork crown to reduce drag.

Giant also provides bikes for the Rabobank development squad, which has already produced successful riders such as Lars Boom and 2012 graduate Jetse Bol. There is the women's squad, too, and the incomparable Marianne Vos. Vos wins races off-road and on. She has won gold medals in the Olympic Games on the track; she has also won national, European, and world championships. She has won the Flèche Wallonne Féminine four times; in 2011 she won the Giro d'Italia Femminile (Giro Donne). At the Giro, she sealed her claim to the *maglia rosa* by dropping Garmin-Cervélo's Emma Pooley on the Passo di Mortirolo. In the Netherlands, if manufacturers want their bikes to sell, all they have to do is persuade Vos to ride them and they will fly out the door.

Forty years after the creation of the company by King Liu, Giant has risen from nowhere to become king of the hill. It is not the biggest bike maker in the industry, but it is not far off the mark. Getting to the top was hard work. Staying there will be harder still because the advantage that Giant had in its earlier years—cheap labour—has now passed to China, and Giant's prices are being undercut. Building and badging bikes for others is still an important part of Giant's business, so pricing matters.

In order to counter this, Giant has shifted some of its production to China and expanded its business. It has looked down the supply chain and bought one of its aluminium suppliers. However, Giant is also moving sideways, and electronic bikes are leading the company into producing electronic cars. The future is, after all, green. Within a few years, it is possible that a Giant-sponsored pro team will be supported by a fleet of Giant-made e-cars. **FMK**

1972	1980	1986	1996
King Liu establishes the Giant Manufacturing Company in Taiwan.	Eight years after starting the business, Giant is the largest bicycle manufacturer in Taiwan.	Giant expands its business in the Netherlands, and—over the next eight years—sets up in the United States, Japan, Canada, Australia, and China.	The company opens a production facility in the Netherlands; it is its first in Europe.

"Our bicycles are born with a spirit of adventure, and they offer our riders companionship wherever they may be going."

ANTHONY LO

■ The stunning 2012 Giant TCR Advanced SL ISP Rabobank (team issue).

■ Marianne Vos (in orange) in the 2010 Women's Omnium at the UCI world track cycling championships.

1997	1998	2002	2007
With an eye firmly on expansion, Giant creates the Chuansin Metal Products company in China.	Giant produces 2,840,000 bicycles in a year.	The company smashes its production record by manufacturing 4,730,000 bicycles in a year.	Giant manufactures five million bikes and the company is valued at US $1 billion.

ONCE TEAM'S 1997 GIANT TCR

When the Spanish ONCE team arrived at races in August 1997 with Giant TCR road bikes, it raised more than a few eyebrows. Until then road bike geometry conformed to a pattern of measurement and design, with frames typically built with long, flat top tubes. In order to improve stiffness frame-builders would simply use stiffer materials, even if that negated elements of comfort and power displacement.

But ONCE—pronounced "On-say," named after its sponsor, the Spanish charity for the blind, and dubbed the yellow peril for the colour of its kit and all-conquering performances—was an innovative, forward-thinking team. And so it was characteristic of the Spanish squad to form an alliance with the Taiwanese company Giant, who broke the mould with its new, mountain bike–influenced frame design.

British bike designer Mike Burrows—responsible for Chris Boardman's carbon fibre Lotus—had moved to Giant in the mid-1990s, and he was the man who came up with the TCR, or "Compact" road frame. The sloping top tube allowed for the size of the front and rear triangles to vary, which shed weight and improved stiffness without compromising comfort.

Laurent Jalabert, Abraham Olano, and Carlos Sastre were among the first riders to race on the TCRs and, although ONCE folded in the early 2000s, Giants were used subsequently by T-Mobile and Rabobank. Many have attempted to copy Giant, but the yellow bike that raised eyebrows in 1997 easily retains its status as a landmark machine.

Giant was one of the first manufacturers to use micro-adjustable aero seatposts, which were bladed for better aerodynamics.

The original TCR frames came in only three sizes, small, medium, and large, but the portfolio has since been increased to six sizes for men and four for women.

Giant sourced components from Italy, with Cinelli and Campagnolo adding the finishing touches to its TCR machines.

Giant pioneered the sloping downwards top tube. The idea came from mountain bike design and proved popular on the road scene.

DESIGN DETAILS

BRAKE LEVERS

Ergopower, Campagnolo's integrated gear and brake system, was launched in 1992. The ONCE TCR frames were equipped with Campagnolo's Record groupset, featuring hidden brake and gear cables.

CRANKSET

The TCR is equipped with a top of the range C-Record crankset manufactured by Italian component giant Campagnolo. It has 6.89-inch (175-mm) cranks and 53/39 chainrings.

■ Riding for Brooklyn,
Roger De Vlaeminck
and Aldo Gios make
last-minute adjustments.

■ Alfredo Gios
photographed in
1979 working on
the prototype of
his "Lite" model.

Gios

An Italian bike manufacturer with a Belgian flavour, Gios made the distinctive blue frames and earned fame and notoriety in the 1970s when it supplied the Brooklyn Racing Team, an Italian squad that dominated the tough Classics of northern Europe.

In the 1970s and 1980s, if a bike shop added Gios frames to its range, it could spark a mini riot. Bike fans would arrive in numbers to drool over these fantastic Italian imports, and no wonder—a brand new Gios frame, seen for the first time, is a thing of beauty, a study in elegant simplicity. The lustrous blue paint job was enough in itself to take one's breath away, but, back then, there were other details to suggest that this was a frame like few others. It was carefully packed in its polystyrene home, together with several matching accessories, including a Gios jersey, *casquette*, and *bidon*; a new Gios would also typically come with an engraved Cinelli Record 1R handlebar stem, a Campagnolo seatpost and chainring, and, finally, and most appealingly, a small tin of "Gios blue" paint.

Like Henry Ford before it, Gios would build its customers a bike in any colour they wanted— as long as it was blue. But what a blue! It is as distinctive to Gios as celeste green is to Bianchi.

Unlike Bianchi, however, the reason for the standard paint scheme is generally agreed upon.

Tolmino Gios was born on March 4, 1916, in Vittorio Veneto in the province of Treviso. When he was two years old, the family moved to Turin, the town that would become inextricably linked with Gios bicycles. The roads around there provided the perfect terrain for Tolmino to ride his bike, and in 1931, at the age of fifteen, he joined the rank of "cadet riders."

Over the next few years Tolmino enjoyed success in many races, culminating in an extraordinary victory in the 1936 edition of the "Kings Cup," a big amateur race in Milan. Young Gios reportedly finished the race with an average speed of more than 26 miles per hour (42 km/h), a performance that should have resulted in selection for the world championships in Bern and the Berlin Olympics. However, a major disagreement with the national team manager resulted in his exclusion from both. It was Italy's loss, because France dominated the Olympic road events and Italy returned with only a silver medal in the team pursuit. Despite this setback, Tolmino still made the professional ranks and competed in several Giri d'Italia alongside some of the greats of Italian cycling, although he never quite matched his feats as an amateur.

After the end of World War II, in which Tolmino served as a corporal major, he returned to Turin and set up a bike shop in 1948. Although he originally focused on building practical bikes for city use, it was inevitable, given his background, that he would gravitate towards the construction of lightweight racing cycles. But it took a while. Over the next ten years the shop prospered, and it became home to the Velo Club Gios, which nurtured local cyclists, the best known of whom was the tall, lithe Italo Zilioli, who joined in 1958. Zilioli won the national championship aboard a

Gios, and would go on to win five stages of the Giro throughout his career.

During the late 1950s and early 1960s Gios's frame production flourished, but Tolmino could not run the factory forever and, in 1958, when he was fifty-two, he handed over the day-to-day running to his three sons, Adrian and Alfredo, who would attend to administration, and Aldo, who would look after the manufacturing and development side of the business.

Not that Tolmino walked away, far from it. He guided his boys and passed on the lessons that he had learnt, thus ensuring that the business was in safe hands. The plan worked because in the hands of the three Gios sons the brand developed well. Their success owed much to a chance encounter at the 1971 Milan Trade Show. In fact, the brother's decision to exhibit there was a turning point in the destiny of "Gios Torino."

"Like Henry Ford I will sell you a bike in any colour you like, as long as it's blue!"

ALDO GIOS

■ This 1970s bicycle features the distinctive colouring, described by Gios as "electric, vivid, almost surreal."

■ Four-time Paris–Roubaix winner De Vlaeminck, seen here in 1973 in his distinctive Brooklyn jersey.

■ A promotional poster from the 1970s proudly shows De Vlaeminck astride his Gios.

The chance encounter was with Giorgio Perfetti, the owner of Brooklyn Chewing Gum. Perfetti's eye was caught by a Gios bike and he wandered over to visit the stand. He had spotted the "Easy Rider"—a bike that was only there to stimulate interest in the rest of the range. Perfetti claimed that he was "struck by lightning" the moment he saw it. He was convinced that this bicycle would be perfect to give away as a prize in his "Brooklyn Chewing Gum cycling competition." Catching the Gios brothers off-guard, he ordered one hundred Easy Riders on the spot.

Alfredo would later cite that meeting as vital in influencing the future direction of the Gios brand. This was because Giorgio Perfetti, in addition to running competitions, also set up a professional cycling team with Franco Cribiori, who had been a distinguished racer the previous decade. The Brooklyn Racing Team was unusual for an Italian squad because it specialized in the Classics, but it captured the imagination as much for its distinctive jerseys as for its many victories.

Gios's involvement went beyond mere bike sponsor. The smitten Perfetti insisted that the company supplied customized bikes in the same shade of blue as the Brooklyn jersey. The jersey was reminiscent of the US flag: red stripes on the lower half, with the top and shoulders a striking royal blue. Brooklyn stood out for more than its jerseys. The team signed the Belgian superstar Roger De Vlaeminck and his countryman, the track racing legend Patrick Sercu. Known as the "Gypsy" on account of his travelling family's roots, De Vlaeminck was also called "Monsieur Paris–Roubaix" for his four victories in the cobbled Classic—all bar one, his first in 1972, ridden on a beautiful blue Gios.

1948	1971	1972	1978
Returning to Turin after serving in World War II, Tolmino Gios opens a bicycle shop.	Alfredo Gios meets Giorgio Perfetti, owner of the Brooklyn Chewing Gum brand. Perfetti orders one hundred bikes to give away as prizes.	Perfetti establishes his Brooklyn Racing Team using Gios bikes and expertise. The team, which included Roger De Vlaeminck, would go on to win multiple titles.	Alfredo Gios signs with Gustav Janssens, an ice cream maker. Dietrich "Didi" Thurau claims some significant victories for the team.

1980

Dutch bike dealer François Vermeer and Alfredo Gios create Vermeer-Thiys-Gios. Riders for this pro team include Michel Pollentier and Alfons "Fons" De Wolf.

1990s

The Kelme team has six seasons of victories for Gios from 1994 to 1999, including Fernando Escartin's podium place in the 1999 Tour de France.

2004

The Relax team is created, and it goes on to ride Gios bikes for three seasons under the management of Jesus Suarez Cueva.

2010

The Gios brand is sold to its Japanese distributor, and the company concentrates on mid-market models.

The Paris–Roubaix successes were arguably the best advertising for any bike manufacturer. The "Hell of the North" is the toughest of the Classics, with its tortuous sections of pavé dishing out a relentless, brutal punishment to both man and machine. De Vlaeminck negotiated these with incredible grace, and made it appear as though his Gios was floating over the cobbles.

De Vlaeminck, Brooklyn, and Gios all featured prominently in Danish filmmaker Jorgen Leith's film, the highly rated *A Sunday in Hell*, which documented the 1976 edition of the race. Although he only managed to finish third that year, De Vlaeminck's style and panache won him many more admirers—and probably sold a few Gios bikes as a result.

The following year brought an end to the Brooklyn team, but Gios did not disappear from top-flight racing. The company was now firmly established as one of the best manufacturers, and recognized the benefits of operating in the shop window offered by the pro teams. Its next major partnership began in 1978 when it agreed to supply bicycles to a Belgian racing team sponsored by the ice cream manufacturer IJsboerke. The roster included German star Dietrich "Didi" Thurau, who scored many memorable victories during his career, including the 1979 Liège–Bastogne–Liège.

The next memorable association between a Gios bike and a star rider was Alfons "Fons" De Wolf, who had been tipped as a successor to Eddy Merckx and was another stylish Belgian who oozed class aboard his blue machine. Although De Wolf never lived up to the pressures placed upon him in cycling-mad Belgium, he took a solo victory in the 1981 edition of Milan–San Remo, with De Vlaeminck making it a Belgian one-two as he won the bunch sprint, eleven seconds back.

The roll call of Gios riders is impressive, including Giro winners Michel Pollentier, Roberto Visentini, and Stephen Roche, as well as Laudelino Cubino, Fernando Escartín, Roberto Heras,

■ Fernando Escartín and his Gios battle through stage fifteen of the 1999 Tour de France.

■ The Gios Gress 105 features a carbon monocoque frame, carbon forks, and a Shimano groupset.

and, more recently, the Italian sprinter Ivan "Il Ghepardo" (The Cheetah) Quaranta, who won five stages at the 2001 Giro.

Aldo Gios was at the heart of the company's bike development and he introduced many interesting and novel refinements to his frames over the years, without detracting from the purity of the craftsmanship. He was one of the first to introduce microfusion cast elements to his frames, including a bottom bracket shell that was rigid enough to do away with the traditional chain stay bridge. This area was always difficult for any frame-builder because excessive heat during manufacture could result in critical tube failure. Gios also produced a micro-adjustable dropout to a frame that he introduced as the Compact. This allowed for extremely precise alignment of the rear wheel and introduced a replaceable gear hanger, which proved useful if the frame was damaged in a crash, because it avoided having to return it to the factory.

In 1998 Gios celebrated its fiftieth anniversary with the introduction of the Cinquantenario

frame, built from a custom-drawn Dedacciai 7003 alloy tubeset, and instantly hailed a "modern classic."

It is the distinctive bright blue, recognized by cognoscenti the world over, that is the Gios trademark. However, the paint scheme—and even the name—might not signify quite the same craftsmanship as it did in the past. It has become more difficult for quality frame-builders such as Gios to compete in a marketplace that is increasingly dominated by mass manufacturers, so the company has had to change.

In 2010, the Gios name was sold to its Japanese distributor. This has resulted in a sprawling range of middle-market bikes that, in truth, only share the blue paint job with the old Gios frames. Today, it is Aldo who is the keeper of the flame. He continues to work in his factory in Volpiano with his son, Mauro, building high-quality frames badged "Original GIOS Torino." Reportedly, the split between the brothers was not caused by a family feud, but by a legal dispute with a Belgian dealer. The Sogno Blue lives on. **RD**

"The point was that we made the bikes, my brother and I. Even if we could not build every frame, nothing ever left this factory without us first seeing it."

ALDO GIOS

■ The 1976 catalogue
showcased the Gypsy
Sport general purpose
bike, Gitane 600 tourer,
and the Interclub racer.

■ Gitane made this
unused prototype
design for Fignon's 1987
Hour record attempt.

Gitane

An array of cycling legends, including Greg LeMond, Bernard Hinault, Laurent Fignon, and Jacques Anquetil, made French company Gitane one of the most prominent and most prestigious manufacturers in the history of the sport.

Gypsy women. Cigarettes. Tough men and steel bikes. These are the associations that many people make with the word "Gitane." In the cycling world, most people associate Bernard Hinault with Gitane, because together they sum up a particular era: an era of men for all seasons, when riders could win the Tour and the Classics, and would race and win from March to October.

The first Gitane bikes began to appear in the late 1920s. A few years earlier, Marcel Brunelière had set up shop as a blacksmith in the town of Machecoul; as well as shoeing horses and fixing farming equipment, he began to assemble bicycles, and then started to build his own. In the 1950s he added motorcycles to his range, and the company name became Micmo (Manufacture Industrielle de Cycles et de Motocycles).

When he started to make his own bikes, Brunelière chose the name "Gitane" but the reason is not clear. For twenty years Gitanes had been the name of a popular brand of cigarettes, whose blue box featured a tambourine-playing gypsy. The word itself is French for gypsy woman,

and so has a certain air of romance and freedom associated with it. And, in the 1920s, cycling was all about romance and freedom.

Brunelière started sponsoring cycling teams in the 1940s but did not have much success until the 1960s. Riders such as José Beyaert, Roger Piel, and Roger Walkowiak passed through the squads in their early years. In 1960 Gitane, after a brief hiatus, returned to the sport with the Rapha-Gitane-Dunlop squad. Ab Geldermans won Liège–Bastogne–Liège. Roger Rivière won a couple of stages in the Tour de France. Jo de Haan won Paris–Tours. The next year Tom Simpson won the Ronde van Vlaanderen. This gave Gitane an admirable but not momentous record.

In 1963, everything clicked into place. Three teams merged into one and formed the Saint-Raphaël-Gitane-Géminiani supersquad. Raphaël Géminiani and Raymond Louviot were the team bosses, and their riders were some of the most memorable in the sport's history: Jacques Anquetil, Rudi Altig, Guy Ignolin, Roger Hassenforder, Jean Stablinski, Shay Elliott, Ab

Geldermans, and Jo de Rooy. Wins included the Tour, Paris–Tours, the Giro di Lombardia, and Paris–Nice.

The following year Arie den Hartog joined the team and victories included Ghent–Wevelgem, the Ronde van Vlaanderen, the Giro d'Italia, and another Tour. A year later, with Ford France as the sponsor (and British rider Vin Denson on the squad) it added another Paris–Nice win along with victories in Milan–San Remo, the Critérium International, and the GP des Nations. Furthermore, Anquetil pulled off his Critérium du Dauphiné Libéré/Bordeaux–Paris double.

Within three years the word "Gitane" had become synonymous with French cycling. But then it stopped. In 1966 Brunelière sold up and retired. Micmo was sold again in 1970. In 1974 Renault acquired 30 percent of the company, and then bought Micmo outright in 1976.

Gitane bikes returned to the pro peloton in the 1970s and started small. In 1973 Joop Zoetemelk won stages in Paris–Nice and the Tour. Britain's Michael Wright also won a Tour

stage. In 1974 Gitane became the co-sponsor of the Sonolor squad, where Jean Stablinski was *directeur sportif*. Stablinski had been a Gitane rider in the 1950s, and also in the 1960s as part of the superteam built around Maître Jacques (Anquetil). Among Stablinski's riders at Sonolor in 1974 were Lucien Van Impe, José De Cauwer, Willy Teirlinck, and Bernard Hinault. They won nothing. The following year was more successful. Hinault won the pro-am Circuit de la Sarthe and Van Impe won the King of the Mountains jersey in the Tour.

A year later Stablinski left the company and Cyrille Guimard took over. Guimard had been a cyclist of some renown before injury forced him to retire. He actually started the 1976 season as a Gitane-Campagnolo rider and won a couple of cyclo-cross races before taking over as *directeur sportif* when the road season began. At the end of the Tour, Lucien Van Impe was the man in the *maillot jaune,* and the legend of Cyrille Guimard was born: the *directeur sportif* told his rider that if he did not attack he would drive him off the road. Van Impe attacked and won the Tour. However,

the lightweight Belgian climber did not have the core of steel that Guimard was looking for in a rider and quit the team at the end of the season. No one cared because in 1977 Hinault won Ghent–Wevelgem, Liège–Bastogne–Liège, the Dauphiné Libéré, and the GP des Nations, and Bernard Quilfen was one of three Gitane riders to bag stages in the Tour that year. Dawn had broken on Gitane's golden age.

In 1978 Renault became the lead sponsor for the team, and it was a relationship that lasted through to 1985. These were Guimard's glory years. As well as nurturing Hinault's talent, Guimard brought Laurent Fignon through the ranks and introduced Greg LeMond to Europe. During those years, there were few races that Gitane did not win, because if a race was worth winning, Guimard's team would win it: all three Grand Tours, all five Monuments, and most of the important one-day and multi-day races of the time. And the team won with style, class, and panache.

Fignon's autobiography, *We Were Young and Carefree*, goes into great detail about those years. Richard Moore's *Slaying the Badger* and Sam Abt's *LeMond: The Incredible Comeback* also offer fascinating detail and insight. It is most important to understand that all these stories have four men at their core: Guimard, Hinault, LeMond, and Fignon. All are men of fiery temperament. All are men of character: men with a steel core, hard and uncompromising.

Clearly the bikes played an important role in these victories, too. Although Gitane was not particularly cutting edge in its use of materials—Reynolds and Columbus tubing still ruled the roost—its bikes were solid, reliable, and functional. They were not fancy works of art, but

1925	1926	1940	1957
Marcel Brunelière opens a mechanics shop and forge in Machecoul, France.	Brunelière opens a bicycle manufacturing shop in a horse stables on Rue des Redoux in Machecoul, and produces two to three bikes a day.	Frame production begins in earnest, and the company now produces complete bicycles.	Jacques Anquetil scores the company its first major win when he rides a Gitane to victory in the French national championships.

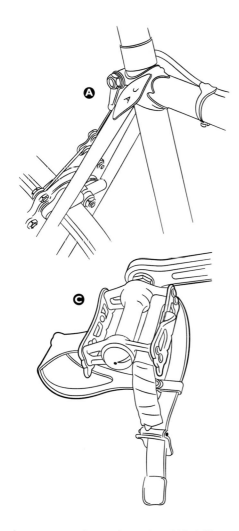

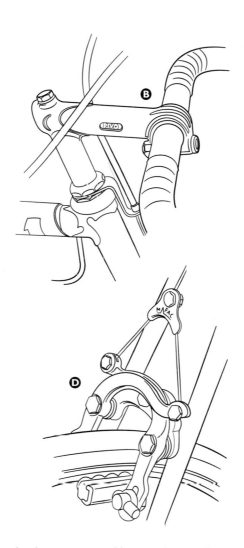

■ Jacques Anquetil won
the 1962 Tour de France
at a speed that was not
bettered until 1981.

■ Detail drawings of
Jacques Anquetil's 1964
Tour de France bike:
Ⓐ seat lug
Ⓑ alloy stem
Ⓒ Campagnolo pedals
Ⓓ MAFAC brakes.

they were good enough to win cobbled Classics, and good enough to ride day after day in the Grand Tours. The bikes were, in many ways, not unlike the men who rode them to glory; they had a character that grew on you.

One area in which Gitane did innovate was time trial bikes. In 1979 Guimard had special low-profile bikes built for his riders. Other developments saw cables routed internally, or the front brake placed behind the fork. Every aerodynamic advantage was considered. Being part of the Renault group—and so having access to Renault's wind tunnel—had its advantages.

However, Gitane's winning streak came to an end when Renault began to face business problems and in 1985 sold Micmo. Gitane was

1972	1974	1992	2012
Micmo, as the company was renamed in 1960, is France's biggest exporter of bicycles, sending more than 185,000 overseas per year.	Renault buys a 30 percent interest in the company. Two years later it is fully annexed into its Renault Factory Group, only to be dropped in 1985.	Gitane, Peugeot, and BH cycles combined to form Cycleurope, the largest manufacturer of bicycles in Europe. In 2000, Cycleurope is purchased by Grimaldi.	Today, Gitanes produced in Machecoul are only available in France. A Taiwan-made Gitane is available in Australia.

Hinault in the yellow
jersey during the 1981
Tour de France. He
won by an almost
fifteen-minute margin.

able to stay involved with the sport for another
few years and provided the bikes for Guimard
and Fignon's new squad, Système U, but that
ceased at the end of 1988. In 1992 Micmo was
sold yet again—the fifth time in twenty-six years—
to Spanish bike manufacturer BH (Beistegui
Hermanos). BH also acquired Peugeot's bike
business, and Gitane became part of a portfolio
of brands operating under the umbrella of
Cycleurope. The Swedish group Grimaldi then
acquired Cycleurope in the early 1990s. Today,
Gitane is just one brand in a portfolio that also
includes Legnano, Bianchi, and Puch.

Gitane had some involvement with top-level
cycling at the end of the 1990s and in the early
2000s, providing bikes for La Française des Jeux
(1997–2001) and then BigMat-Auber (2002–03).
The Madiot brothers, Marc and Yvon, were
Française des Jeux's *directeurs sportifs* and had
themselves been part of Guimard's squads in the
1980s and had ridden Gitanes. In 2010, the Gitane
brand returned to the peloton and provided bikes
for the Pro Conti squad Saur-Sojasun, where
Stéphane Heulot was *directeur sportif*. Heulot had
been a rider with Française des Jeux. Despite all
the gaps in Gitane's sponsorships through the
years, there remains a sense of continuity.

This continuity exists in the way that the
bikes are built today, with steel and aluminium.
Gitanes are still produced in Machecoul and also
in Peugeot's old factory in Romilly sur Seine. Most
of Gitane's bikes, though, are for the urban and
recreational market. Cycleurope's star brand
is Bianchi, and it is through this that they stay
involved with cycling at the elite level.

Today, the thought of a Gitane being ridden
to victory in the Tour—or in any of the major
races—seems more remote than that of a French
rider finishing in Paris in the *maillot jaune*. One
day it may happen. Until it does, there is more
than enough nostalgia from the days of Cyrille
Guimard and the exploits of Hinault, Fignon, and
LeMond to keep the Gitane flame alive. **FMK**

*"Gitane bikes were
handcrafted in
the factory. The
best workers were
assigned to the
professional bikes."*

BERNARD HINAULT

Guerciotti

Versatility is a Guerciotti hallmark, but, unusually for an Italian bike company, these Milanese frame-builders have developed a reputation for excellence in a discipline more popular in northern Europe: the winter sport of cyclo-cross.

The fact that a top professional cyclist rides a particular brand of bike should not inform anyone's choice of machine when looking for a new model. Professional riders are paid to race on whatever bike they are supplied with, after all, and will say that it is the finest bike they have ever ridden, that it handles like a dream, and does everything and more that is asked of it. However, the whole team equipment sponsorship relationship would break down if the public did not respond to advertising.

It is almost impossible not to be impressed by British cyclo-cross champion Helen Wyman racing aboard her Guerciotti, for example. When questioned about her machine, Helen did indeed

claim that it really was the very best she had ever ridden. This may be a predictable response, but there is no point denying that the Guerciotti does feel fast. It also looks cool, and it is Italian.

In 1964 company founder Italo Guerciotti opened his small shop in Milan with his brother, Paolo (a talented rider himself), and advice and guidance from the great Cino Cinelli. The company expanded rapidly through the 1970s and produced the usual range of road and track frames alongside its renowned off-road versions. Today the modern frames, mostly in carbon, lack the charm of their steel forebears but also, importantly, the weight: the top of the range Eureka comes in at less than half the poundage of the lugged steel Record. The only model in Guerciotti's portfolio that comes in for criticism is the Team Replica, which has an integrated seatpost that many people regard as pointless and infuriating.

Guerciotti's statistics are very impressive: its bikes have been ridden to ten cyclo-cross world championships, including by the likes of Radomir Simunek and Roland Liboton, both of whom are great riders, and that extreme rarity, an Italian winner—Daniele Pontoni—who was cyclo-cross amateur world champion in 1992 and elite world champion in 1997. The brand has also made an impact on the road. In 2008 the Serramenti PVC Diquigiovanni-Androni Giocattoli team rode Guerciottis. The first season saw a cluster of small wins, but the 2009 season was a different story, and the team claimed three stages of the 2009 centenary edition of the Giro d'Italia. Having missed out on invites to the Tour de France and Vuelta a España that year, the team regarded the Giro as its most important race of the season, and it did not disappoint. Operación Puerto refugee, Michele Scarponi, took the first win. On stage five, the Italian lost five minutes in the general classification but bounced back the following day to seal a notable win in Mayrhofen, Austria. It set the team on a winning streak, and Leonardo Bertagnolli took a stage before Michele Scarponi bagged his second win of the race on stage eighteen to Benevento.

The following year the team returned to the Giro on Guerciottis, and Scarponi took home another stage victory and fourth place in the general classification. The sponsorship deal with Androni Giocattoli soon came to an end, but in 2011 Guerciotti put its name to the Miche-Guerciotti race team, to supply bikes and become joint sponsor. This confirms that Guerciotti's output is still going strong and while the muddy conditions of cyclo-cross may not appeal to everyone, there is no doubting the quality of these bicycles from Milan. **IC**

■ Paolo Guerciotti was a dedicated 'cross rider who competed in the 1979 world championships.

■ The 1979 Guerciotti Oro features, from top to bottom, a gold-plated anodized finish below the seatpost, curved forks, seat stays, and the company's star logo on the head tube.

LeMond makes adjustments to his saddle in his home workshop.

Research and development in 1989, aided by LeMond and a wind tunnel at the St-Cyr Aerotechnical Institute in France.

LeMond

Greg LeMond, the United States' pioneering three-time Tour de France winner, was always fastidious about his bikes and he adopted the same approach to the machines produced in his name, until a dispute with Trek stopped the company in its tracks.

"I was looking at a lot of different bikes out there and things weren't great and things hadn't really advanced."

GREG LeMOND

Greg LeMond's name is synonymous with more than innovation—more like revolution. LeMond was the American who arrived in Europe in the early 1980s and was at the forefront of the massive changes to the sport that followed, from equipment to riders' pay, during a decade in which the European stranglehold was broken by an invasion of English-speaking riders.

At the head of that invasion was LeMond. He was the first rider to sign a million-dollar contract, the first non-European to win the Tour de France (in 1986), and the first to do so on a carbon fibre bike. For his second Tour victory

in 1989, he became the first high-profile rider to use "triathlon" handlebars as he raced to the narrowest win in Tour history, and, following that success, he took cyclists' wages into the stratosphere, signing a three-year contract worth US $5.5 million. The circle was completed for his third and final Tour win in 1990, when he rode one of his own LeMond-branded bikes.

It was in 1985 that LeMond and his father, Bob, first began discussing the possibility of setting up a family-run bike company. It was an obvious direction for him to take: LeMond was fascinated by bicycle design and biomechanics, and the LeMond name was both unusual and very marketable. His 1986 Tour victory had resonated back home in the States, with major coverage in the mainstream press and magazines such as *Sports Illustrated* and even *Rolling Stone*, not to mention an invitation to the White House from President Reagan.

The original plan had been for the bike company to be established once LeMond retired from racing. However, the plans were accelerated when the American moved to the French superteam, La Vie Claire, in 1985, and became the first "million-dollar cyclist" (it was reported that he earned US $1 million over three years). However, on the French team, dominated by Bernard Hinault, he found himself riding a Hinault-branded steel bike. It was clunky, heavy, and sub-par, and LeMond, ever the perfectionist, was not happy. Even when he looked elsewhere, he could not find what he wanted: a perfect bike, in terms of fit and weight.

"I was looking at a lot of different bikes out there and things weren't great and things hadn't really advanced," LeMond explains. "Carbon fibre was beginning to make waves so in 1986 I had La Vie Claire add into my contract that I could have my own bike deal. That was mainly because I wanted a competitive advantage. In most instances a pro is confined to ride a [certain] bike based on sponsorship, but for me it was all about finding out who the best manufacturer was. I wanted the best equipment and that became the very essence of my company."

A deal was done by LeMond and his father with the US manufacturer Huffy, who had developed bikes for the US Olympic team in 1984. However, the bikes were unusable. "Huffy made me this bike and had it shipped to us and I remember the mechanic pulled on the fork and it literally came out like a rotten tooth," LeMond recalls. "So I ended up using the Look team bikes in 1986, which were in fact made by TVT." It was on just such a bike that LeMond won that year's

The LeMond team works on frames and makes adjustments to the chain stays.

LeMond tube parts, used to connect the chain stays with the down tube, seat tube, and seat stays.

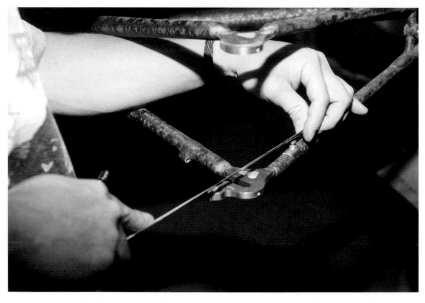

Tour de France and beat his teammate Bernard Hinault after a bitter three-week battle.

Behind the scenes, LeMond was developing his own line of bikes. However, he suffered a terrible setback the following spring when he was accidentally shot while hunting in the United States. He was lucky to survive, but he missed more than a year of racing and found himself scraping around for a team. He may have been a Tour de France champion, but only two squads were willing to offer him a chance, PDM and Carrera, and he eventually settled for the former.

Within a year LeMond had moved again, to the Belgian squad ADR. By now his stock had plummeted—he was no longer in a position, for example, to demand that he could ride his own choice of bike. But 1989 turned his career around: by the end of the season he was a champion again—his bike business and his racing career flourished side by side.

Although he rode a Bottecchia bike in 1989 for his second Tour win—which was also the closest ever, with LeMond pipping Fignon by eight seconds—it was on a LeMond bike (once again made with TVT carbon tubes) that he rode and won the world road race title in Chambery later that same year. It had one feature that he had craved: an extra long top tube, which allowed LeMond, with his long back, to stretch out and achieve a more aerodynamic position.

After his Tour and world championship double, LeMond was once more at the top of the tree and in a position to dictate. As well as signing a US $5.5 million contract with Z, he was able to demand that his new team (not just him) use LeMond bikes. "I was now in the driver's seat," he stated, "and we sponsored the teams I was on for the next five years."

1986	1986	1987	1990
Greg LeMond becomes the first American, and the first non-European, to win the Tour de France. He repeats the feat on two other occasions in his career, in 1989 and 1990.	Greg LeMond and his father set up the rider's own bike brand, LeMond Bikes.	Two months before the Tour de France, a shooting accident leaves LeMond close to death. His brother-in-law had fired a shotgun into his back at close range.	LeMond wins his final Tour de France onboard a LeMond-branded bicycle.

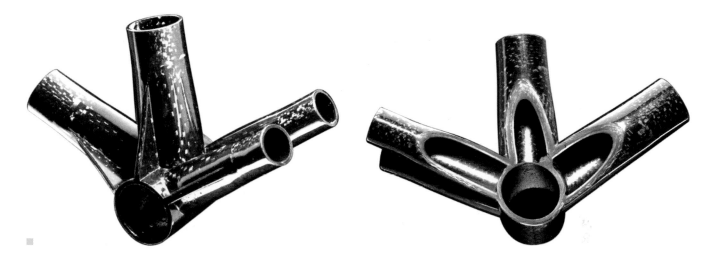

The zenith came in 1990 when LeMond not only defended his title at the Tour, but also did so on a LeMond bike. Having been the first American to win the Tour in 1986, now he became the first to do so on an American-engineered machine. A year later he would be the first to ride an all-carbon road bike at the Tour de France.

His contribution to the racing bike was therefore considerable. "When I came into the professional ranks very few manufacturers were replicating what the professionals were actually riding," LeMond says. "There was a huge disconnect. What they were making were essentially touring bikes."

However, things slowly began to unravel for LeMond, and for LeMond Bikes, after 1990. The next year he was off the pace as a new generation broke through, and at the same time the new wonder drug, EPO, began to distort the sport. The LeMond bike company also began to struggle, and the strain was evident in the relationship between LeMond and his father, who had been running the business.

LeMond had cut a deal with Japanese investors worth close to US $2 million in capital. But the deal was affected when the Japanese economy began to stutter. LeMond says only US $6,000 came through, which left the company short of funds, but running full staff and production in the United States. Road and mountain bikes were being built, all to LeMond's specifications: racing bikes, designed for speed, rather than touring bikes.

The company suffered as the relationship between LeMond and his father began to buckle. It was, says LeMond now, "one of the most painful things in my entire career." He explains: "When I turned pro at eighteen, I was just a kid. I had my dad manage things and he really helped me get some really good contracts. During negotiations I used to be the good cop and he'd be the bad cop. People used to say 'your dad's a hard ass,' but behind the scenes it was me being demanding and he was just the bearer of bad news. We were like teammates."

The fallout from the Japanese shortfall was devastating. "It put my dad in an impossible

"When I came into the professional ranks very few manufacturers were replicating what the professionals were actually riding."

GREG LeMOND

1994	1995	2004	2008
LeMond bows out of cycling and into retirement. At the time he links his deteriorating performances to mitochondrial myopathy, but later blames overtraining.	Trek and LeMond sign a ten-year licensing deal, which was amended in 1999. The agreement allows Trek to use the Greg LeMond Cycles brand.	LeMond is interviewed and tells reporters, "If Armstrong's clean, it's the greatest comeback. And if he's not, then it's the greatest fraud."	After a hard-fought legal battle Trek and LeMond privately settle. A donation is made by Trek to 1in6.org, a charity with which LeMond is affiliated.

position. He committed to people, hired them, and then this capital wasn't coming in. My dad was right in the middle. I saw right away that we weren't in a good position and I told my dad we needed to cut back, but he was so connected with people in the company that I had to make a decision: bike racing or the company.

"My dad became so overwhelmed and I lost all contact with him. I said to him, get someone else to manage the company and that he should come back to me. My parents felt that I didn't trust them, but that wasn't it, and there were a lot of emotions involved, but essentially I had to fire him. But all I really wanted was my dad back."

LeMond put new owners in charge as the company downscaled to the bare minimum. Bikes were still produced and LeMond's team—Z, which became Gan—used his bikes until LeMond hung up his wheels in 1995.

While manufacturing slowed down, an olive branch appeared in the spring of 1995 when Trek offered to become a licenser of LeMond's bikes. At the time Trek was struggling to penetrate the European market. Trek and LeMond signed a ten-year licensing agreement. "A huge mistake," says LeMond now. The agreement turned sour when LeMond had a public disagreement with Lance Armstrong, who put Trek on the map with his seven Tour de France victories. When LeMond questioned the veracity of Armstrong's successes, it left Trek in a difficult position. LeMond, meanwhile, claimed that Trek's response to his rift with Armstrong was to stop promoting his bikes.

A legal case finally ended the dispute between LeMond and Trek in 2008. It also effectively brought the curtain down on LeMond Bikes. Thus, a marque that, with LeMond's interest in technology, materials, and biomechanics, could have become synonymous with top-end racing bikes, ended in bitter acrimony, and an out of court settlement that saw Trek donate an undisclosed sum to a charity of LeMond's choosing. **DB**

■ LeMond heads for his third Tour de France victory in 1990, riding for Team Z.

■ Handmade LeMond frames feature, from top to bottom, Greg's signature on the top tube, ergo handlebars, Campagnolo rear brake, and Campag crankset.

■ Armstrong and his
Eddy Merckx-branded
Litespeed win the
individual road race at
the 1993 world cycling
championships.

Litespeed

While most other manufacturers were experimenting with aluminium and carbon,
Litespeed pioneered the use of titanium in bicycle frames and produced bikes that were
as revered for their sumptuous brushed silver finish as their durability and light weight.

Over the last twenty years, this Tennessee-based
company has been one of the world's leading
manufacturers of titanium bikes. However, in
a similar way to BH and Orbea in Spain, its
manufacturing grounding was not originally
related to bikes at all.

Litespeed's foundation dates back to 1986,
but its roots go back another two decades, to
1962 to be precise, to the establishment of
the Tennessee Machine Works. One of the
many satellite businesses that worked with the
aerospace and chemical companies based in
and around Chattanooga, the company became
a niche supplier of specialized alloys. It might have
remained in that niche market if David Lynskey,
one of the sons of company co-founder Bill, had
not switched to cycling after damaging his knees
through running. Lynskey was an engineer in the
family business and he began to tinker with bike
design using off-cuts of titanium. Working with
his friends, he initially produced frames for their
own use, but in 1986 one self-designed project
developed into a frame that appeared at the Long
Beach Bike Show.

Another three years passed before bike
design and construction were allocated time

and space within the Tennessee Machine Works
factory. Seven years on from that, Litespeed was
established as a bike manufacturing company in
its own right.

Although during certain periods Litespeed
has produced bikes using aluminium and carbon
fibre—and has returned to doing so today—
titanium has always been the company's material
of choice. Indeed, Litespeed's reputation as a
leading manufacturer of high-end frames is almost
totally down to its titanium models. For a long
time that reputation was linked to the frames
that the Tennessee company produced for other
brands, including Bianchi, Merckx, De Rosa, and
Trek. These collaborations enabled Litespeed's
designers to work with many well-established
bike manufacturers and to trade Litespeed's
experience of working with titanium with the
insight that seasoned manufacturers could
provide into the ride characteristics required
by both on- and off-road bikes.

Undoubtedly the best known of these
collaborations was with Trek in 1999. Looking for
a time trial bike that would give Lance Armstrong
an edge going into his first Tour de France after
his return from cancer treatment, Trek opted

*"I figured if I'm
going to spend
that much time on
a bike training and
racing, it better be
a healthy bike."*

BRYCE WALSH
ultracyclist

to paint a Litespeed Blade in the colours of Armstrong's US Postal Service team and rebadged it as a Trek, which was the team's bike supplier at that time. Armstrong not only won that Tour, but he also bagged all three time trials along the way. Interestingly, Armstrong's first major success, at the 1993 world championships in Oslo, also came on a Litespeed that had been rebadged as an Eddy Merckx when he was riding for the Motorola team.

The problem of working with others was that they ended up taking most of the credit for the end product. Initially, though, this suited Litespeed, because the company built up its knowledge and expertise in working with titanium within the bike industry. However, the company was by no means operating completely under the radar. In the mid-1990s, Litespeed enjoyed a highly successful period as bike supplier to the Chevrolet-LA Sheriffs team that featured British sprinter Malcolm Elliott as its leader, a young Bobby Julich as one of its upcoming talents, and was the leading domestic outfit on the North American scene for a number of seasons. Although not big budget, the team looked very much the part with its strikingly stylish green and yellow kit matched with the shiny brushed silver finish of its Litespeeds.

In 2002—by which point David's brother Mark Lynskey had become the company's president—Litespeed stepped into the big league, becoming bike supplier to the Belgian Lotto-Adecco team led by Australian sprinter Robbie McEwen and Belgian Classics specialists Andrei Tchmil and Peter Van Petegem. Litespeed provided the Belgian team's twenty-six riders with a variety of bikes: the Vortex as a general steed, the cutting-edge Blade for time trials, and the superlight Ghisallo for more mountainous races and also some time trials.

McEwen and Tchmil were among the nineteen riders on the Lotto-Adecco roster who rode stock frames that season, emphasizing the

■ Robbie McEwen (left) and Erik Zabel sprint to the finish line of the eighteenth stage of the 2002 Tour de France.

■ The Litespeed Archon CIR, sculptured in a wind tunnel, is designed to minimize drag. The frame features, from top to bottom, a stealth-fighter matt finish, SRAM's top of the range components, size variable tubing, and a fully integrated seat mast design.

accuracy of Litespeed's sizing and geometry. Did it hold them back? McEwen enjoyed one of the best years of his long pro career, so it seems not. The highlight for the Australian, his team, and Litespeed was McEwen's victory in the points competition at the Tour de France. Winner of two stages, including the most prestigious of the race on the Champs Elysées on the final day in Paris on July 28, McEwen ended German sprinter Erik Zabel's run of six consecutive green jersey successes as the winner of the points title. He also claimed another seventeen sprint wins in 2002, including two stages at both the Giro d'Italia and Paris–Nice.

The bikes in the Litespeed range combined lightness, comfort, and durability, earning them very favourable reviews from their professional users. The fact that they could also be bought ready-made meant that everyday riders were quickly won over as well. In fact, a decade on from Lotto's partnership with Litespeed, it is not difficult to find Vortexes and Ghisallos from that time that still look immaculate and offer a perfect ride.

The secret to this success arguably lay in Litespeed's use of 6/4 titanium, comprising 6 percent aluminium and 4 percent vanadium, as opposed to the more usual 3/2.5 mix, in its top of the range frames. Although the 6/4 alloy is harder to work with, it has a better strength to weight ratio than the 3/2.5 alloy or raw titanium. Working with the 6/4 alloy set Litespeed apart from most other manufacturers that were working with titanium, partly because the alloy was not available as tubing at that time. Instead, Litespeed had to cold-work sheet titanium until the desired dimension of tube was formed, at which point the seam could be welded. Although

very time-consuming, this technique meant that all tubes could be made to Litespeed's required specification and provided the company with expertise that others were quick to admire but unable to replicate. The neatness of the welds was very impressive; the skill of Litespeed's finish welders was so well honed that they did not need to be finished, filled, or sanded. The final touch was the transformation of the frame's appearance in what the company described as "BufferWorld" from a dullish finish to a shiny silver that was so eye-catching that it made the need for a paint job totally unnecessary.

Litespeed's innovative approach to bike design using titanium continues to this day. Its top of the range T1 titanium frames, including the Archon road and the Citico mountain bike frames, are reputed to be the most technologically advanced titanium bicycle frames ever produced, based on knowledge gained from research partnerships with NASA and other leading scientific research organizations. As a result of Litespeed's proprietary WRAP technology—which increases the weld area and "wraps" the tube to be joined—these frames are also stiffer and stronger than ever because stresses at the joint are better dispersed. Litespeed bicycles continue to be at the forefront of innovative aerodynamic design, with a distinctive American DNA.

The cutting-edge technology that carried McEwen and his teammates to glory in 2002 is available within Litespeed's T3 designs, such as the Xicon and the Pisgah. Created to be lightweight and nimble workhorses with exceptional handling for the serious rider, these frames, like all those in Litespeed's range, are still built by hand in Tennessee.

1986	1993	1999	2000
David Lynskey begins making bike frames, the first of which is unveiled at the Long Beach Bike Show.	Lance Armstrong wins the world road race in Oslo. He takes the rainbow jersey on a Litespeed bike badged with an Eddy Merckx emblem.	Armstrong wins the Tour de France after beating cancer. He rides a Litespeed bike, painted as a Trek, during the time trials of the race.	The company buys up rivals Merlin and triathlon specialists Quintana Roo. Lance Armstrong had previously used a Quintana Roo Superform bike.

Every Litespeed frame is built by hand at the facility in Ooltewah, Tennessee.

The 2010 Archon C3 uses a 3K weaving pattern in the surface layer of the carbon fibre.

Since 2010, Litespeed has stepped back into composite design and construction with a range of carbon fibre bikes and frames. They are more aerodynamic than the time trial bikes that performed with such resounding success at the Tour de France at the turn of the century. Furthermore, Litespeed's use of reactive pressure moulding brings with it weight reduction, increased stiffness, and improved durability as a result of the technology's ability to control the internal structure and wall thickness of the carbon frame during manufacture.

As well as being very active on the design side, Litespeed was quick to consolidate and bought up rival titanium manufacturer Merlin and triathlon bike specialists Quintana Roo in 2000. The companies came together under the umbrella of the American Bicycle Group, which was the

name given to Litespeed after JHK Investments purchased it in 1999. The company sold Merlin in early 2011 and now focuses on its Litespeed and Quintana Roo brands.

The Lynskey family's long association with Litespeed ended in 2005 when Mark Lynskey stepped down from his position as vice president of sales and marketing of parent company American Bicycle Group. He soon established a new brand under the Lynskey name in partnership with his brothers Tim, Chris, and David, along with their mother, Ruby. They have gone on to produce a wide range of road and mountain bike frames—all built with titanium—under the name Lynskey Performance. The silver finish to most of the Lynskey Performance frames will be familiar to Litespeed fans. And the company is still based in Chattanooga, Tennessee. *PC*

"What I've got going for me is more desire, I keep going at things."

DAVID LYNSKEY

2002	2002	2005	2008
The company steps out of the shadows in professional racing and supplies Belgian team Lotto-Adecco with an array of frames, including the Vortex, Blade, and Ghisallo.	Riding a Litespeed, Australian Robbie McEwen wins the green jersey at the Tour de France.	The Lynskey family association ends when Mark Lynskey steps down as the vice president of the parent company, American Bicycle Group.	At the Beijing Olympics, mountain bike rider Geoff Kabush races on an Ocoee, and Portuguese triathlete Vanessa Fernandes competes on a Ghisallo.

■ A Look promotional
postcard taken in the
mid-1980s features
Bernard Hinault.

■ Tapie, Hinault, and
LeMond in 1985. Each
played a key role in
the promotion of
the Look brand.

Look

This French company helped to revolutionize professional cycling in the 1980s with its mass market clipless pedals and carbon fibre frames, first used by the great Bernard Hinault and his US challenger, Greg LeMond.

By every measure, Look's influence on road cycling has been extraordinary. Twice in two years, at a time when road racing had an embarrassment of great champions, the company unveiled new technology that revolutionized the professional sport and made it the recognizable pastime that it is for millions of people around the world today.

Cycling would be quite different without clipless pedals and carbon fibre frames. Look made the first marketable versions of both and popularized them through two Tour de France champions, who, apart from being incredible athletes, were polar opposites in every way. There was the brilliant, belligerent Bernard Hinault, steeped in the traditions of cycling, and Greg LeMond, the young US naïf who became the archetype for the growing number of clean-cut New World professionals coming to the sport.

Look's early ventures into cycling were bound in the successes of Hinault and LeMond, but its history stretches back to 1951. Until the mid-1980s, however, the only time the brand would be seen at the great summits that the Tour

Bernard HINAULT

JOSÉ ALVAREZ **LOOK**

de France habitually visited was during winter on the ski slopes. The company, based in Nevers in the heart of France, became well known for ski bindings. It was established by Jean Beyl, an engineer and irrepressible inventor. His original company was a rubber manufacturing business called Le Caoutchouc Manufacturé, which made, among other things, the internal bladders for footballs. In 1948, though, Beyl was put on a new path. He broke his leg in a skiing accident and he realized that the fracture was caused by the rigid bindings that did not allow the leg and ski to move independently in a crash. When he hit upon a marketable ski safety binding he founded Look, named after a US photo magazine popular on the continent in those post-war years.

Eventually, Beyl realized that a version of his binding could be transferred to cycling. Other companies had tried to solve the engineering puzzle through the 1970s but failed. Stephen Roche, the Tour winner in 1987, remembers representatives from small engineering firms approaching riders with their various contraptions in the early 1980s, but none took root. Initially Beyl's technology looked like it would go the same way, because he did not have the capital to develop his *pédale automatique*.

This changed in 1983 with the arrival of a multimillionaire businessman with the Midas touch. Bernard Tapie was a well-connected tycoon who grew up in a tough Parisian suburb. His reputation for having a finger in every pie was only superseded by his ability to take failing businesses and make them profitable again. He acquired a 66 percent stake in the company and left Beyl, on a tiny budget, to tweak the design.

Tapie had a problem, however. For all his business *savoir faire*, he knew little about cycling and how he was going to market the new product. In *Slaying the Badger*, Richard Moore's book about the 1986 Tour de France, he describes how three years earlier Tapie had

heard Hinault giving a radio interview during which he discussed his plan to set up a new squad for the 1984 season. Tapie liked the sound of the tough, focused Breton coming over the airwaves and immediately contacted him with an eye to offering his shop chain, La Vie Claire, as the main sponsor. Within a week of their first meeting in September 1983, Tapie and Hinault convened a press conference to tell the assembled journalists a new team was in town.

It was a perfect match for both. Tapie recruited Hinault primarily as a consultant to assist with the clipless pedal's development and as a rider second, because it was unknown whether the Frenchman, forced to sit out the 1983 Tour with an injury, could return to the level that had brought him four Tour titles. Hinault, who by now was twenty-eight and perhaps even

- Released in 1984, the PP65 clipless pedal introduced Look's three-hole cleat pattern.

- The Keo Blade pedal with a carbon blade and enlarged cleat platform to improve power transmission.

- The carbon fibre Keo Blade weighs just 3.3 ounces (95 g) and was designed to improve cleat engagement and disengagement.

> *"It was probably the biggest innovation in cycling of the last thirty years, but there wasn't a lot of hype when Hinault used them that first time."*

STEPHEN ROCHE

contemplating retirement, found himself at the centre of a powerful new team with a sound exit plan if he could not recapture his form.

At the beginning of 1984, the pedal was on sale but Hinault did not use them at that year's Tour. Instead, the focus was on the impending battle with a precocious young talent called Laurent Fignon, the 1983 winner. Hinault and his team were immediately recognizable in the La Vie Claire jersey with its bold Piet Mondrian–inspired cubic design, and it is testament to the synonymy that Look developed with La Vie Claire that the pedal manufacturer would incorporate the blue, red, and yellow squares into the logo it has today.

The fairy tale return for Hinault did not materialize in 1984. He was defeated at the Tour by his former teammate, Fignon. True to character, Hinault tried all he could to dislodge his rival, but Fignon answered his every move. His dominance was so total that he declared afterwards: "I'll win five or six and then stop."

However, in 1985, it was Fignon's turn to be sidelined by injury. It meant that Hinault went to the start in Plumelec in his home region of Brittany as the favourite. At his side was LeMond, whom Tapie had recruited with a salary that promised to make him the sport's first million-dollar cyclist. As well as a bolstered team, Hinault had a secret weapon: he wore a pair of strange-looking cycling shoes with cleats on the soles that clipped into even stranger Look PP65 clipless pedals. There was not a toe-clip to be seen and all around him opponents were now in a previous era, using standard metal and leather toe straps. Hinault talked up the new pedal combination, claiming that it was safer, more efficient, and more comfortable than traditional pedals.

1951	1984	1986	1988
The company is established in Nevers, France, by Jean Beyl as a ski equipment manufacturer producing bindings.	More than thirty years after the invention of Beyl's ski binding, the technology is applied to bicycle pedals and the PP65, the first clipless pedal, is launched to great acclaim.	Greg LeMond wins the Tour de France on a Look KG 86, the first carbon frame with TVT tubes, providing a high level of rigidity.	The Look KG 96 is the first carbon frame entirely built by hand. It uses Campagnolo components, including the crankset, derailleurs, seatpost, and rims.

Tour veteran Stephen Roche remembered that for all their novelty and the revolution they precipitated, Look's pedals had a low-key introduction. "It was probably the biggest innovation in cycling of the last thirty years," he said, "but there wasn't a lot of hype when Hinault used them that first time. I think people just thought it was another bit of new equipment and it took time to realize their importance."

Although Look had created the market, the original designer, Beyl, got tired of working on the minimal budget imposed by Tapie. He left in the late 1980s for a new company, Time Sport International, to develop the mechanism further and incorporate "float," a degree of horizontal travel to accommodate a given individual's unique pedal stroke.

Roche was one of the last to turn in his toe-clips, doing so in 1993. He was disinclined to make a major change to his equipment he said—especially following a couple of injuries—but when he did, with compatriot Sean Kelly, the revolution was complete: clipless pedals had become as standard as Lycra shorts.

However, inside the Look factory in Nevers in the mid-1980s, the engineers were working on other projects besides fancy new pedals. Riding high on Hinault's success at the 1985 Tour, Tapie wanted to build a name for Look—and quickly. The next opportunity arose at the 1986 Tour and the engineers had a special frame to debut.

The Tour would be a hard-fought battle—one of the hardest ever—but La Vie Claire was in with a strong chance of winning. The last thing the team needed was for the equipment to fail. Nevertheless, Tapie transferred the team from Hinault-branded bikes to the Look brand in order to attract all the exposure he could.

1996	2008	2010	2011
The company's carbon track frames triumph at the Atlanta Olympics, claiming four gold and two silver medals.	Look claims fifteen medals at the world track championships and five medals at the Beijing Olympics, ridden by one of the company's star riders, Arnaud Tournant.	The 695 single-piece carbon frame is launched, with innovations such as inclinable carbon C-Stem, ZED2 single-piece carbon crankset, and the HSC7 carbon fork.	For the second time the company is awarded the French INPI Trophy for Innovation, this time for the Keo Power—the first pedal to measure pedalling power.

■ Despite both riding
for the Look-equipped
La Vie Claire team
at the 1986 Tour de
France, Hinault and
LeMond became bitter
adversaries.

A change of bikes was not the only big adjustment taking place in the team—a change of leadership was due, too. The year before, Hinault had publicly pledged to help LeMond, after the American helped him in 1985. It was one of the most captivating Tours in history as Hinault and LeMond appeared locked in battle. On the first stage in the Pyrenees to Pau, Hinault launched an unexpected break, which LeMond, languishing at the back of the peloton, did not learn about until the leading group had an unassailable lead. It was symptomatic of Hinault's approach to the race and it looked remarkably like he was doing the dirty on his teammate.

The internecine strife lasted for two whole weeks. Finally, on a valley road between the Col de la Croix de Fer and the final ascent to Alpe d'Huez, the battle for supremacy came to an end. Hinault was a spent force from a final desperate attack on the Galibier and he was being shadowed by LeMond. The final scene began when a La Vie Claire car containing Tapie pulled up alongside them. After a few words from Tapie, the pair rode in unison all the way up the claustrophobically crowded Alpe, with Hinault shepherding the yellow jersey–clad LeMond around the hairpins. The American gave his teammate the stage victory. It was an apt and timely gesture that confirmed 1986 as a year of transition: the Tour had its first English-speaking winner, and moreover, one who had beaten the most established and cherished French star of the era.

And then, of course, there were the bikes. The 1986 Tour was memorable not only because it heralded the arrival of the first New World champion but also because it marked a technological revolution in bike equipment. Both LeMond and Hinault rode state-of-the-art Look KG 86 frames that were made with a brand new material: carbon fibre.

The frame was the product of a collaboration with the Kevlar specialists, TVT, who provided

■ Laurent Jalabert in the 2002 Tour. Upon retirement he became a consultant for Look.

■ The Look factory in France. The company's innovations have won numerous awards, including the 2010 IF design prize.

the tubes. Engineers in Nevers had solved the challenge of binding the tubes into aluminium lugs to create a stiff, light, and comfortable frame.

The Look KG 86 that went on sale had a label that proudly informed the new owner: "This exclusive frame and fork has been produced and designed by Look in collaboration with the La Vie Claire pro cycling team of the Bernard Tapie Sport Group and created by TVT, the technological leader of the Carbon Kevlar compound. This unique dampening unbreakable tubing is made of a Kevlar carbon fibre. Enjoy the ride." The American tone of the message is unmistakable—and another sign, perhaps, of cycling's changing times.

It was a testament to quite how far ahead of the competition Look was that carbon frames did not become de rigueur for more than a decade. All through the 1980s and early 1990s, Look was at the vanguard of technological development. It was the first to make carbon lugs that allowed the first all-carbon frame to be built. In 1990 it produced one of the first moncoque carbon frames, with the structure formed as a single piece. The list of firsts is admirable, but they all pale in comparison to the engineering achievements of the first two years.

In 1989 Tapie sold Look to a Swiss pension fund with what should have been a solid legacy. However, sales gradually failed to cover the costs of its research and innovation programmes. The rise of major US brands with cheaper manufacturing facilities in the Far East also hit Look hard. In 1998 the company filed for bankruptcy, but was rescued by a management buyout led by Dominique Bergin. He is still the chief executive today and has returned the company to its enviable form.

Bergin restored innovation to the heart of the business and reaffirmed Look's presence in the pro peloton. In 2002 Look sponsored no fewer than three top-tier teams—Kelme, Crédit Agricole, and CSC-Tiscali. Laurent Jalabert, who rode for CSC, has become synonymous with the brand and he remains involved as a technical consultant. Between 1998 and 2009 the company lodged 169 patents connected to new generations of pedals and frames. In the last decade it has received multiple high-profile awards for its bikes and has twice been awarded the INPI Trophy for Innovation, marking it as one of the most inventive manufacturing companies in France.

The brand has also remained resolutely French. While other companies have relocated their manufacturing facilities out to the Far East, each Look frame is still made—crafted—at the factory in Nevers, where it all began. **SD**

The Look 695 IPACK was the official bicycle of Team Cofidis at the 2010, 2011, and 2012 Tours de France.

The Tradition of Endurance
and Excellence... Goes On.

Masi

Faliero Masi—the Italian craftsman behind Masi frames—was known as "The Tailor" for his ability to build bikes to fit their rider as neatly as any bespoke suit, and the clients on his books testify to his genius.

Beneath the transfer stickers of Eddy Merckx's 1968 Giro d'Italia winning bike, Frederico Bahamontes's 1959 Tour frame, and Tom Simpson's Peugeot was the workmanship of a man who dedicated his life to bikes: Faliero Masi. The list of riders who sought out his exquisite expertise in his workshop below the Vigorelli velodrome in Milan is long and illustrious, but his name rarely featured on the great pros' bikes—that honour was reserved for the more muscular brands who mass-produced frames and sponsored the teams for whom the champions rode.

Faliero Masi's life was dedicated to racing bikes. In his prime he rode the Giro d'Italia and then became a mechanic, a role he thrived at

and kept up long after he began building his own bikes. Masi would often tell the story of Antonio Maspes, the champion Milanese sprinter who required his bearings to be boiled to wash all the grease out because he thought it would lose him a vital advantage.

However, the event with which Masi is most closely associated is the Hour record—the ultimate test of man and machine against the clock. Between Fausto Coppi's attempt on the record in November 1942 in the Vigorelli, and Ferdinand Bracke's effort in the Olympic velodrome in Rome in 1967, Masi handbuilt five of the six successful record attempt bikes.

It is said that Bracke only rode his bike once before his attempt, earlier in the day around the

■ A 1970s catalogue
cover highlights the
proud hsitory of Masi.

■ Antonio Maspes in
September 1955,
at the world track
championships in Milan.

*"Maspes was the
most difficult. He
was a meticulous
racer. He even boiled
his ball bearings in
English oil."*

FALIERO MASI

velodrome. With Masi's precision, one ride was enough. He became known as "The Tailor"—the man who made bikes that fitted their rider as sharply as any bespoke suit produced in the city's fashion houses.

Perhaps because of the thin deception that riders were aboard the stock frames of their sponsoring manufacturer, Masi's name became synonymous with championship quality. This allowed him to begin selling his bikes to the public well beyond the confines of European cycling.

In 1972, Masi left his son, Alberto, in charge of the shop below the Vigorelli and moved to California to take advantage of the growing market for Italian bike frames there. Alas, it was not a happy experience for him. He returned to Italy after selling the brand Cicli Masi to a US consortium led by Ted Kirkbride. There was reportedly a falling-out over production volumes, but Masi also disliked the Californian lifestyle. Their divergence meant that Kirkbride continued making high-quality frames in the Carlsbad factory for the US domestic market, while Alberto kept the family flame alive making custom bikes in the Milanese workshop.

After many years spent making frames that were covered in the stickers of other brands, Masi did finally get the long-lasting exposure that its artisanship deserved—a role in a US movie. In *Breaking Away*—perhaps the seminal English-language feature film about cycling made in 1979—the hero of the piece, the Italo-phile Dave Stohler, chases road racing success with a group of friends. For him, only one bike would do: a bright red Masi Gran Criterium. It was the sort of exposure that other brands craved but could not hope to obtain.

Nowadays the famed Masi workmanship has been made redundant by the advancement in production line technology, but the name and the feel of the bikes will always evoke memories of peerless quality and a long line of cycling's great stars. **SD**

> *"The Masi is to the bicyclist what Ferrari is to the autobuff."*
>
> BICYCLING MAGAZINE

■ Belgian pro Ferdinand Bracke, seen here in the 1970s, rode a handbuilt Masi bike.

■ A Masi Gran Criterium dating from between 1972 and 1974, restored by Ray Dobbins, featuring, from top to bottom, Campagnolo brakes, steel frame, Campag hub, and Reynolds tubing. The frame has been refinished by CycleArt restorers in Vista, California.

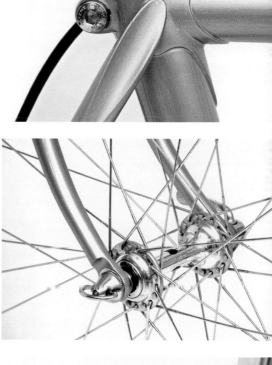

■ Antonin Magne was the first professional cyclist to use Mavic's aluminium rims in a Tour de France.

■ Mavic's aluminium Dura rim was illegal for racing in 1934; the company disguised it as wood.

■ A 1934 poster advertises the advantages of Mavic's "Apron Mudguard."

Mavic

The Mavic company name is synonymous with radically new racing wheels. However, in addition to introducing the first aluminium rim in 1934 and the first disc wheel in 1973, its innovatory designs include 1994's Zap Mavic System electronic gear shifter.

In 1934, Antonin Magne won the Tour de France for the second and final time in his career. At a time when the Tour was contested by national teams, Magne and his French compatriots dominated the event and won victories in nineteen of the twenty-three stages, including two by Magne himself.

Unknown to his competitors, Magne's 1934 Tour victory was aboard a bicycle that incorporated a revolutionary technological innovation: an aluminium rim. Illegal at the time, it was camouflaged to resemble the wooden rims used by the rest of the peloton. The new rim's manufacturer was the French company Mavic. Although its early initiation into professional racing was surreptitious, today the company enjoys a ubiquitous presence. Mavic-equipped professionals are easily recognizable by the iconic and extremely visible yellow and black elliptical logo that appears on the company's featherweight carbon wheels. Yellow Mavic neutral support vehicles are always seen in the peloton's race convoy, too.

Mavic is one of the elder statesmen of the cycling world. The company was founded in

1889 by Charles Idoux and Lucien Chanel. The company's name is an acronym of Manufacture d'Articles Vélocipédiques Idoux et Chanel. Acronyms are still popular at Mavic, and its stable contains numerous acronym-laden technological innovations.

The French company was first known for its bicycle mudguards, soon followed by pedal-powered children's cars. Mavic was bought by Henri Gormand in 1920, after which it focused its attention on bicycle rims. The company's first true innovation, however, was nearly eclipsed in 1934 by a like-minded Italian who was a hair's breadth quicker on the draw. Mavic had developed a duralumin dished rim using eyelets to distribute the stress of spokes on both the upper and lower walls. It was a new concept that produced a rim that was both lighter and stronger than typical steel rims. However, a mere two hours before Mavic could patent the design, an Italian named Mario Longhi beat the company to it with an identical prototype that he had developed independently.

Luckily for Mavic, Longhi allowed it to use his design under licence, and later in 1934 Magne

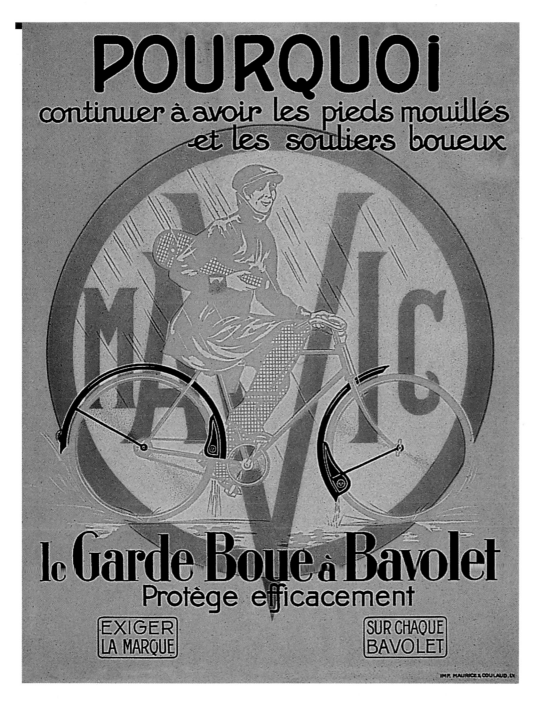

rode a cycle with a disguised pair of the
wheels to Tour de France victory. Mavic considered this to
be a wondrous portent of future success, and the
rims went on to the market not long after.

It was not until 1964, however, when Henri
Gormand's son, Bruno, took over the reins at
the head of the company that Mavic blossomed
into its position at the forefront of technological
innovation within the pro peloton. Bruno
Gormand was to Mavic what Tullio Campagnolo
and Ernesto Colnago were to their respective
companies—its heart, soul, and driving force for

innovation, excellence, and quality in the realm of professional-level cycling equipment.

"Bruno Gormand was a typically French entrepreneur," said Richard Goodwin, sales and marketing director for Mavic in the United States in the late 1980s, and founder of Mavic's US Neutral Support Programme. "He smoked, drank, loved good food, and lived the life of a playboy. He knew absolutely everyone in the European world of cycling. He took the reins of the company in 1964 and put in place the team that would be with the company until the end of the century. His visions were neutral race support, components, and hard anodized rims. Although Mavic components had limited success in the market, many of their innovations are now omnipresent in the world of cycling components."

The bright yellow Mavic neutral assistance vehicle was the brainchild of Bruno Gormand. At the 1972 Critérium du Dauphiné Libéré he lent his own car to a team director whose vehicle had broken down before a stage, and this chance event triggered the idea for a neutral support vehicle—Mavic-branded, of course—that would drive with the race convoy and provide assistance to anyone in need.

The 1973 Paris–Nice was Mavic's first foray into neutral support. The initiative was groundbreaking, not only in its approach to giving mechanical assistance to all riders but also in its use of radio liaison between all the vehicles involved. Efficient communication was now possible between organizers, doctors, sports managers, and journalists. Mavic's presence within the race caravan even prompted a switch from a red to a yellow logo, as Gormand was advised that yellow would be a preferable colour for television viewers.

1889	1923	1933	1952
Léon and Laurent Vielle start a nickel-plating business, and Charles Idoux and Lucien Chanel begin to sell bicycle parts. The president of both companies is Henri Gormand.	The first iteration of Mavic's distinctive logo is created. It includes a large central "V" and is set in a circle.	The company branches out into pedal cars for children. Only a small number are made, making them extremely rare collector's pieces today.	Using Mavic products, Ferdinand Bracke sets the world Hour record at 29.88 miles (48.09 km).

■ A Mavic catalogue from 1980 shows the company's impressive range of rims.

■ In 1975 Mavic introduced the Mavic 500: the world's leading cartridge-bearing hub.

In this way, the Mavic neutral assistance vehicles became inextricable in the eyes of the public with professional cycling's marquee event, the Tour de France. In 1977, the Tour itself recognized Mavic's innovative role and honoured the company by starting stage nineteen of the race outside Mavic's factory in St Trivier sur Moignans.

Mavic's relentless pursuit of stronger, faster designs for bike wheels triggered innovations in componentry during the 1970s. They included cartridge-bearing hubs; the first anodized rims; and the patented Module E rim, the first clincher with a double "hook" bridge to seat a high-pressure tyre. The Module E rim ushered in the era of high-performance clincher wheels in a market dominated by the less convenient tubular rim.

All this development ended in 1979 with a complete, professional-level *gruppo* called Tout Mavic. Former Mavic vice president Art Wester said, "When Mavic started neutral technical support in 1973, they saw a lot of problems in servicing the components that were available at the time. We thought we could do better." Mavic reasoned that riders need reliable components, and mechanics need equipment that is easily serviceable. Hence, the Tout Mavic *gruppo* components were designed to be strong and rebuildable, such as derailleurs that were easily disassembled into a pile of castings, springs, pivot pins, and bearings.

Professional cycling legends such as Sean Kelly, who enjoyed his best form in 1984 on a Mavic-equipped Vitus for the Skil-Sem squad, would be forever linked with Mavic componentry.

1973	1979	1989	1994
In response to studies in aerodynamics, Mavic shifts focus and produces its first branded wheel. In the same year, it introduces Mavic neutral assistance vehicles.	The Mavic brand's best-known and arguably most important innovation goes on the market: the Tout Mavic *gruppo* of components.	Just eight seconds ahead of Laurent Fignon, Greg LeMond wins a Tour de France of nail-biting tension and excitement using Tout Mavic.	Cutting-edge work in wheel systems gives birth to the aluminium Cosmic and the Cosmic Carbone.

■ Lance Armstrong rides
on Mavic wheels during
his first Tour de France
win in 1999.

■ Team GB rides in the
men's team pursuit
qualifying for the 2011
track cycling European
championships.

of their Cosmic and Helium, however, Mavic
engineers looked at what they considered to be
their ideal wheel and then designed a system that
would accomplish their goals without regard to
current restraints or compromises. The dream
list from the engineers included the following
qualities: stiff, light, serviceable, reliable.

Mavic had already created a very light,
serviceable, and reasonably durable wheel in
the Helium. The internal bearing and axle design
of the Helium hub was good, and the engineers
saw no reason to change it. However, the Helium
was not as stiff as it wanted, and that was where
it saw the most room for improvement. Mavic
figured that, while an improvement in rim design
would increase lateral stiffness, the biggest limiting
factor was neither the rim nor the hub, but the
traditional steel spoke design. If it could make
the spokes more rigid, without a weight penalty,
it would dramatically improve responsiveness. It
was known that oversized aluminium could be
more rigid than steel, and was potentially lighter,
too. The resulting oversized alloy spoke was
exceptionally stiff and strong, but there was one
big problem—there was no way to attach it
to the hub and rim using existing technology.

This is where Mavic's system-based design
came in once more. The engineers set about
designing hubs and rims that would work with the
revolutionary new spoke. Making creative use of
machined alloy, they took the proven and reliable
alloy hub internals and bearings from the Helium
and put them into a hub specifically designed
to maximize the new spoke's potential. Then
they paired up the new hub with a totally new
rim design, built from an advanced alloy called
maxtal, which had been utilized in the French
TGV trains. Maxtal is much stiffer than standard
6061 aluminium alloy and this enhanced strength
allowed the engineers to design an innovative,
oversized spoke nipple that threaded directly
into the rim. Instead of traditional stainless steel
spokes and nipples, Mavic used a superheated bit

that melts threads right into the Maxtal alloy rim. Special oversized nipples on the bladed aluminium spokes then thread directly into the inner wall of the rim, leaving a solid outer rim wall that adds strength and rigidity and leaves an airtight cavity. The resulting wheel achieved all the objectives that the engineers had set out to accomplish. In the 21st century, right up to the present day, virtually every major professional race has been won by a Mavic-wheeled professional.

Carbon is the material du jour for wheel construction. Mavic began to employ it in 1985 for its Comete disc wheel; in 2011 Philippe Gilbert racked up victories all season long with the aid of Mavic's current flagship wheel system, the Cosmic Carbone Ultimate.

Mavic continues to innovate with its wheel technology. It also develops tyres, computers, pedals, helmets, footwear, and technical apparel, which all showcase the quality on which the French company has built its reputation. As the demands of professional racing continue to push the boundaries of equipment, undoubtedly Mavic will continue to be at the vanguard. *PH*

Mavic

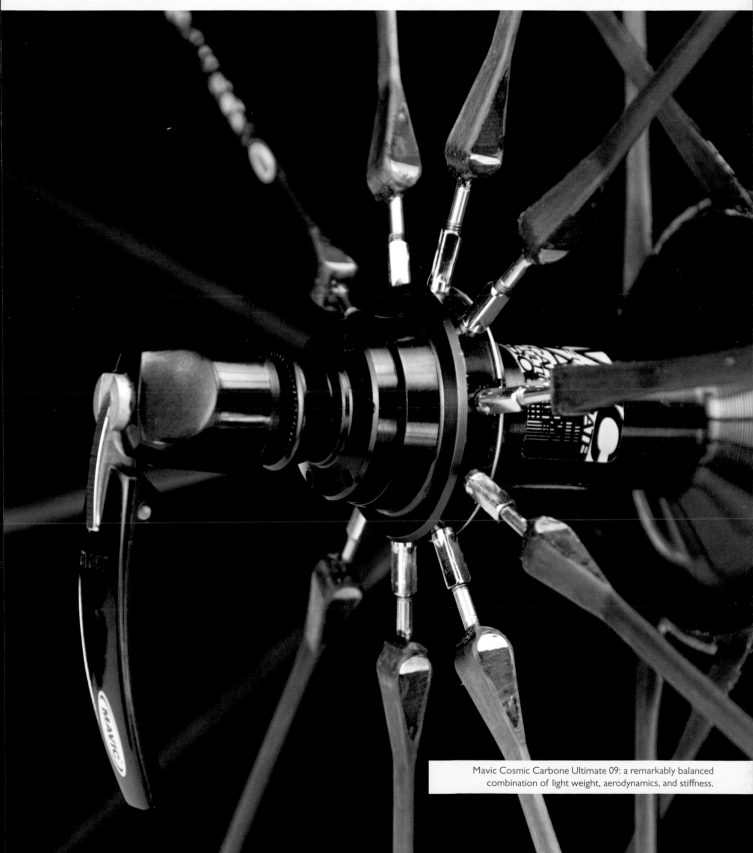

Mavic Cosmic Carbone Ultimate 09: a remarkably balanced combination of light weight, aerodynamics, and stiffness.

CHRIS BOARDMAN'S
LOTUS 108

When Britain's Chris Boardman appeared at
the Barcelona Olympics in 1992 with his striking
space-age Lotus bike, he took the world by surprise.
That, of course, had been the intention. Prior to
the Games, although he had spent six months testing
the design in a wind tunnel, Boardman had not yet
used the bike in competition. Instead, a less well-
known member of the British team—Bryan Steel—was
selected as the guinea pig and rode the Lotus in a
meeting in Leicester, east Midlands.

The reason for this was not to find out how
the bike fared; Boardman already knew it was fast.
It was to ensure that it was legal. In the event, it raised
barely a flicker of interest and passed the officials'
inspection without any fuss—but this may have
been because it was being ridden by the relatively
unknown Steel.

The carbon composite monocoque frame was
not entirely new, but Lotus's version was developed
by designer Mike Burrows when cycling's governing
body, the Union Cycliste Internationale, revoked its
ban on monocoque frames in 1990. Two years later,
when Boardman won the Olympic pursuit title, setting
a new world record in the process, the so-called
"Superbike"—and Lotus—received as much attention
as the rider, although the extremely aerodynamic
position that Boardman was able to adopt was arguably
just as significant. Using the same position—but not the
Lotus—he went on to enjoy many more successes on
the track and road.

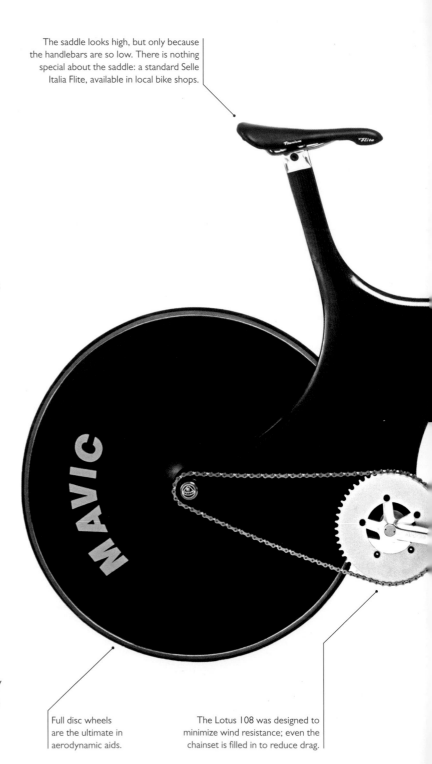

The saddle looks high, but only because
the handlebars are so low. There is nothing
special about the saddle: a standard Selle
Italia Flite, available in local bike shops.

Full disc wheels
are the ultimate in
aerodynamic aids.

The Lotus 108 was designed to
minimize wind resistance; even the
chainset is filled in to reduce drag.

Boardman used tri-bars popularized by Greg LeMond at the 1989 Tour de France. The steering column of the Lotus was titanium. The forks were twin-blade with aerofoil cross-sections.

DESIGN DETAILS

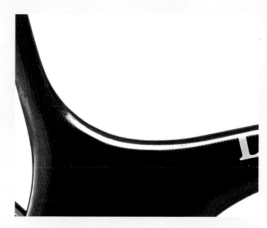

MONOCOQUE FRAME

The Lotus 108 bike is an aerofoil-section composite monocoque moulded out of advanced materials, mainly carbon fibre. It was constructed with aerofoil cross-section, formed with unidirectional and balanced-weave carbon fibre plies in epoxy resin.

MAVIC 3G

The Mavic 3G tri-spoke carbon wheel is more aerodynamic than standard spokes, and more stable than a full disc wheel. The deep section blades also produce a fantastic sound when moving at speed.

The Mavic tri-spoke carbon: more aerodynamic than standard spokes.

■ The Velocita features a carbon rear end to soak up shock, carbon chain stay, and Dedacciai carbon forks. Despite the new technology the Velocita incorporates handbuilt fillet brazing.

■ This stylish Mercian features Reynolds 753 tubing, and the "barber's pole" paint job as an optional extra.

may never match carbon for lightness, but it will always be more durable, and repairable. In the event that a Mercian is damaged, the company has an inexhaustible list of repair options to put its bikes back on the road. It is also reassuring to know that a tired and shabby-looking Mercian can be restored to its former glory. These are bikes for life, or even longer.

With the modern Mercian range, it is worth noting how little has changed over the decades. With the exception of the Velocita and its carbon forks and rear triangle (an almost unwelcome hint at modernity), the Derbyshire artisans remain true to their roots. The gorgeous, intricate hand-cut lugs of the Vincitore is a feature that appeals to true aficionados of the bicycle. The Miss Mercian, with its dropped crossbar, might appear to be commercially unviable because it appeals to such a niche market, and yet it lives on. Paint schemes, with contrasting panels and lined lugs, are classic and unfussy. "I think the barber's pole will always be popular," said Mosley of the helter-skelter down tube design that, although not unique to Mercian, is synonymous with the brand.

One model where the intricacy of the colour scheme is most evident is the Paul Smith, a collaboration between bike-builder and clothing designer that, not surprisingly, puts attention to detail at the top of the list of priorities. Sir Paul is a lifelong Mercian rider and was a keen racer until a teenage accident ended any hopes of making it as a professional cyclist.

Smith's designs for his track-equipped Mercian feature a unique colourway with separate shades on opposing sides of the frame, intended to mirror the "flip-ability" of the single speed or fixed options to stunning effect. Hand-cut spearpoint lugs, Reynolds 631 tubing, and

1946	1950s	1963	1965
The cycle shop opens in London Road, Derby. The chosen name relates to the ancient Anglo-Saxon kingdom of Mercia, the capital of which is nearby in Repton.	The Special Tourist, Campionissimo, and Super Vigorelli models are introduced; the latter features Reynolds 531 double-butting.	With a well-established reputation, the company introduces the New Superlight, weighing 17 pounds 8 ounces (7.937 g)	After a change of premises in the 1950s, Mercier moves to a larger workshop on Pontefract Street, off Ascot Drive, Derby.

engraved signatures are topped off with Smith's hand-picked finishing kit—matching Brooks saddle and bar tape, naturally. The result is almost too beautiful to ride.

In an age when so many UK-based frame-builders have ceased trading (a notable exception being the prolific Merseyside frame-builder Terry Dolan), it is a wonder that Mercian has not only kept going, but also managed to thrive. There has certainly been a backlash against the disposable nature of modern mass-produced bikes and the disadvantages of alternative materials over their forebear: the "steel is real" idea.

"We have always been busy really," Mosley has stated, "but the move back towards steel has certainly helped. We have orders coming in from all over the world: the United States, Singapore, Australia. The Mercian name travels well."

Advertising the brand has never been a priority. And nor does it seem to have been a necessity. Apart from the old-school catalogues that have been produced by Mercian since the very early years, it is difficult to find any publicity in cycling publications. "We don't need to advertise," Mosley said, proudly. "I think the website with the Online Frame-builder and the internet generally have certainly helped, but we are busier than ever. We have just taken on a new frame-builder, so that is four we have now."

When an order is placed, one of those four builders will take tubing and lugs and emerge with a fully formed frame some time later. "All of the builders have their own little signatures so I can pick up a newly made frame and know who has built it. It is good to know one person has worked on your frame from start to finish," Mosley has said, and he is, of course, quite right. Perhaps that is the secret of Mercian's success.

"We still have a jig in the shop so customers do have the option of being measured here, but many are happy to use the Online Frame-builder. They are encouraged to come in with their existing bike so we can assess their current position and correct any anomalies—sometimes they can be quite a way out, so you have to gently persuade them to get in the right position."

The idea of using an online builder to order a custom-made machine may sound risky, but Mosley is confident that, with a few select body measurements and using the "personal spec" option to make any required change to angles, exactly the same results can be achieved as with a personal fitting. Indeed, Mercian won a UK Trade and Industry award in the Innovative Exporter category for its online tools and received an invitation from the queen for tea at Buckingham Palace for its efforts.

Mercians move in glamorous circles. Sir Paul Smith has one. We are not sure about the queen, but if she did ride a bike, what could be more fitting than a Miss Mercian in purple? *IC*

"All of the builders have their own little signatures so I can pick up a newly made frame and know who has built it."

GRANT MOSLEY

1971	1981	2002	2006
The company moves again, to The Cavendish, Normanton. In 1984 it moves to larger premises at 7 Shardlow Road, Alvaston.	The Strada Speciale, lightened by using drilled lugs, goes on general release. The Tourist Tandem uses Reynolds 631 tubing and is advertised as "suitable for racing as well as touring."	Mercian Cycles is purchased by Mercian frame-builder Grant Mosley and his wife Jane.	A staple since the 1950s, Mercian stops producing the Superlight model. It is now a collector's item.

Mercier

One of the great names of French cycling, Mercier equipped some of the country's top riders, most notably Raymond Poulidor, who spent his entire career on bikes whose name survives in the history books but not, sadly, in the marketplace.

Although only a little more than 3 miles (5 km) long, there are few climbs on the Tour de France to match the Puy-de-Dôme, with its unyielding final climb averaging 13 percent. It was here that one of the sport's most iconic battles was staged, when Raymond Poulidor, the "eternal second," went elbow to elbow with the great Jacques Anquetil. Locked in battle, neither was able to break the other as they wound their way up in tandem. This image of Anquetil and Poulidor would come to epitomize the Tour and divide a nation's loyalties.

It was a defining moment for both riders, but it also represented the essence of the Mercier team, with whom Poulidor spent his entire career. The man who captured public affection far more easily than his great rival pulled clear at the finish, but it was not enough: Anquetil still led the Tour

heading into the final time trial, his speciality. For Poulidor, defeat only heightened his fame and that of his team: Mercier, a bastion of cycling for more than thirty years. It was in the Mercier purple that Poulidor crossed the line after his epic battle with Anquetil, and it was in the same acclaimed purple that he ended the Tour, missing out on the yellow jersey by less than one minute.

Poulidor was one of Mercier's best-known exponents and was particularly popular in France because of his perennial little guy status, but he was by no means Mercier's only star. Cyrille Guimard nearly took the team to the *maillot jaune* in 1972 when he matched Eddie Merckx in the mountains, only to be forced to withdraw two days from the finish. Joop Zoetemelk rode for the team, but had his sponsorship withdrawn at the end of 1979, which prompted a switch to the TI-

■ Poulidor was considered stronger than Anquetil in the mountains, but victory was far from assured.

■ An iconic shot of Anquetil and Poulidor battling elbow to elbow in the 1964 Tour de France.

Raleigh squad with whom he would win the Tour the following year.

The Mercier story begins with its founder Emile Mercier, born in 1899 in St Etienne. At the age of twenty, Emile began making crank shafts and bowls alongside brothers Paret and Ribaud. Five years later, in 1924, he bought his two partners out, and by 1930 he had converted the outfit into a frame manufacturer and assembler.

Having dabbled with professional racing from as early as 1920, it was inevitable that Emile would decide to fully enter the professional arena. In 1933 the first Mercier team was established in conjunction with Francis Pélissier and Hutchinson, an outfit based near Montargis that had been producing cycling tyres since 1890. Notable success arrived courtesy of Albert Barthelemy, who beat Alcyon-Dunlop's Alfons Ghesquiere to victory in Paris–Brussels; and Henri Pomeon, who won the Circuit des Monts du Roannais.

Mercier became the sponsor of the team two years later in 1935, although Hutchinson's tyre supply ensured that it continued to have a presence within the squad. Maurice Archambaud, in his fourth year as a professional, led the team to a stage victory in the year's Giro d'Italia and later to victory in two stages of the Tour de France; he eventually finished seventh overall.

The wait for Tour glory lasted only two more years, when Roger Lapébie profited from the withdrawal of the Belgian team and the much-fancied Sylvere Maes to beat Italy's Mario Vicini by a little more than seven minutes. Lapébie won four stages along the way, while Archambaud won the second stage to Charleville.

This victory did not only boost Mercier's reputation as a manufacturer, but also it was, in many ways, a personal vindication for Emile, who

1924	1933	1937	1946
Emile Mercier buys out brothers Paret and Ribaud from the company that all three founded, and by 1930 the business concentrates on frame construction.	Emile enters the world of professional racing by establishing the first Mercier team in conjunction with Francis Pélissier and Hutchinson tyres.	Mercier gets its first Tour de France victory with Roger Lapébie becoming the first rider to win using a "modern" derailleur. He beats favourite Mario Vicini by some seven minutes.	The iconic purple jersey is adopted, becoming synonymous with the Mercier brand. The yellow collar and cuffs are added in 1950.

■ The Netherlands' Joop Zoetemelk, racing for Gan–Mercier, was second overall in the 1976 Tour de France.

■ The fixed-gear Mercier Kilo TT Pro track bike, seen here in luminous tangerine yellow, has a double-butted and tapered Reynolds 520 cromoly frame.

had been involved in a long legal battle with the Tour de France's first organizer, Henri Desgrange. Desgrange, a former cyclist who set twelve world track records, fell out with Mercier in spectacular style after a dispute over the career of Andre Leducq.

After two years (1926 and 1927) with the Thomann squad, Leducq moved to Alcyon, headed up by Edmond Gentil. In 1934, however, he was persuaded to move to Mercier, and the team name changed to acknowledge his presence. As retribution, Gentil asked Desgrange to leave Leducq out of the French squad for the Tour, and—whether by coercion or chance—the request was agreed to, much to Mercier's chagrin. He engaged lawyers in an attempt to reverse the decision, but found Desgrange intransigent in his views and happy to help the situation deteriorate

further by ordering his staff not to mention the Mercier name. The publication *L'Auto*, facing a dilemma, opted to misspell Mercier's name, and when corrected by Mercier or his legal team would print a recorrection with a new variation. "Monsieur Cermier," one issue stated, "insists that in fact he is known as Monsieur Merdier"—a delicious, if aggravating, wordplay. Consequently, when Lapébie finished fourth in the crucial Vire–Caen time trial, to establish the platform from which he claimed victory in the 1937 Tour, Mercier was delighted not only to collect the spoils of victory, but also to see his bike—with its name finally spelt correctly—splashed across the front cover of *L'Auto*.

Mercier continued to meet with success over the following years, as Luducq, Archambaud, and Raymond Louviot in particular excelled in the

"The more unlucky I was, the more the public liked me and the more money I earned."

RAYMOND POULIDOR

1959	1964	1975	1985
Bernard Gauthier discovers unknown rider Raymond Poulidor and signs him to Mercier. In 1961 Poulidor wins the Milan–San Remo in his second season as a professional.	Watched by half a million spectators, Poulidor battles his arch rival Jacques Anquetil up the slopes of Puy-de-Dôme, but is narrowly beaten.	Joop Zoetemelk joins Mercier and is second to Bernard Hinault in the 1978 and 1979 Tours de France. He and Mercier would part ways four years later.	After five years of financial difficulty, Mercier is declared bankrupt and the business is sold.

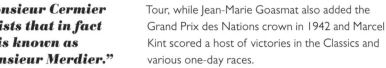
Tour, while Jean-Marie Goasmat also added the Grand Prix des Nations crown in 1942 and Marcel Kint scored a host of victories in the Classics and various one-day races.

The year 1946 was unspectacular, but it marked the emergence of one of Mercier's most enduring legends: the purple jersey. At the same time, chosen riders within the Mercier family opted to ride under their own names—in 1947, for example, Leducq rode what was technically classified as his own frame, and for the Mercier-Leducq team. Other riders, such as Archambaud and Lapébie, followed suit. With frames now rebranded, it was the purple jersey that became the symbol of Mercier's presence in the peloton. By 1950 the distinctive yellow collar and cuffs had been added, a design that would endure until 1970. The jersey found its best-known wearer when Raymond Poulidor joined the team. He was discovered while riding as an independent in criteriums, and was offered a deal by Antonin Magne, the team's sporting director. Poulidor went on to spend his career with Mercier, and imprint both it and himself on the nation's consciousness following his dramatic duels with Jacques Anquetil.

The rivalry existed as much in column inches as it did in genuine feuding. Anquetil boasted the superior record, particularly in the Tour, but Poulidor could command the same appearance fees—to Anquetil's annoyance—because of the public demand to see the pair do battle. While Anquetil's resentment towards Poulidor can be debated—the two later became friends—the issue of money was certainly a source of irritation and only fanned the flames in the eyes of the public. There was also the matter of character: Anquetil was often regarded as haughty or arrogant, and mastered the craft of winning a race by doing just enough. Poulidor inspired the greater affection, both for his open manner and his maverick, attacking style. "The more unlucky I was," Poulidor reflected, "the more the public

■ The Kilo TT features, top to bottom, threadless 1" headset, the TruVativ Touro crankset, Mercier 4130 cromoly forks, and TrackSpec high flange aluminium hubs with stainless spokes.

■ Sean Kelly rides a Mercier and wears the green jersey in the 1985 Tour de France.

liked me and the more money I earned." The rivalry reached its zenith on a mountain pass in 1964, when Anquetil managed to hang on to Poulidor's tail. Some thought Poulidor too reticent in attacking Anquetil, who was weaker in the mountains, but both riders were at the very limit of their physical ability. Arms and elbows sometimes clashed as they wound up the Puy-de-Dôme, with Poulidor inching ahead at the very finish. An image of the two locked in battle, Poulidor in the iconic Mercier jersey, became ingrained in Tour history.

Poulidor, who finished second in three Tours, continued to ride at a top level through to his final Tour in 1976, when, for the fifth time, he was third. In that time Fagor became the team's main sponsor for 1970 and 1971, before GAC was brought in as title sponsor the following season. Cyrille Guimard emerged as a stage contender, while Dutchman Joop Zoetemelk joined for 1975 and was second to Bernard Hinault, the successor to Anquetil's crown, in the Tour in 1978 and 1979. Zoetemelk also swelled Mercier's trophy cabinet by winning Paris–Nice on three occasions and claiming victory in the 1979 Vuelta a España.

However, Mercier's fortunes plummeted, and 1980 marked the beginning of a descent into bankruptcy. The company folded in 1985, two years after making its final appearance in the Tour. The cycling division was sold and sold again, and today still produces road and speciality frames, although its bikes have not returned to the Tour.

Much like the photograph of Poulidor and Anquetil fighting side by side up the Puy-de-Dôme, Mercier's imprint on the sport is consigned largely to the annals of history and legend. Yet it remains one of the most romantic names to be associated with the Tour, thanks to its fifty-year involvement and to the riders who came through the Mercier stable. In Poulidor and the purple jersey, it found a way to ensure that its presence was felt even after the team itself folded, and so it has left a permanent imprint upon the greatest race. ***ST***

Olmo

"Gepin" Olmo had been one of the top riders of the 1930s—with an Olympic gold medal, twenty stages of the Giro d'Italia, and the Hour record—before he picked up his tools and started a frame-building business that remains at the forefront of the industry.

In common with many of the great Italian frame-building names, Olmo's history is rooted in pre-war racing, in this case through the exploits of Giuseppe "Gepin" Olmo. A gold medal winner in the team time trial at the 1932 Los Angeles Olympics, Olmo went on to have a stellar career as a professional. In 1933 he took the first of twenty stage wins at the Giro d'Italia, where he finished runner-up to the legendary Gino Bartali in 1936. He also recorded two victories in Italy's biggest one-day race, Milan–San Remo, while his ability on the track enabled him to set a new mark for the world Hour record in October 1935. Riding on the fabled Vigorelli track in Milan, Olmo recorded a distance of 28.01 miles (45.090 km), breaking the record held by France's Maurice Richard by more than 984 feet (300 m).

In 1939, as Olmo's competitive career drew towards its close, he joined his three brothers—

Franco, Giovanni, and Michele—in founding Olmo Cicli in their home town of Celle Ligure. Within a decade, the four brothers' company was receiving high acclaim for the durability and quality of its bikes. The company's backing of a top-line pro team in the post-war years boosted the brand's status even further. However, unlike most other Italian brands, Olmo began to look to expand outside, as well as inside, the bike industry. In the 1950s, the brothers established a series of other businesses involved in the production of specialized plastics for a variety of other industries, including cars, textiles, and footwear.

However, bike production continued to be where Olmo's heart lay. Building on the knowledge he had gained from competing in and winning some of the sport's greatest races, Gepin Olmo played a key role in developing cutting-edge designs using state-of-the-art materials. Many of

■ Joaquim Agostinho powers his Olmo uphill at the 1972 Tour de France.

■ An Olmo Bicycle promotional poster from the 1940s recalls Giuseppe's heyday on the track.

■ The Olmo Soon, introduced in 2010, features Toray T700 high modulus carbon.

the bikes produced by the company in the 1970s and 1980s are regarded as design classics, their notoriety based on the quality of the ride they offered to both pros and amateurs. Indeed, this period was a golden age for Olmo; its backing of squads such as Magniflex, Gis, and Alfa-Lum brought a host of titles, including Milan–San Remo. During this period, Gepin Olmo, by now into his seventies, continued to have a hands-on role with design and production right up until his death in 1992, and his expertise and knowledge ensured that the qualities that had made Olmo's top of the range bikes so desirable were maintained.

Towards the end of the century, Olmo re-entered the professional side of the sport as bike supplier to the Spanish Vitalicio Seguros team, a link that brought the company's biggest success when Oscar Freire won the world road race title in Verona in 1999. A year later, the Vitalicio team claimed four stage wins on Olmo bikes at the Giro d'Italia.

Although Olmo's bikes are mass-produced, the meticulous focus on design detail and development, added to the care taken in the production process, has maintained Olmo's tradition for producing beautifully crafted and extremely rideable bikes. Never a company to sit back on its laurels, Olmo has produced road, off-road, and city bikes using new, lighter materials and cutting-edge production techniques. These new ranges have carried this great name successfully into the 21st century. *PC*

Orbea

The Basque company began making guns, but in the 1920s turned to bicycles. Today it is a firm fixture in the professional peloton and has supplied leading Spanish riders from 1988 Tour de France winner Pedro Delgado to 2008 Olympic champion Samuel Sánchez.

Basque cycling conjures up images of the bright orange team colours of Euskaltel, enthusiastic crowds lining steep, rain-washed mountain roads, superfit climbers (often writhing on the ground after crashes), and the cooperative bike manufacturer that is so often at the heart of all of this—Orbea. From Pedro Delgado escaping from the pack on the penultimate stage of the 1985 Vuelta a España, coming from six minutes behind race leader Robert Millar to win the race, to Samuel Sánchez winning the 2008 Olympic road race from a six-man break, to many other remarkable stories from road, track, mountain bike, and triathlon, Orbea continues to have a special place in cycling history.

The story began in 1847 when brothers Juan Manuel, Casimiro, Mateo, and Petra Orbea Murua set up Orbea Hermanos y Compañía in Eibar, in the Basque region of Spain. They manufactured guns and hunting equipment, and the business soon took off. It embraced new technologies and in 1890 built a hydroelectric plant that enabled it to sell electricity as well as power its factory. That same year the company, now run by Jacinto, Valentín, and Juan, sons of the original founders, changed the name to Orbea y Compañía.

Business was good until family disagreements turned into a full-blown feud, and the company divided in 1926: one part continued to make gun cartridges, and the other kept the name Orbea y

■ Iban Mayo riding his Orbea in 2004, during stage thirteen of the Tour de France.

■ Prototypes are assembled by hand, and robots in hermetically sealed rooms are used to paint the frames.

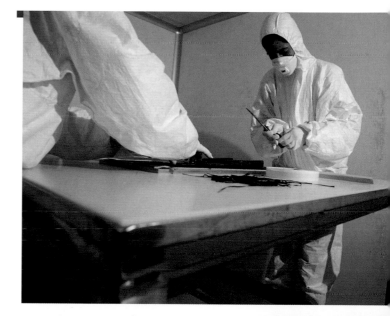

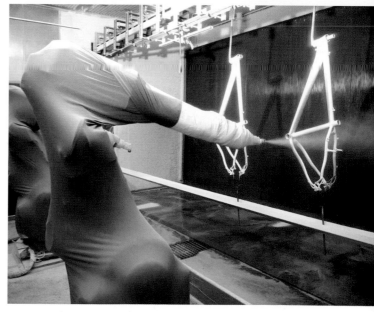

Compañía and began to make bicycles. It made good business sense, in a part of the world that passionately adores cycling, and the company took off. Four years later it began to sponsor professional riders, and between 1932 and 1936 sponsored the first of many cycling teams. It continued to sponsor teams throughout the 1940s, 1960s, and 1970s.

Like many bicycle companies, Orbea developed a motorized bicycle in the 1950s. However, as with other European bike companies that branched out in this way, it caused problems. The company could have folded, but instead, in 1960, it became a worker-owned cooperative and in 1964 joined the Mondragón Corporación Cooperativa, a huge federation that now has more than 250 cooperative members. The decision paid off, and Orbea continues to make bikes, including professional-level road, track, and mountain bikes, as well as bikes for the children's, touring, and leisure markets. From 1998, Orbea expanded globally, and now has more than 70,000 employees in Spain, Portugal, and China, with every bike continuing to be assembled and finished in its factory in Basque Country.

It also continues as a major sponsor— Euskaltel-Euskadi, the unofficial Basque national team, and its development team, Orbea, and Andalucía CajaGranada on the road; the Orbea Racing Team and Luna Chix mountain bike squads; and Australian triathletes Emma Moffatt and Courtney Atkinson—as well as supporting road and mountain bike races across Spain. It remains a company that talks about taking its traditional ethos and culture into new markets across the world, but whose roots remain firmly planted in Basque Country. *sc*

Pegoretti

Pegoretti frames are among the lesser known but most sought-after bikes on the market, with each creation a labour of love that can take up to two years to complete and can cost as much as a sports car.

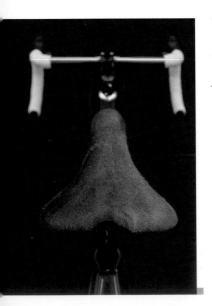

When cyclists order a Pegoretti frame they have little idea when it will arrive—or exactly what it will look like—which for many people makes the idea of owning one very appealing. The name alone inspires this kind of confidence because Dario Pegoretti is one of the very few frame-builders in business today who produces frames that combine technical quality with characteristics that make his creations more like objets d'art. Most owners agree that the bikes are well worth the wait—even if this can be up to two years.

Pegoretti started his career in 1975, and studied under another celebrated Italian frame-builder, the late Luigino Milani, who is credited with producing bikes for countless champions, even though many of these frames bore the

name of the rider's sponsor rather than that of Milani. Luigino taught his student well. Pegoretti's understanding of frame design goes much deeper than the jaw-dropping paint finishes that adorn many of his creations. He is so highly regarded in the industry that he collaborates closely with tubing manufacturers, and therefore enjoys a level of control and customization that is almost unheard of.

It is no surprise to discover that the cost of his frames can be steep. Yet the amount that riders would pay for a Pegoretti frame is not dramatically different to the cost of a mass-produced, relabelled carbon fibre frame that is imported from the Far East. In contrast, Pegoretti's frames are lovingly made by a master craftsman, one at a time.

All of the frames in the Pegoretti range have a story to tell and there has been a steady evolution in Pegoretti's designs and methods—within the industry, he is credited as being a pioneer of tungsten inert gas welding. He works with aluminium, but it is steel that represents the majority (80 percent) of his output. His decision, as frame materials and frame-building trends changed, was to stick to what he knows. Not that his frames are museum pieces; in their own unique way they have moved with the times over the past three decades.

The only feature that Pegoretti frames really share is that they are all different—almost all of Pegoretti's creations are destined for a particular customer and built to their exact dimensions. The paint job is as much a part of the Pegoretti experience as are the technical details, such as the non-standard cross-sections and profiles of the frame's tubes. Generally, when ordering, only a guide to personal colour preference is required; the rest is left to Dario, his mood, and imagination. Consequently, the result is a truly personal interpretation. Many owners claim that they can feel something of Dario, and something of themselves, in their frames. It is one reason, perhaps, why you rarely, if ever, see second-hand models on the market.

Officially, Pegoretti has not supplied any of the great champions. However, like his mentor Milani, he is secretly in high demand. Miguel Indurain, Marco Pantani, and Mario Cipollini are among those who have favoured Pegorettis. Big brand graphics may have adorned the frames of these and other top riders' bikes, but a closer look at the tell-tale details will reveal a different story. Dario cannot, for obvious reasons, name names in his marketing, but his reputation is such that he does not need to.

Today, Dario Pegoretti works from a small workshop in Caldonazzo, tucked away in the Dolomites, with a couple of close friends. A singular man, a singular frame-builder. **RD**

- There are thirty Love #3 frames produced per year. They are made from aluminium.

- The Day is Done bike features a painting technique called the "Venizia" finish.

- Frames from top to bottom: Luigino; Baci; Duende; and a different view of the Luigino, so named after Pegoretti's mentor.

DARIO PEGORETTI'S BIG LEG EMMA

There is no one in the world who blurs the lines between bicycle frame-builder and artist to the same extent as Dario Pegoretti. However, he is quite clear: he is a frame-builder first, and his priority is to build a high-quality, technically sound racing bike. Aesthetic considerations come second, but are still very important.

Pegoretti's reputation is forged on both aspects. Without doubt he is one of the world's leading frame-builders: his mentor was the great Luigino Milani, and Pegoretti has followed a similar path. He has devoted himself to his craft and built frames under his own name, and also for countless champions who have preferred a Pegoretti, among them Miguel Indurain, Maurizio Fondriest, Mario Cipollini, and Marco Pantani.

To the uninitiated, it is the designs of Pegoretti's frames that sets them, and Dario himself, apart. Having been inspired "to try to change some of the conventional rules," he has been heavily influenced by 1960s street art. Many of his frames, therefore, feature wild, exuberant paint schemes, with detail and texture added by his innovative use of other materials, such as bits of newspaper, powder, coffee grains, and watercolour paints.

Music is a major influence. Pegoretti says that the sound system is switched on in his workshop first thing in the morning and it plays until late at night. Indeed, many of the frames are named after his favourite songs. Featured here is Big Leg Emma by Frank Zappa, whereas other Pegoretti frames include Day is Done (Nick Drake) and Love #3 (Charles Lloyd Quartet).

The Italian-made fi'zi:k Aliante saddle, with carbon rails.

Components are a mix of Italian and Taiwanese brands, with Campagnolo Record and FSA.

For some of his wilder designs, Pegoretti uses newspaper, powder, and coffee grains to achieve his unusual finishes.

The only part of the frame that is not steel is the fork; Big Leg Emma features the Reynolds Ouzo Pro carbon fork.

DESIGN DETAILS

FRAME

Although it might look aluminium, with its fat tubes, Big Leg Emma is a steel frame, with horizontal reinforcing struts inside the tubing for torque response. The tubeset itself is unique to Pegoretti, who remains a big fan of steel.

CHAIN STAYS

The barcode spells out Big Leg Emma on enormous 1.3-inch (35-mm) chain stays, which are internally strutted for extra strength and rigidity. At one of the major stress points of the bike, it means less flex and more responsiveness.

Peugeot

From penny farthings in the 1880s to carbon fibre racing frames a century later, the roaring lion of Peugeot stood as an emblem of French manufacturing excellence and racing success, with ten victories in the Tour de France before decline set in.

Saturday, May 11, 1985 will forever be etched into cycling lore as the day when circumstances, bad weather, and a Spanish cartel combined to deprive Robert Millar of overall victory in the Vuelta a España. As Pedro Delgado slipped undetected into a breakaway, Millar found himself out of allies and severely compromised, with those around him choosing not to ride. As accusations of foul play and spoiling tarred the race, they also deprived not only Millar but also

his Peugeot team—one of cycling's oldest and most decorated—of victory. It was the last time the team would be in contention for victory in a Grand Tour, because less than one year later it succumbed to financial ruin. For one of cycling's behemoths, it was an ignominious end.

Given Peugeot's history, it is more important to remember its triumphs rather than its final breaths. The team can count ten Tour de France victories, three Vuelta wins, three world road

race championships, six wins in Milan–San
Remo, and five in Paris–Roubaix. History also
records that Peugeot handed Eddy Merckx, the
greatest rider of them all, his debut in 1966—to
devastating effect.

Robert Millar is by no means Peugeot's best-
known rider, but he does illustrate a legacy that
extends past a bursting trophy cabinet to the very
fabric of the sport itself. Fourteen years after the
team gave Merckx his opening as a professional,
it recruited Millar and several other Anglophone
riders—including Phil Anderson, Stephen Roche,
and Allan Peiper—from the amateur Athletic
Club de Boulogne Billencourt. Their subsequent
success contributed immeasurably to cycling's
growth from a niche sport contested by a handful
of nations into a truly global enterprise. Peugeot's
history can be measured, therefore, not only in
the gleam of silver, but also in the very shape of
cycling today; the rare mark of a team able to
transcend the sport in which it made its legend.

Peugeot's success is all the more remarkable
given its humble beginnings, which sprang from
the early 19th century and from the vision of
Jean Pequignot, Jean-Pierre, and Jean-Frederic
Peugeot. The three brothers forged a business
in wooden water mills and steelworks, but as
competition increased they began to diversify and
made coffee grinders and razors in their factory
in Montbeliard. In order to distinguish their
products, a Montbeliard engraver was tasked
with designing a trademark, and so, as far back as
1858, the Peugeot lion was born. It adorned the
first bicycle—"Le Grand Bi," a penny farthing—
produced by the Peugeot brothers at their
Beaulieu facility in 1882, which marked the birth
of the Peugeot cycling legend. (Peugeot would
also become—and remain—a car manufacturer,
although the bicycle and auto divisions separated
in 1926.)

Eight years after producing its first bicycle,
Peugeot collected its first trophy when Paul
Bourillon became the world sprint champion in

■ The Peugeot direct-
drive "Grand Bi"
penny farthing dates
from 1882.

■ These crest and decals
were used between
1970 and 1976. The
logo changed three
times in the 1970s.

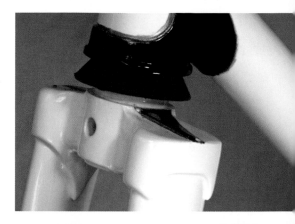

■ Lucien Petit-Breton was the first to win the Tour de France twice, in 1907 and 1908, riding a Peugeot.

1882	1907	1926	1955
The first Peugeot bicycle—a penny farthing called Le Grand Bi—is released. It is handbuilt by Armand Peugeot.	Peugeot dominates the Tour de France: Lucien Petit-Breton takes first place and the next four positions are all held by Peugeot riders.	After making 9,000 cars for use in World War I, the expanding auto business is separated from its bike efforts. In 1930, bicycle production reaches 162,000 units a year.	The facilities at Beaulieu (Mandeure), France, turn out 220,000 bicycles a year and employ 3,500 workers.

Copenhagen. At the turn of the 20th century the Peugeot cycling team was created, and in 1904 it contested only the second ever Tour de France. Hippolyte Aucouturier, twice a winner of Paris–Roubaix (1903 and 1904), finished fourth only to be later disqualified, when victory was awarded to Henri Cornet for his Cycles JC team.

Aucouturier stayed with the team for 1905 and won three stages in that year's Tour, which placed him second in the general classification. The star of the show, however, was another Peugeot rider, and arguably its first great—Louis Trousselier, or "Trou-Trou" as he was known to the French public. The son of a wealthy family, Trousselier took leave from national service to compete in his first Tour in 1905 and marked the occasion by winning the opening stage, and five stages in total, finishing with the yellow jersey and with thirty-five points to Aucouturier's sixty-one. It is said that victory brought him contracts to race around France and a bonus from his team, which he duly gambled away in a game of dice that night.

Trousselier won four more stages in the following year's Tour, including in a punishing 298-mile (480-km) ride between Marseille and Toulouse, but this time could only finish third and victory went to another Peugeot rider and one of the Tour's best climbers, René Pottier. The Frenchman was first in the second and then third stage, a mountainous climb between Nancy and Dijon that took in the Ballon d'Alsace. He won three further stages on his way to what would be his only Tour win. Two years later he committed suicide, and a steel statue at the top of the Ballon d'Alsace remains a monument to his memory.

The following two seasons saw Peugeot's dominance of the Tour continue as Lucien

Petit-Breton recorded back to back victories, winning seven stages along the way. In many respects Petit-Breton's hopes looked slim in 1907 when he lost contact with the leaders on the Col de la Porte, but the points system used in the Tour's formative years meant that time was irrelevant and he was able to eventually claim a maiden Tour win. One year later, he made history by becoming the first rider to win the Tour twice, having finished outside the top four in only one stage. Peugeot's fourth Tour crown was completed in emphatic fashion, when its all-conquering squad claimed the first four places. Peugeot achieved two further Tour wins before the outbreak of World War I. Belgian Philippe Thys secured back to back wins in 1913 and 1914, and 1913 was also notable for a new world Hour record—27.045 miles (43.525 km) set by Oscar Egg on a Peugeot bike.

Success followed shortly after the war's end, when Belgium's Firmin Lambot led Peugeot to a massive forty-one-minute win in the 1922 Tour—the team won all of the opening ten stages and eleven in total during the race. However, it was the final Tour triumph for forty-five years and began a barren run, which was broken by various national road race championships and, in 1948, the Vuelta a España, the first of Peugeot's three wins in the Spanish tour.

The following two decades saw a Peugeot renaissance, however, as a wave of new riders helped to return more frequent success to the marque embodied by its roaring lion logo. Gaston Plaud became the new sporting director of the team, and, under his stewardship, Charly Gaul, Tom Simpson, Roger Pingeon, Eddy Merckx, and a host of other riders came through the Peugeot ranks.

1963	1980s	1986	2001
Peugeot introduces its now-famous black and white checkerboard team strip. The PX-10 bike is released, one that Eddy Merckx would ride for the Peugeot team early in his career.	A difficult decade for the marque sees Peugeot cycles and motorbikes suffer competition from Asia. The Peugeot team ends its winning streak.	Despite its formative successes the Peugeot team is disbanded because of budget problems.	Peugeot enters a partnership with Cycleurope to distribute its branded bikes throughout Europe.

The upturn in results coincided with a new team strip that was introduced in 1963—the recognizable black and white checkerboard design that, like the purple of rivals Mercier, would become a symbol of Peugeot's presence in the peloton. It was in the black and white that Tom Simpson won Bordeaux–Paris that year, Milan–San Remo one year later, and in 1965 added the world championship and the Giro di Lombardia to his collection of victories.

One year later and the arrival of Eddy Merckx, "The Cannibal," was announced in typical fashion. In total the Belgian won twenty races that year, including victory in the Milan–San Remo Classic, and finished on the podium a further sixteen times. A similar pattern emerged in Merckx's second season with the team when he took twenty-seven wins and twenty-four additional podiums, including victory in the world race championships and again in Milan–San Remo. As Merckx attacked every race he entered, a more focused approach from Roger Pingeon saw him triumph in that year's Tour with a narrow three-minute advantage over Julio Jiménez Muñoz, thus cementing a dominant year for the Peugeot team.

Pingeon won the second of Peugeot's three Vuelta a España titles two years later in 1969, when his victory on the stages from San Feliu to Moya proved critical. Two years after that came Peugeot's third—and final—Vuelta win, this time courtesy of Ferdinand Bracke. It was the Belgian's only major Tour victory, although he was twice crowned world pursuit champion for Peugeot in 1964 and 1969.

Victories continued to flow in national championships, but it was eight years until Peugeot claimed another major triumph in the 1975 Tour de France. With Maurice De Muer taking over as sporting director, the Tour turned out to be a fight between Bernard Thevenet and Eddy Merckx, now riding for Molteni-RYC. As the Tour approached its zenith, Thevenet took two key victories on the fifteenth and sixteenth stages,

■ Robert Millar finished fourth in the 1984 Tour de France and won the King of the Mountains.

■ The Peugeot Vitus ZX1, launched in the early 1990s, had Dura-Ace 7400 components and Mavic carbon wheels.

and gained more than three minutes on Merckx, thus paving the way for overall victory when the race reached the Champs-Elysées.

A change of co-sponsor occurred in 1976 when BP was replaced by Esso, but the oil giant was rewarded with one more Tour victory, which again came courtesy of Thevenet in 1977. It was the last time that Peugeot would wear yellow on the final podium.

After 1977, Peugeot took only three more major wins in national championships as it fell into a slump from which it did not recover. At this time it began to recruit Anglophone riders, initially to consternation from traditionalists until the newcomers' hunger and ability manifested itself in results. Still the wait for Tour glory went on. In 1983 Pascal Simon wore yellow for Peugeot after stage ten, but one day later broke his collarbone in a crash. He persevered for six days, but eventually had to abandon the race, and his departure signalled the last time a Peugeot rider would wear the prized *maillot jaune*. The team continued to fight for success, and in

1985 it had its final chance for silverware when Robert Millar led the Vuelta. Hostile crowds and a general desire to see a Spaniard win combined with devastating effect, however, as torrential weather exploited a lack of nous on behalf of Peugeot director Roland Berland and handed Pedro Delgado the crown on the penultimate stage. Millar bore the Spaniard no ill will, but felt aggrieved by the lack of guidance he received.

It was an ignoble end for Peugeot's legendary team. It entered and competed in 1986, but ran out of budget before the end of the year and folded. Consequently, the story of a cycling behemoth came to a close almost a century after it was first created. Fittingly, Peugeot's influence in the cycling world continued to be felt long after its demise, particularly in the policy of looking abroad for the next generation of riders. The history books, and a bursting trophy cabinet, certainly attest to innumerable glories during Peugeot's time in cycling. Peugeot's legacy cannot yet be relegated to the past and, even today, its influence continues to be felt. *ST*

Spain's Miguel Indurain
pictured during a time
trial in the 1995 Tour
de France.

increased. Marino Basso won two stages of
the 1967 Tour de France with the GPT logo—
Giovanni Pinarello, Treviso—on his bike and
helped to boost the company's sales still further.

It was 1975 before a Pinarello was ridden to
overall victory in the Giro, when Jolly Ceramica's
Fausto Bertoglio took the final *maglia rosa*,
only a year after Pinarello had started backing
the team. Six years later Pinarello was no
longer only a supplier of bicycles to teams; the
company also had its name on a jersey as one
of the co-sponsors of the Inoxpran squad. It
was a wise investment, and Giovanni Battaglin
unexpectedly doubled victory in the Vuelta a
España and the Giro. In those days, the Spanish
tour preceded the Giro, with rarely more than
a week separating the end of the Vuelta and the
start of the Giro. In 1981 it was just three days,
which made it a double worth celebrating.

By this point, Pinarello's sponsorship had
brought home to Treviso two of the three
Grand Tours, along with Tour, Giro, and Vuelta
stage wins and victories in lesser races. In 1984
an Olympic gold medal was added when Alexi
Grewal rode a Pinarello to victory in the road
race at the Los Angeles Games. The same
year saw the beginning of Pinarello's Spanish
adventures when the company hooked up with
José-Miguel Echávarri and Eusebio Unzue's
Reynolds squad. In 1988 Pedro Delgado romped
home to victory in the Tour de France on a
Pinarello. When Reynolds became Banesto
and Delgado was surpassed by his *domestique*,
Miguel Indurain (Big Mig), Pinarello entered
a golden age.

Pinarello claims that all five of Indurain's
Tour victories were won on its bikes. The reality
is a lot more complicated. In 1991, the Banesto
squad was riding bikes from a Spanish marque,
Razesa. Although the team rode Pinarellos for
the next four Tour victories, most of Indurain's
bikes were actually made by the frame-building
gun-for-hire Dario Pegoretti. In those days, it

**"I didn't feel
I had to prove
anything more."**

MIGUEL INDURAIN

> *"A winning bicycle brings together the expert of the artisan, the latest in technological innovation, a passion for the sport, and a fanatical attention to perfection."*

FAUSTO PINARELLO

1952	1960	1981	1984
In Treviso, Italy, Nane Pinarello is paid not to start the Giro by his bosses at Bottecchia. He uses the money to set up his own bike business.	Pinarello begins to sponsor its first professional team, Mainetti.	Now on a jersey as a co-sponsor with Inoxpran, the brand enjoys huge success as Giovanni Battaglin wins the Vuelta a España and Giro d'Italia in one season.	Alexi Grewal wins the Olympic road race in Los Angeles on a Pinarello bike. Sixteen years later in Sydney, Jan Ullrich repeats the performance.

was still the custom for the most successful riders in the peloton to have their rides made by specialists and badged with the name of whoever had the contract for supplying the rest of the team's bikes.

The years of Big Mig's reign were years of glory for Pinarello. Nane may have been the slowest rider at the 1951 Giro, but his bikes were now firmly associated with the fastest men in the peloton. As well as successive Tour wins, Indurain delivered Pinarello time trial victories at the world championships and the Atlanta Olympics. Banesto also brought home to Treviso victories in Paris–Nice, the Critérium International, the Critérium du Dauphiné Libéré, and the GP des Nations.

The most important victory of them all, though, was the Hour record in 1994. It was significant not so much for the prestige, although back then, before the UCI got around to pressing the reset button, the Hour garnered much attention. The win was important in the field of technical excellence.

The Hour bike that Pinarello built for Indurain—the Espada, the Blade—was an eye-catching carbon monocoque frame that cut through the air with ease. Even purists, who believe that a diamond frame is an essential feature of bicycles, acknowledge its beauty. Riding the Espada, Big Mig added 1,072 feet (327 m) to Graeme Obree's record, pushing it out to 32.95 miles (53.04 km). Although his record only lasted for about five weeks before Tony Rominger added another 2,598 feet (792 m) to it, the bike that Pinarello built for Indurain was a thing of lasting beauty: a bike that perfectly married form and function, aesthetically pleasing and fantastically fast.

Banesto was not the only team riding Pinarello bikes to glory in those years. Pinarellos were being supplied to the Italian Del Tongo squad, where a young, flamboyant sprinter started to make his mark. With his blonde hair and film star looks, Mario Cipollini was bound to be memorable. However, it was his sprinting that earned him his fame. At Del Tongo, and later Mercatone Uno, Cipo was able to make an impression riding Pinarellos. The company was also finding success in the women's peloton in those years: Diana Ziliute won the road race at the world championships in 1998, and Edita Pucinskaite won the Tour Féminin.

Pinarello also supplied the extremely successful Telekom team. Indurain's run of Tour victories ended in 1996, when Telekom's ageing Dane, Bjarne Riis, sealed victory by storming up the Hautacam on a Pinarello bike. A year later Riis's teammate, Jan Ullrich, made it a seventh consecutive Tour victory for Pinarello. However, the sprint sensation from Germany, Erik Zabel, surpassed the overall Tour victories of Riis and Ullrich when he won six back to back green jerseys at the Tour between 1996 and 2001. The first two victories showed just how strong a cycling powerhouse Telekom was, because the team landed the yellow, green, and white jerseys. Zabel also added victory in Milan–San Remo to Pinarello's palmarès.

By the early years of the new millennium, Nane had turned his initial investment of 100,000 lire into a multi-million-euro company. Cycling's biggest races were the shop window for his bikes: bikes that were ridden by the stars of the sport. His own palmarès may have been modest, but the palmarès of his bikes helped make Pinarello one of the pre-eminent bike

Jan Ullrich powers through stage thirteen of the 1997 Tour de France.

1991	1994	2010	2011
Miguel Indurain wins his first Tour de France. It sparks a seven-year winning stretch for the Italian company that sees Indurain win five Tours in a row.	At the height of his prowess, Indurain sets a new world Hour record on Pinarello's Blade carbon monocoque frame.	Team Sky is launched in London with key signing Bradley Wiggins on hand to unveil the team's Pinarello bikes.	Current world champion Mark Cavendish signs with Team Sky for the 2012 season.

■ Riis in yellow and Zabel
in green in the 1996
Tour de France, both
riding a Pinarello.

■ The Pinarello Dogma
carbon frame is
asymmetrical, aiding
balance. It also features
Campagnolo wheels.

brands of the last three decades. It was time
to hand over the business to his children—
daughter Carla and son Fausto. A younger son,
Andrea, was also involved in the business for a
short time, but died of a heart attack, aged forty,
after completing the first stage of the amateur
Giro del Friuli in 2011.

Through the first decade of the new
millennium, the victories continued to
accumulate. A year after Ullrich had landed
the rainbow jersey at the world championship
time trial in 1999, the Telekom team delivered
more Olympic glory at the Sydney Games, with
Ullrich winning the gold medal in the road race
and his teammates Alexander Vinokourov and
Andreas Klöden landing silver and bronze in a
Telekom/Pinarello lock-out on the podium. At

Fassa Bortolo the victories piled up, too, when
the team added Tirreno–Adriatico and the Giro
di Lombardia to Pinarello's palmarès, along with
more stages and jerseys in the Grand Tours and
other races. In the women's peloton, in 2004,
Nicole Cooke won the Giro d´Italia Femminile
as a member of the Safi-Pasta Zara squad, riding
a frame from Pinarello's Opera line.

Pinarello's successes involve getting the
best riders and the best teams to ride its bikes.
Sadly, too many of them have been linked with
doping, particularly in the EPO era. However,
a bike manufacturer cannot be held ultimately
responsible for doping, and the calibre of the
teams—Banesto, Telekom, and Fassa Bortolo—
that have chosen to ride Pinarellos shows the
esteem in which the brand is held within the

peloton. That esteem has been earned by moving with the times, adapting to the shift from steel to titanium, aluminium, and carbon. In 2002, the company introduced a frame made entirely from magnesium, the Dogma. Magnesium offers a marvellous mix of lightness and rigidity, but the manufacturing process is complex and expensive. Fassa Bortolo's Alessandro Pettachi returned the investment in 2004 by winning nine victories on a Dogma and another fifteen on a Prince.

The latest iteration of the Dogma series sees magnesium superseded by carbon, but still claims another first: an asymmetric frame, the driveside seat stay and the off-side chain stay built to take different stresses than their opposite parts. In 2011, in the pro peloton, the Dogma was the bike of choice for Movistar, the latest part of the collaboration between Pinarello and Eusebio Unzue, and at Unzue's Caisse d'Epargne in 2006, Alejandro Valverde added Liège–Bastogne–Liège to Pinarello's list of races won.

The Dogma was also the preferred ride for Team Sky, and in 2011 it helped deliver victory in the Critérium du Dauphiné for Bradley Wiggins, and stage victories in the Tour de France and the Vuelta a España for the team. Having been associated with two of the sport's great sprinters—Cipollini and Zabel—Pinarello is now linked to a third one, Mark Cavendish, after he signed with Sky in 2012.

There are still two of cycling's Monuments, the Ronde van Vlaanderen and Paris–Roubaix, that are missing from Pinarello's list of victories. Grace Verbeke won the women's Ronde van Vlaanderen in 2010 on a Pinarello, thus throwing down the glove to the men to match her achievement on the cobbles and see that Pinarello's palmarès finally includes all of the most important one day-races, as well as the Grand Tours. Nane Pinarello celebrates his ninetieth birthday in 2012, and those elusive wins would make a perfect gift. **FMK**

Pinarello made four Espada bikes,
all for Miguel Indurain.

- Frank Bowden established the Raleigh Cycle Company in 1888.

- Raleigh, "the all-steel bicycle," is reviewed in an early edition of *Cycling* magazine.

- Raleigh racer Arthur Zimmerman pictured in 1893, his world championship year.

Raleigh

The British and world market leader for all kinds of bikes, from BMXs to high-end racing models, Raleigh became the first and only UK manufacturer to win the Tour de France when Dutchman Joop Zoetemelk won the 1980 edition of the world's greatest race.

At one time, in many British households, Raleigh meant bicycle as automatically as Hoover meant vacuum cleaner and Biro meant ball-point pen. For any makers of anything, this is the holy grail: having the name of your product mistaken for the name of the thing you make. Yet such ubiquity has not always served Raleigh well, especially in its efforts to build and sell the kind of top-end road bikes to which the company aspired.

In the 1970s and early 1980s, although Raleigh supplied bikes and lent its name to the continent's most successful pro team—the all-conquering TI-Raleigh team—the company cultivated a very different image back home. In Britain, Raleighs were family-oriented, with a range of children's models (first the Bomber, then the Grifter) that were experimental and

fun, while the adults' bikes were noted for their reliability and affordability.

Meanwhile, on the other side of the English Channel, the TI-Raleigh team was ripping the sport asunder. It was cycling's first superteam, and the first to apply the Dutch "total football" philosophy to cycling. With Peter Post, an autocratic, slightly abrasive Dutchman, at the helm, it was a winning combination: Dutch flair coupled with British engineering. On mainland Europe, the TI-Raleigh team was huge, but in Britain, the rather significant British contribution went virtually unnoticed.

It seems remarkable now, but even the formidable Post appeared powerless in the face of Raleigh's entrenched "brand values," and its reputation for family and functional bikes. Other than a few notable individuals, the company

did not seem all that interested in the team it sponsored. Perhaps it was unsure how to capitalize on TI-Raleigh's successes; or maybe, given that its core market was not particularly interested in continental road racing, it was uncertain whether the company even wanted to.

The best example of this attitude came in 1980, when Joop Zoetemelk won the Tour de France on a Raleigh and became the first—and still the only—British bike to win the world's biggest race. It was a landmark achievement, but one that few noticed. Raleigh, it seemed, had decided that the British public did not, could not, and would not understand the Tour de France. At the time it was probably right, but things have changed considerably. With the emergence of Mark Cavendish, Bradley Wiggins, and Team Sky, cycling has finally found an audience in Britain, but these British stars ride Italian (Pinarello) bikes. The greatest name in British bicycle manufacturing is conspicuous by its absence. At a boom time for cycling in Britain, Raleigh—who at a couple of points in its history was producing one million bikes a year—seems to have slipped into the margins. In order to understand such a state of affairs it is necessary to go back to the beginning, and to understand something of how cycle racing in Britain developed, or rather did not.

In Raleigh's case, the story begins in 1887, when a prosperous, thirty-eight-year-old lawyer, Frank Bowden, bought a bike from a small workshop, owned by Messrs. Woodhead, Angois, and Ellis, on Raleigh Street, Nottingham. Bowden had been advised by his doctor to take up cycling, but he so enjoyed it, and he was so impressed by his new bike, that he returned to the workshop and bought the company. His first decision was to name it after the street: Raleigh.

1887	1903	1932	1948
Frank Bowden buys an interest in a bicycle company on Raleigh Street, Nottingham, and three years later the Raleigh Bicycle Company is formed.	The Sturmey Archer three-speed gear hub—the world's first practical gearing system—goes on sale. In association with Raleigh, Sturmey Archer will also later produce a Dynohub lighting set.	Company director Harold Bowden retires. Production under his direction had reached 62,000 cycles a year.	Reg Harris turns professional for Raleigh, winning four world sprint titles on the track, and on a Raleigh bike, in a ten-year association.

■ The Duke of Edinburgh
visited Raleigh in 1952,
to open a factory
extension.

■ The £1.2 million
expansion at the factory
in 1952 featured an
overhead conveyor-
based production line.

1970

Raleigh launches the Chopper
to great success in Britain and
the United States.

1980

Joop Zoetemelk of Holland,
riding for TI-Raleigh Creda,
wins the Tour de France.

2001

Management of Derby Cycle
Corporation, led by Alan Finden-
Crofts, acquires Raleigh after a buyout.

2012

Raleigh celebrates its 125th birthday
and releases a new range of classic
models, such as the Clubman, Sojourn,
and Classic De Luxe, as well as new
mountain and BMX bikes.

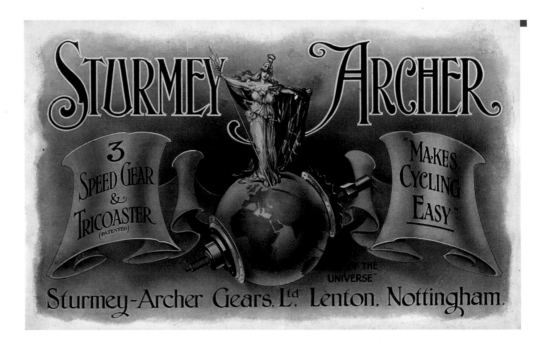

Bowden was also responsible for Raleigh's heron logo—a heron adorned his family crest.

Over the next six years, the company went from producing three bikes a week to become the biggest bike-maker in the world, occupying a five-storey factory. It also boasted the first ever world cycling champion, Arthur Augustus Zimmermann, who won two titles, in the sprint and 6.2 miles (10 km) races, in Chicago in 1893.

Zimmermann, from New Jersey, had raced in Britain in 1892, but when he returned as world champion a year later he ran into controversy when Raleigh, who had given him two bikes, featured him in its advertisements. The National Cyclists' Union took a dim view and ruled that he had broken rules on amateurism, and banned him from racing in Britain. Zimmermann went to race in France and turned professional the following year. It was a portent of the divide that would open between Britain and continental Europe.

By the early 1920s Raleigh was producing 100,000 bikes a year, rising to 500,000 by 1938.

It was at the vanguard of bicycle manufacturing throughout this period, particularly with its Sturmey Archer gearing systems. It built the full gamut of machines, ranging from lugless racing frames to folding bikes for paratroopers in the war, and continued to thrive even after the death of Bowden in 1921, when his son, Harold, took over.

While the company was establishing itself as the world's biggest cycle manufacturer, with production hitting a million "units" in 1951, there was a divergence between Britain and Europe when it came to racing. Most of the great road races—the Tour de France (1903), Giro d'Italia (1909), Paris–Roubaix (1896), Milan–San Remo (1907), Tour of Flanders (1913)—were born in the early years of the 20th century, or just before, but British roads were a no-go area. Early events were repeatedly disrupted by the police, and the National Cyclists' Union, concerned about the legality of racing on public roads, banned it, thus restricting cycle sport to closed roads or velodromes.

A rival organization, the Road Time Trials Council, came up with a solution: clandestine individual time trials, held at dawn, with the riders dressed in black. This meant that a culture of time trialling developed in Britain, which, in every conceivable way, was at odds with the colourful, exuberant spectacle of mass-start road racing. On the roads of France, Italy, Belgium, Holland, and Spain, the great races had already woven themselves into their respective country's sporting fabric, whereas in Britain cycle racing was underground. One exception was Reg Harris, the colourful and charismatic track sprinter, who turned professional with Raleigh in 1948 and won four world titles in a ten-year association.

The demand for sleek road racing bicycles was stronger overseas than it was at home in Britain, where the market was dominated by functional or leisure machines. After World War II, Raleigh's production continued to rise, but the majority of the bikes, all built in its factory in Nottingham were exported.

Like most manufacturers, Raleigh suffered through the late 1950s and 1960s as cars became more affordable. In 1960 the company was taken over by Tube Investments (TI), who already owned the British Cycle Corporation, including bike manufacturers Phillips, Norman, Sun, and a name well known in racing circles Hercules. Hercules had backed a professional team and, according to some historical accounts, it was the first British team to ride the Tour de France. Although six of the ten-man team rode for Hercules, they represented England at the 1955 Tour, not Hercules.

When TI took over Raleigh, it gave the British Cycle Corporation 75 percent of the British market. But that market was still dominated by utilitarian and leisure bikes. In fact, Raleigh had all but stopped building quality lightweight racing bikes. Instead, it spent the 1960s figuring out how to take on Alex Moulton

■ The Sturmey Archer three-speed gear hub first went on sale in 1903.

■ A Sturmey Archer catalogue from 1910 featured the three-gear hub that "fits any bicycle, new or old."

■ An exploded view of Sturmey Archer's AW hub gear, introduced in 1936. Still on sale today, it is the survivor of a larger range of "A" model three-speed hubs, which included the AM, AC, AR, and ASC models.

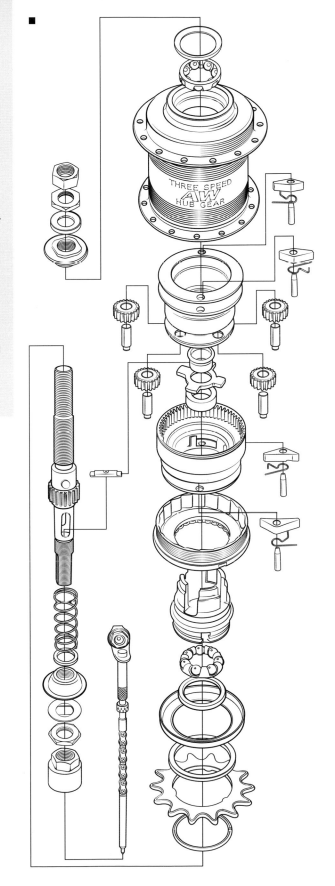

> ## "The head tubes are black, so that the Raleigh badge shows up—you can always spot them in a bunch picture."
>
> GERALD O'DONOVAN

and his popular, small-wheeled "shopping" bikes. It looked across the Atlantic for inspiration and introduced the California-influenced Chopper in 1969.

It was another TI-Raleigh acquisition, Carlton, that helped to put racing bikes back on the Raleigh map. Taking over Carlton gave Raleigh an opportunity to establish a small department to handbuild racers; Carlton had been producing 2,500 such frames a year under its owner and master frame-builder, Gerald O'Donovan.

O'Donovan remained in charge when Carlton became part of Raleigh, and he remained committed to handbuilding lightweight racing bikes. He was a skilled and meticulous craftsman—many of the 1960s Carltons have ornately beautiful lugwork—but also an innovator. Raleigh clearly saw some potential in the racing market and set up O'Donovan in a new Special Products Division in 1974. It was based in Ilkeston, Derbyshire, with six frame-builders hand-picked from the Raleigh factory.

Initially the bikes were branded "Raleigh-Carlton," and from 1963 they got involved in team sponsorship, which worked as a testing ground and shop window: a concept recognized by continental manufacturers some years earlier. The opening of the Special Products Division coincided with Raleigh's most ambitious racing venture: the TI-Raleigh professional team. It saw O'Donovan's department—which was soon building thirty frames a week—charged with producing the stylish, steel-framed red, yellow, and black bikes ridden by Peter Post's new team. Considerable thought had gone into the paint scheme, as O'Donovan explained: "The choice of team colours was because they photographed clearly in colour or black and white. And the head tubes are black, so that the Raleigh badge shows up—you can always spot them in a bunch picture."

The TI-Raleigh team manager, Peter Post, had been a formidable rider; he had won the fastest-ever Paris–Roubaix in 1964 and was known as "Emperor of the Sixes" for his domination of the winter six-day track races.

This F frame Raleigh Carlton was created between 1970 and 1971, and featured highly tensiled steel tubing.

In 1980, Zoetemelk won his—and TI-Raleigh's—only Tour de France.

Post was certainly an inspired choice as boss, even if his hard-as-nails manner and headmaster-esque approach to discipline was not to everyone's taste.

With Post at the helm, after years of regarding the sport's major races from the perspective of an outsider, Raleigh and its Dutch-based squad were now big players. They were soon winning: more than fifty victories in their debut season—and they were winning big: fifty-five stages in the Tour de France over the next decade. Raleigh dominated the Classics and won most of them. But the peak came in 1980 when, among 120 wins, Zoetemelk claimed the greatest prize, the Tour de France, after the pre-race favourite, Bernard Hinault, dropped out with a knee injury. If this suggests an element of good fortune, TI-Raleigh's tally of victories in the 1980 Tour suggests utter domination; it won eleven of the twenty-five stages.

Post brought a new philosophy: his "total cycling" was adapted from the style of his favourite football team, Ajax, in which every player had a clearly defined role. Cycling squads were traditionally hierarchical, led by one rider, with a team of *domestiques* behind him. Post recognized the weaknesses in this model. Problems occurred if the leader was off-form, and a rider who was capable of winning could be prevented from showing his potential because of his responsibilities to his leader. Post allowed different riders to lead, and to win. In fact, TI-Raleigh was arguably professional cycling's first real team.

Yet Post's team seemed almost divorced from the company whose flag it flew with such distinction, and on whose bikes it won. One reason for this was that, although Post started out with a team of Dutch and British riders, he soon got rid of the British ones. Some complained about an apparent Dutch bias, but few could argue with the results. Post could be diplomatic, too, and told O'Donovan, on a visit

to Raleigh's Special Products Division in 1982: "We are perhaps the best team in the world because we have the best bikes in the world."

However, the venture did not last much longer as TI-Raleigh. Post brought in a new title sponsor, Panasonic, and Raleigh stayed as co-sponsors. O'Donovan explained, "Finally the ante was so high that we moved out. We just could not meet the cost of their sort of budget."

O'Donovan's department continued to produce high-quality racing bikes, and in 1986, with a burgeoning British professional scene, the company lured Tour veteran Paul Sherwen to lead—and then to manage—a domestic team. It also briefly returned to continental professional racing in 1989 and supplied Laurent Fignon's team (Super U-Raleigh) when Fignon recaptured his form and won the Giro d'Italia and came within eight seconds of giving Raleigh its second Tour de France.

Raleigh is still racing: the latest incarnation, Team Raleigh, came into being in 2009 to contest domestic races. However, the company has experienced huge change. In April 1987, Raleigh was sold by TI to Derby International, which stabilized the company. It continued to sell lots of bikes in the 1990s, with the British, Canadian, and Irish operations the biggest-selling manufacturers in their respective countries, but other changes followed. In 1999 it stopped mass-building frames in Britain. By 2003, after a management buyout, bike assembly on home soil had stopped, too.

Raleigh was always different from some of its continental counterparts. The name is iconic, but not for the same reasons as Bianchi, say, or Colnago, whose names are synonymous with some of the great champions and great races. Raleigh always produced high-quality racing bicycles. It says a lot for the culture of cycling in Britain, however, that it is better known as a great producer of bikes, rather than as a producer of great bikes. **RM**

"We are perhaps the best team in the world because we have the best bikes in the world."

PETER POST

■ Riding for Raleigh, Fignon was favourite to win the 1989 Tour de France, but lost by eight seconds to LeMond.

■ A beautifully
understated Reynolds
trade catalogue from
the 1920s.

■ The sign over the
company's entrance in
Birmingham, England. In
1923 the Patent Butted
Tube Co Ltd changed
its name to Reynolds
Tube Co Ltd.

Reynolds

The foremost name in steel bicycle tubing for more than a century, Reynolds invented
the butting process that resulted in bikes that were both stronger and lighter. With the
resurgence of steel, it remains in the vanguard when it comes to lightweight racing bikes.

A visit to the Reynolds factory evokes a sense
of wonder similar to an excursion to a whisky
distillery. The setting is very different, with the
Talisker distillery, for example, sitting in a remote
corner of the Isle of Skye, whereas the Reynolds
factory is on an industrial estate on the outskirts
of Birmingham, England. However, they do have
something in common: in these unassuming
buildings, staffed by small teams of skilled
workers, the products that emerge have a name
that is respected worldwide. In the same way
that a bottle of Talisker single malt may be found
in bars from Moscow to Mogadishu, a Reynolds-
tubed bike can be found anywhere in the world.

Today, even with the popularity of materials
such as carbon, aluminium, and titanium,
95 percent of all bikes are still constructed with
steel. Most of these are made in China and India

from "mild steel," which is the cheapest, heaviest
form of the alloy. High-quality, handmade bikes,
on the other hand, are made with senior grade,
light, and strong iron alloys. There are several
noted marques producing steel tubing: Columbus,
True Temper, Dedecciai, Tange, and Ishiwata to
name a few. If you are British and of a certain age,
however, it is the Reynolds name that resounds.

It is a global brand, and the name is known
worldwide. Keith Noronha, Reynolds's current
managing director, tells a story of being asked
his line of business by US customs officers. "We
make cycle tubes," he explained. "Not Reynolds,
is it?" the officer asked. Most companies
would give an arm and a leg for such a level
of recognition. In order to appreciate how
remarkable this achievement is, it is necessary
to understand how the tubing is made. Today,

that is. Today, an experienced team of around ten does this specialist work. Some have worked for Reynolds for thirty-plus years.

Again like whisky distilleries, there is a certain mystique to the Reynolds factory. The techniques they use are unique, the "recipe" guarded as closely as that of Coca-Cola, but they continue to produce tubesets that are sought-after by some of the world's top frame-builders.

For their first fifty years Reynolds, founded in 1841 by John Reynolds, made nails. It was his son, Alfred John, who became interested—as did so many people in the 1890s—in bicycles. He was concerned with a problem that troubled the burgeoning bicycle industry: how do you join together thin, lightweight tubes without weakening the joints? The problem was in attaching the thin tubes to the heavy lugs required to join them together. Some inserted liners to reinforce the joint; others resorted to thick, heavy tubing. Neither was satisfactory: either the joints were weak or the bikes were too heavy.

Reynolds' solution was radical: he made tubes of varying internal thickness. Externally they were the same diameter throughout; inside, they were thin in the middle, thick at the ends—where they needed to be stronger. Thus were born "butted" tubes: it was a breakthrough for the industry.

Today, in Reynolds' cabin-style office housed within the factory, the original Patent certificate is displayed on the wall. Alfred applied to the Patent office on October 27, 1897, it was approved exactly a year later, and on December 20, 1898, the Patent Butted Tube Company Limited was incoporated. It was the process that was patented. As the patent certificate states, "the invention… consists of improvements relating to the manufacture of seamless steel and other tubes for boilers, for cycle construction, and for other purposes, our object being to readily produce such tubes with a varying distribution of metal, or with the ends or other required parts of a greater thickness than the body of the tubes."

The advantages, in weight reduction and strength, were significant and within five years Alfred's invention was established as the ultimate in tubesets. Bikes were safer, too. "The joints, hitherto the weakest points in cycle construction, are under this system the strongest," stated the early sales literature of the Patent Butted Tube Company. Its machinery could also produce tubes of pinpoint accuracy, with the diameter of each guaranteed to 1,000th of an inch.

In order to achieve this, Reynolds would take delivery of steel tubes and then "draw" them. First, the rough tubes, made by a hot process at other factories, would be de-rusted and de-scaled in long tanks of diluted sulphuric acid. While immersed in these tanks, they would be "agitated," which, according to the company's official history, "usually involved a man standing over the immersed bundle, moving the tubes about with a long bar." The "drawing" process was a two-man job, with one person gripping the tube and the other hammering the hot ends on an anvil.

Praise flooded in for Reynolds's tubes, from cyclists, frame-builders, and the cycling media. "Whatever the process, a wonderful degree of accuracy has been obtained," was the verdict of *Cycle Referee*. "The interior is beautifully smooth," said *Cycle Trader*, "and the graduation of the butted portion such as to be almost unnoticeable to the eye. The metal is very tough and close in grain, and should prove the ideal material for cycle frame construction."

It was not until 1923 that the company name was changed to the Reynolds Tube Company Ltd. Five years later it became part of a bigger concern and voluntarily joined Tube Investments; Reynolds was not taken over by the Tube Investments conglomerate, under whose umbrella it would remain until 1996.

The year 1935 saw the arrival of the tubeset that would ensure Reynolds a bright and enduring future: 531. By that time there was a new man at the helm, the colourful, Eton-educated Austyn

■ This Reynolds factory worker rakes fork blades by hand in the 1970s.

■ The Reynolds manufacturing plant and warehouses in the 1970s and 1980s.

Reynolds and it was he who decided on the name of the new tubeset. The reason is not clear. The current managing director, Keith Noronha, admits that the famous Reynolds numbered tubing (with 753, 853, and 953, among those to follow) is, above all, "clever marketing", though he adds that there are at least two possible explanations for the original: one, that "531" referred to the ratio of the three main elements in the steel's chemical compistion; or, two, that it referred to its strength: 53 tonnes per square inch (53:1).

However they were arrived at, those numbers—531—came to stand for the very highest quality in racing cycles. It also helped immeasurably that Austyn reached out to the continent, making contact with Roger Dupieux in Paris, who, according to Reynolds' official history, "helped Reynolds 531 become a household name on the continent." As for the tubes themselves, they were developed through the company's burgeoning knowledge of aircraft technology, using Swedish steel. The tubes where thinner than the earlier versions: 0.090 in (2.3 mm) at the ends, just 0.062 in (1.6 mm) in the middle.

The tubes were so delicate that Reynolds issued *A Few Points of General Guidance* to frame-builders: "Brazing should be carried out in clockwise sequence… When brazing frames made from 531, the joints should be pre-heated, and after brazing the cooling should be controlled. Brazing must be carried out in shops free from draughts."

Reynolds 531 was an instant hit, though the company's manufacture of cycle tubing was suspended completely a few years later. When World War II broke out Reynolds employed 1,000 people. That climbed during the war to 2,055, with the company producing 25,000 miles

1897	1928	1935	1958
Alfred Reynolds patents the invention of butted tubing for use in bike manufacture. A year later The Patent Butted Tube Company is incorporated.	Reynolds become part of the Tube Investments (T.I.) holding company, with whom they remain until 1996.	Using Swedish steel the company introduces the ultimate steel tubeset: Reynolds 531, which dominates the market for more than fifty years.	Charly Gaul wins the Tour de France on 531. Twenty-four of the next twenty-five Tours are won by riders using 531 tubing.

and steel tubing for various applications, including 18,037 tubular wing spars for Spitfires: £2 million worth of business.

After the war it was back to bikes, although Reynolds was always keen to apply its expertise to other challenges. Over the decades it produced 531 tubing for the E-Type Jaguar sub-frames as well as equipment for NASA, and some unusual one-off projects included the structure for a trapeze circus act and oxygen cylinders for two Everest expeditions.

Incredibly, by the 1970s, Reynolds 531 remained the tubeset of choice—and of champions. One of the first high-profile successes was the climber Charly Gaul's 1958 Tour de France victory, and, from then, 531 tubing claimed twenty-four out of twenty-five successive winners of the Tour, including all of Jacques Anquetil's record five wins. When Eddy Merckx claimed his first, in 1969, it was on 531, and so fond was Merckx of the tubeset that he stuck with it even when its much-heralded successor was unveiled in 1976. Heat-treated 753 tubing was 50 percent stronger than 531; it was also lighter, with "tube walls so thin that the frame design, choice of lugs, joining techniques, and other aspects are especially critical. The finished frame, naturally, is intended for special purpose only."

Reynolds 753 replaced 531 as the racers' frame of choice, with the exception of the big, powerful Merckx who preferred his bikes to be (relatively speaking) strong and sturdy. Among the riders to enjoy success on 753 were Bernard Hinault, who joined Anquetil and Merckx as a five-time Tour winner in 1985, and also the fourth member of that exclusive club, Miguel Indurain.

Other tubesets have followed—including 653, 708, and 853—and Reynolds has also used titanium, aluminium, and carbon. But the flagship steel frameset is 953, introduced in 2007. It followed an approach from Carpenter Specialty Alloys in Pennsylvania.

As Keith Noronha, who led a management buyout of Reynolds in 2000, explains: "Carpenter specializes in very high strength metallic alloys, generally used in aerospace and armoured plating. They had a specific alloy in sheet form only and had never made a tube with it. They contacted us to see if we were interested in using it, and so we examined the mechanical properties to see if it could be turned into a butted cycle tube. It wasn't easy. We had to research, and we had some complaints from frame-builders at first, because it was chewing up their equipment. But we sorted that out and now it's our flagship tubeset: the ultimate, really. It's our thinnest walled tubeset—only 0.3 mm. But it also has the highest strength to weight ratio: even better than titanium."

"In 953 frames," says Noronha, "you've got the ride and comfort of steel, but, like titanium, if you look after it, it'll outlast you." Indeed, so strong is 953 that it has been used in one of the toughest working environments—drilling for oil.

As for the process, Noronha explains that the flat sheet metal, manufactured to aerospace standards by Carpenter in the United States, is turned into tubing by a sub-contractor before it is delivered to Reynolds in Birmingham. Once there, it is engineered for bike tubing. Remarkably, this process is essentially the same—albeit with more sophisticated machinery—as the one that was patented by Alfred John Reynolds in 1897.

"In principle," says Noronha, "what Reynolds invented in 1897, is what we still love. The treatment might have changed, but, over a century later, the same mechanical principles apply." **RM**

■ Charly Gaul's 1958 Tour de France victory on a 531 tubeset was a first for Reynolds.

■ A 1971 advertising card shows that Reynolds was clearly proud of its sporting accomplishments.

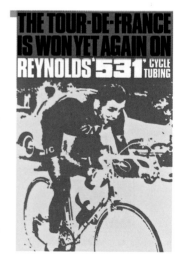

THE TOUR-DE-FRANCE IS WON YET AGAIN ON REYNOLDS' 531 CYCLE TUBING

1976	1996	2000	2007
Reynolds 753 is launched and billed as the ultimate lightweight racing tubeset.	The company is taken over by US-based Coyote Sports Inc. and two years later celebrates one hundred years as the world's leading bicycle tubing manufacturer.	A management buyout sees the company renamed Reynolds Cycle Technology Ltd. Reynolds Composites LLC remains a separate entity based in California.	With steel returning to fashion, Reynolds 953 is launched, made from high-strength steel that is used in aerospace applications and armoured plating.

GRAEME OBREE'S OLD FAITHFUL

Scottish cyclist Graeme Obree had an epiphany as he sat in his bike shop in Ayrshire, contemplating the bike before him. It was the late 1980s and the machine was conventional, although Obree was anything but.

As he put it: "I thought, I'm going to ride a bike as though for the first time in my whole life. I went out and pretended I'd never ridden a bike before. I tried to forget everything I knew. And my first thought was: these pedals are too far apart, and why is the top tube in the way of my knees? I hadn't noticed that in fifteen years, because my mind had been closed."

Having opened his mind, Obree set about reimagining his bike. Central to his design was narrowing the distance between the pedals—the only ball bearings he could find for the new, narrow bottom bracket were in his washing machine. Later, this would be what his bike, christened Old Faithful, became best known for, but its ingenuity extended much further. His position was revolutionary. Inspired by a downhill skier's tuck, Obree leant forwards with his arms folded beneath him.

In July 1993 the unknown Obree rode Old Faithful to the world Hour record in Norway; his 32.060 miles (51.596 km) beat Francesco Moser's mark by 1,459 feet (445 m). As other riders were inspired to copy the Obree position, cycling's governing body, the UCI, declared it dangerous and banned it. In 1995 Obree returned with the Superman position—this time with his arms outstretched in front. After winning the world pursuit title in Colombia, inspiring more copycats, Obree's Superman position was also declared illegal.

Obree used a standard saddle: the ever-popular and affordable Turbo, made by Selle Italia.

Specialized tri-spoke carbon wheels were introduced in the early 1990s.

The seat tube was Ishiwata BMX tubing, reinforced in the middle with the side panel from Obree's washing machine.

The narrow handlebars were attached to a long section of Reynolds tubing, level with the saddle, so that Obree could lean forwards on his folded arms.

Obree used a fifty-two-tooth front chainring and twelve-tooth rear sprocket when he broke the world Hour record.

DESIGN DETAILS

FRAME

The main (down) tube was Reynolds tandem base oval; the chain stays were Reynolds 653; the seat stays were Ishiwata; and the forks were Reynolds, which Obree says he "cut open, manipulated, and brazed back together."

HANDLEBARS

Obree created a brand new handlebar position. Although they resemble standard "sit-up-and-beg" bars, they were narrower to reduce drag, with hand grips to enable him to fold his arms beneath his body and adopt the skier's "tuck" position.

Schwinn

The Schwinn brand—at one point the maker of the most prolific bicycle in US history, and a regular in the major international events—is more than one hundred years old and went from boom in the 1970s to bust in the 1990s.

On May 17, 1941, an intrepid Frenchman named Alfred Letourneur mounted his fire engine red motor-pace bicycle on a stretch of highway outside of Bakersfield, California, and rocketed himself into the record books.

Closely following behind a midget race car driven by champion driver Ronnie Householder, featuring a custom-fabricated metal faring at its rear to block the wind, the diminutive Letourneur wound up an inhumanly large 252-inch gear and took 3 miles (4.8 km) to get it rolling. Once he was comfortably spinning the monstrous gear, he sped through a measured mile in 33.05 seconds at an average speed of

108.92 miles per hour (175.28 km/h), 18.01 miles per hour (28.98 km/h) faster than the previous record he himself had set just a few weeks earlier. Letourneur, who in the 1930s enjoyed one of the best six-day careers of the early 20th century with twenty-one victories, now lay claim to the honour of being the fastest man on a bicycle. This record was achieved on a Schwinn Paramount.

In the United States, the word "Schwinn" is synonymous with bicycle, and the company's flagship model, Paramount, was its crown jewel, a handcrafted machine that in its heyday encompassed cutting-edge design, technology, and artistry.

German-born Ignaz Schwinn immigrated to Chicago, Illinois, in 1891 and co-founded a bicycle company four years later with Adolph Frederick William Arnold. Known at that time as Arnold, Schwinn, & Company (in 1968 it changed to the Schwinn Bicycle Company), the firm's genesis fortuitously coincided with a national craze for bicycles. And Chicago was the locus of production.

By the dawn of the 20th century, however, automobiles and motorcycles had moved into favour, which prompted a decline in the bicycle industry. Schwinn was one of the survivors and bought up smaller competitors and expanded into motorcycle production.

By 1928 Schwinn's motorcycle division was third in the country, only bettered by Indian and Harley-Davidson, but it was soon decimated by the stock market crash. On the verge of bankruptcy, Schwinn discontinued its motorcycle line in 1931 to once again concentrate on bicycles. The company came to the fore as a major bicycle manufacturer in the 1930s thanks to the creation of mass-produced balloon-tyred bikes featuring trademark 26 x 2.125 size tyres. (If that size sounds familiar, it will be no surprise to learn that Schwinn laid the groundwork for the rise of mountain bikes in the 1980s.)

Schwinn began as a company that was focused on building racing bicycles, but found itself ramping up production of bicycles for casual and recreational use. Ignaz Schwinn's son, Frank W. Schwinn, who was running the company in the 1930s, saw an opportunity to once again position Schwinn at the pinnacle of professional cycling, at that point synonymous with outdoor and indoor track racing, with winter six-day races the flagship events.

Before long Emil Wastyn, a Belgian immigrant who had already been building bicycles for Schwinn-sponsored professional riders in the 1930s, came on to the scene. He ran a bike shop and frame-building business that was located near

"A bike is perhaps the most demanding mechanical structure that is made by man."

RICHARD SCHWINN

■ The five-speed Schwinn Stingray "Orange Krate" with its iconic banana seat was the must-have kids' bike of the 1960s and 1970s.

■ The 1987 Schwinn Paramount fiftieth anniversary edition by Ray Dobbins. The black and gold model became highly sought-after by fans and collectors and features, from top to bottom, gold-plated front forks, "La Fausto Coppi"—a limited edition saddle by Selle Italia, radial lacing of the front wheel, and beefy seat stays. Each of the 600 framesets came with a burgundy velour pouch to protect the fork.

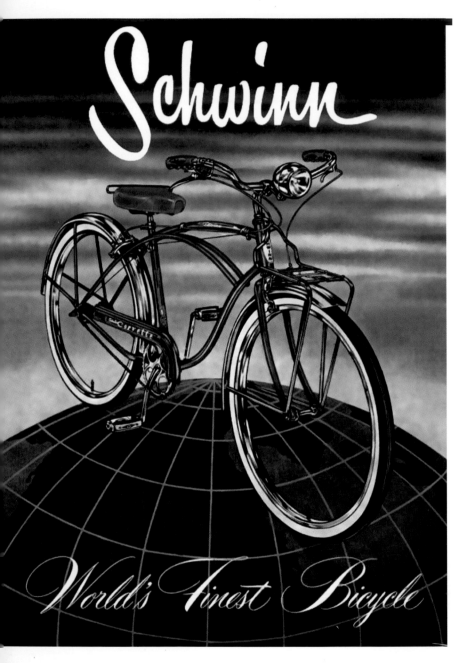

Schwinn

World's Finest Bicycle

Schwinn's Chicago factory and began turning out Paramount-labelled bicycles in 1937. One year later, in 1938, Schwinn officially introduced the Paramount, a professional-quality track bike that was as elegantly constructed as it was tough.

With an increase in the amount of new high-strength steel alloys that were available for bicycle manufacture, Paramounts were soon in the vanguard. They utilized chrome molybdenum steel, exquisitely carved lugs, and brass brazing. Not only did Schwinn build the frames and forks, but also many of the components, including high-flange hubs, stems, handlebars, cranksets, and pedals. For the next twenty years Paramounts would primarily be the bastion of Emil Wastyn, followed by his son Oscar. This was an issue that simmered consistently and became a point of contention as Schwinn strove to bring the production in-house.

Paramount production was born into the glory days of six-day racing in pre–World War II America, but the sport lost all of its lustre in the United States after the end of the conflict. Schwinn tried to keep alive the hope that one day the sport would rise again. However, it was Frank Schwinn who provided the urgently needed financial support to keep competitive cycling afloat in the post-war years. In 1945 a five-year grant from Schwinn enabled the Amateur Bicycle League of America (founded in 1921) to hold national championships that allowed time for the organization to become financially solvent. In addition, when six-day racing briefly tried to re-establish its foothold in the United States in the late 1940s, Schwinn provided event sponsorship. As the only US bicycle manufacturer that was creating racing bikes, the company tried to do its part to keep professional cycling alive.

1895	1912	1938	1941
The company is founded by German-born mechanical engineer Ignaz Schwinn in Chicago.	Ambitious to grow his company, Schwinn purchases the Excelsior Motorcycle Company. In 1917 he adds the Henderson Company to form Excelsior-Henderson.	Schwinn introduces the Paramount series, a bicycle developed from experience gained in racing.	Alfred Letourneur beats the motor-paced world speed record, reaching 109 miles per hour (175 km/h) on a Schwinn riding behind a car on a Los Angeles freeway.

At this point in the late 1940s, one of the stars of US professional cycling who was still operating under the radar found himself on the cusp of a long-term association with Schwinn. Illinois native Joseph Magnani was truly a man before his time as the lone US cyclist to race as a professional in Europe during the era of Fausto Coppi and Gino Bartali. From 1935 to 1948, Magnani raced professionally on the continent where he won several races, performed well in Classics such as Milan–San Remo, and notably finished seventh in the 1947 world championship road race.

In 1948 Magnani returned to the United States where he visited relatives in Chicago and was recruited by Schwinn to race the winter six-day circuit. Magnani felt at home on the roads of Europe as a professional cyclist, but racing on

tightly banked indoor velodromes was a different matter. He was forced into early retirement after sustaining injuries during the opening six-day race of the season held in Buffalo, New York, in October 1948, but found full-time employment at Schwinn until 1972 when he suffered ill-health and stopped working completely. Magnani passed away in 1975.

Befitting his exploits as a professional cyclist in Europe, Magnani assembled all of the Paramount track, road, and tandem bikes for the duration of his employment by the company. He was instrumental in developing the component side of the Paramount, including building wheels and speccing Campagnolo derailleur systems and other pro-level equipment.

While the 1950s and 1960s were the absolute nadir of high-level racing in the United States,

■ The cover of Schwinn's 1955 catalogue shows that the company was not afraid of making grandiose claims.

■ In the 1950s, most Paramounts were built by Oscar Wastyn in his Chicago shop. As demand for racing bikes decreased after the end of the war, Schwinn employed Ovie Jensen to build its frames.

1956	1960s	1979	1992
Schwinn provides Paramount bikes for the US Olympic cycling teams in an arrangement that lasts until 1972.	Schwinn dominates the US youth market with the release of the Stingray in 1963. The Paramount is redesigned with Reynolds 531 tubing.	Schwinn's popularity in the United States is eclipsed by Japanese and European brands. The company fails to capitalize on the BMX and mtb craze.	Squeezed by foreign and domestic competitors, such as US firms Trek, Specialized, and Cannondale, Schwinn is declared bankrupt.

Scott

This US firm started out in skiing and then changed the shape of bicycle handlebars and introduced the skier's "tuck" in 1989. After focusing on mountain bikes and triathlon, it entered the road market with the world's first sub-kilogram racing frame in 2001.

The evolution of technology within professional cycling can be seen in several key innovations. Likely candidates for inclusion in such a list include Tullio Campagnolo's invention of both the quick-release skewer for hubs and the parallelogram rear derailleur; Look's clipless pedal, which signalled the end of the toe-clip and strap-equipped pedals; the creation of the Shimano Total Integration shifter/brake lever, which made down tube gear shifting obsolete; and Scott's clip-on Aero Bar—a design innovation that changed time trialling forever.

Scott's Aero Bar was first used to devastating effect by Greg LeMond on the final day of the 1989 Tour de France. LeMond, who in 1986 became the first American to win the Tour, had been locked in a furious battle for the yellow jersey with two-time Tour champion Laurent Fignon. However, in 1989, the final stage was not a typical final day's road stage into Paris, but a 15.2-mile (24.5-km) time trial finishing on the Champs-Elysées.

After twenty-one days of racing, Fignon entered the final day leading LeMond by a

■ Engineer and racer Ed Scott, founder of Scott Sports, invented the first aluminium ski pole.

■ Greg LeMond, aided by the Scott Aero Bar, races to victory in the thrilling finale of the 1989 Tour de France.

SCOTT **267**

seemingly insurmountable fifty-second margin.
Fignon and LeMond had been evenly matched
in the opening 4.8-mile (7.8-km) prologue, but
LeMond gained fifty-six seconds on Fignon on
the massive 45.4-mile (73-km) stage five time
trial, and beat him by forty-seven seconds in the
23.6-mile (38-km) stage fifteen time trial. These
tiny margins suggested that, over a short distance,
Fignon would be safe.

Professional cycling had already embraced
aerodynamic advantages for time trials, including
disc wheels, wind-cheating teardrop-shaped
helmets, skinsuits, aero-profile frame tubing, and
bullhorn handlebars. But LeMond—the 137th
of 138 riders to start—added a new twist when
he rolled down the start ramp on Sunday, July
23, with clip-on handlebar extensions. Eagle-eyed
observers noticed that shims cut from Coke cans
had been required to help secure them to the
mid-section of his bars.

The clip-on bars, which enabled LeMond to
stretch out his arms in front of him, adopting
a position a little like a downhill skier, were
the brainchild of Boone Lennon, who was the
US Alpine Ski Team coach from 1984 to 1986.
Unsurprisingly, it was Lennon's background in the
aerodynamics of downhill skiing that had inspired
the new bars. Bullhorn handlebars were already
in use for time trials, but Lennon's invention
enabled riders to maintain a narrower and more
aerodynamic riding profile, crucially reducing
frontal wind resistance. Lennon's bars allowed
the rider to support his weight via armrests,
making the position as comfortable as it was
aerodynamic; this in turn encouraged a low
head and horizontal torso, reducing drag even
further. Through a licensing agreement, Lennon's
bars were built by Scott.

LeMond, riding out of his skin for one of the
most remarkable time trial efforts that the Tour
had ever seen, covered the 15.2 miles (24.5 km)
to Paris in twenty-six minutes, fifty-seven seconds
at an average speed of 34.52 miles per hour

(54.545 km/h). Fignon was six seconds down after 3.1 miles (5 km); at 7.1 miles (11.5 km) the gap had grown to twenty-one seconds. It kept increasing: twenty-four seconds at 8.7 miles (14 km); thirty-five seconds after 11.1 miles (18 km); forty-five seconds after 12.4 miles (20 km). Fignon officially lost the Tour a mere 164 feet (50 m) from the finish line; it was here that his deficit went over fifty seconds. Eight seconds later he crossed the finish line, losing the 2,041.4-mile (3,285.3-km) Tour by the smallest margin in history.

The clip-on bars, marketed as Scott DH bars, had already found acceptance in the triathlon community, but LeMond's utilization of them on road cycling's greatest platform broke new ground and set a new global standard for time trial equipment. It is fitting that an innovation that originated in skiing put the Scott company on the map in the cycling world. The company, founded by Ed Scott in 1958, was originally a skiing equipment manufacturer. Scott, a talented engineer and ski racer living in Sun Valley, Idaho, invented the tapered aluminium ski pole, which instantly rendered the existing bamboo and steel poles obsolete. This revolutionary invention launched an eponymous new brand—Scott— which quickly positioned itself as a technical product leader in the skiing market. Ed Scott's initial vision and technical innovation would serve as the cornerstone of company philosophy as the brand matured and expanded into new markets around the world.

Scott next branched into two-wheeled motor sport in 1970 with the creation of the first motocross-specific goggles. In the next year the company produced the world's lightest ski boot, as well as one of the first ski goggles to use

1958	1989	1991	2005
Founded by Ed Scott, an engineer from Idaho, the company starts out in the skiing industry, fast becoming a market leader.	Scott experiences a breakthrough in cycling when Greg LeMond uses its aerodynamic handlebars to win his second Tour de France in thrilling fashion.	Mountain biking is booming and Scott moves its brand with the times, producing its first suspension bikes. A year later full-suspension frames are unveiled.	Scott extends its CR1 technology to time trial bikes with its Plasma frame. As well as aero tubes, the frame features an integrated seatpost.

foam to aid ventilation. In the late 1970s, Scott opened its European headquarters in Givisiez, Switzerland; this was followed in 1986 by the opening of a ski pole factory in Italy, which positioned the company as the global leader in ski pole manufacturing. That same year, Scott made its first venture into cycling with the production of a mountain bike. The Aero Bar made famous by LeMond made 1989 a landmark year in Scott's cycling activities, but the company continued to expand in the burgeoning sport of mountain biking in the early 1990s. In 1991 it produced the Unishock mountain bike suspension fork, which featured a steel unicrown that was simpler than the typical multi-piece crowns that were popular at the time.

The next year—1992—Scott produced its first full-suspension mountain bike and introduced cycling shoes and helmets. However, it was in 1995 that the company really made an impact on mountain biking with the production of the Endorphin, its first carbon fibre mountain bike frame. Fuelled by success in the World Cup and Olympic Games, the Endorphin became a legend and the must-have frame for uphill climbs.

While maintaining its presence in the ski accessory market, Scott continued to experiment with carbon fibre in bicycle manufacturing. In 1998 the company produced the G-Zero, which at the time was the lightest full-suspension mountain bike in production.

It was natural, though, that a forward-thinking company like Scott would eventually progress into the high-end road bike market. In 2001 it released the carbon fibre Scott Team, claiming it was the first frame to weigh less than 2.2 pounds (1 kg). In 2003 came its successor, the carbon fibre CR1, which, at 31.56 ounces (895 g), was the lightest frame on the market. Scott did not stop there: in 2007 it introduced the carbon fibre Addict road frame, which tipped the scales at a featherweight 27.86 ounces (790 g).

In 2002, thirteen years after LeMond introduced the Scott name to professional road racing at the Tour de France, the company made a smaller but arguably more significant impact when Patrice Halgand, of the small Jean Delatour team, rode solo to victory on stage ten of the Tour. This time, he was not only using Scott handlebars, he was on a Scott bike, albeit an aluminium-framed machine rather than one of its superlight carbon fibre models.

Two years later, Scott embedded itself further in the European professional road scene

- Riccardo Riccò during the ninth stage of the 2008 Tour de France, between Toulouse and Bagnères-de-Bigorre.

- The Endorphin, launched in 1995, was Scott's first venture into the world of carbon fibre frames. With its Z1 forks, it is ideal for uphill climbs.

2007	2008	2009	2011/12
The Addict bike bursts on to the scene and is one of the lightest frames in the professional peloton.	The Saunier Duval-Scott team wins three Tour stages. However, Riccardo Riccò and Leonardo Piepoli are stripped of their wins after testing positive for EPO.	Britain's Mark Cavendish wins six stages on a Scott Addict at the Tour de France.	Scott plans to make a return to the professional ranks with Pegasus but the team falls through. A year later they return, with Australian outfit GreenEDGE.

by supplying bikes to a bigger team, the Spanish Saunier Duval squad, for two years. The team enjoyed significant success in those seasons, although several members were tainted by a succession of doping scandals involving the notorious Riccardo Riccò, Leonardo Piepoli, and Iban Mayo. Riccò rode his Scott bike to two stage wins in the 2008 Tour before testing positive. Piepoli, also a stage winner, met a similar fate.

The next team to be supplied by Scott could not have offered more of a contrast. The scandal-free Columbia-HTC were the most prolific winners in the 2009 and 2010 seasons. Mark Cavendish, André Greipel, and Edvald Boasson Hagen, among others, notched up eighty-five victories in 2009, including stages in all three Tours, followed by sixty-four victories in 2010.

In the first year, Cavendish earned the company and its Addict frames some priceless publicity with his stunning win in Milan–San Remo and his dominant sprinting performance at the Tour de France. In the latter, he rode a bike with

an eye-catching customized design. Painted a stylish metallic grey, the bike was made to look like a World War II bomber, complete with rivets, space for marking his kills (or wins), and, at the front end, a glamorous pin-up girl. It worked: he won six stages.

After sitting out 2011, when the Pegasus squad collapsed on the eve of the season, Scott returned to the pro peloton in 2012 with GreenEDGE, Australia's first major professional team. When Scott developed its featherweight carbon mountain bikes—at 31.7 ounces (899 g), the 2011 Scale is the lightest off-road frame ever produced—it became firmly established as one of the big players in the road market.

In fifty years the company has come a long way from its humble origins as a one-man ski-tuning business in Idaho. Scott may now be a worldwide powerhouse in cycling, skiing, and motorsport, but Ed Scott's vision remains true, as does the company's ethos of innovation, technology, and design. **PH**

■ Mark Cavendish rides through stage fourteen of the 2009 Tour. He won six stages that year.

■ The frame Cavendish rode in the 2009 Tour de France featured decals inspired by a World War II bomber.

■ The GreenEDGE Scott Plasma 3 features an IMP5 Technology drivetrain, a carbon saddle, and Shimano Dura-Ace handlebars, disc tyres, and wheelset.

The Plasma 3 has a drag-optimized
profile on its tube sections.

■ This Serotta features a titanium H56 frame, F3 carbon fork, and 404 Firecrest wheels.

■ Bob Roll powers his Serotta Huffy uphill during the San Francisco stage of the 1986 Coors Classic race.

Serotta

The small, independent US frame-builder, with a distinctly Italian name and flavour, handbuilds high-quality road, track, and trail frames that are designed to fit like a glove thanks to the innovative "Size-Cycle." A truly product-driven company.

"The best bike isn't the best bike unless it's the best bike for the person we're building it for."

BEN SEROTTA

Ben Serotta started his frame-building business in Saratoga Springs, New York, in 1972. Since then, an obsession with sourcing the right materials and fitting the frame perfectly to its rider has established Serotta as one of the most desired, bespoke bikes a rider could own.

Serotta learnt the frame-building process at Witcomb Lightweight Cycles in Deptford, London, during the winter of 1971 to 1972, before he returned to the United States to set up his own workshop and to turn his bike-building dreams into reality. Prior to his overseas sojourn, Serotta had worked in his family's general store in Saratoga and was virtually running his own

bike shop by the time he had finished high school, selling components and imported Peugeot frames by the end of the 1960s.

When Serotta started out, frame-building was all about steel frames—a material that he still hails as one of the best. However, the company has also moved with the times and graduated to titanium and then carbon fibre.

Serotta has always been a "Made in the USA" brand, which equally has always been part of the appeal for many of the brand's customers. Moreover, there was plenty to celebrate when, in 1986, Serotta provided the first US team to participate in the Tour de France—7-Eleven—

with bicycles, albeit under a different name. Huffy
was a supermarket brand in need of exposure;
Serotta made a few bucks from helping it out, and
still got its name on the chain stays.

The obsession with the perfect fit led Serotta
to develop the Size-Cycle in 1979—a fully
adjustable rig to get the frame measurements
perfectly dialled to suit the rider—and in turn
came the establishment of the Serotta School
of Cycling Ergonomics in 1998, which allowed
dealers to come to the Saratoga manufacturing
plant and learn from Ben Serotta himself. This
later became the Serotta International Cycling
Institute, and a new generation of Size-Cycle
was developed to ensure the perfect fit. It had
added power measurement to make sure that the
perfect position tallied with the highest possible
power output.

Workers at the Saratoga Springs factory
have always been trained in all aspects of the
manufacturing process, which ensures that
everyone is capable of chipping in and lending a
hand should anyone fall behind. Ben has always
remained hands-on when it comes to the
manufacturing process, constantly checking and
rechecking that everything is just so. It is Ben who
has the privilege of riding, and approving, every
new model before it goes into production.

A period of sustained growth in the mid-
2000s saw Serotta increase production and
offer a range of stock frames, which meant that
those with a lower budget could also enjoy the
painstaking Serotta approach to workmanship and
attention to detail. Today, Serotta has become
the bike of choice for the rich and famous who
care about their machines: Robin Williams, Ron
Perelman, and Ellen Barkin own Serottas, and
senator John Kerry once fell off one during a
presidential campaign. More recently, Serotta
has taken the decision to return to concentrating
solely on its top-end SE custom frames, thus
ensuring that this is a company that produces only
the very best bike frames. *EB*

- The Shimonoseki factory is blessed by Shinto priests in 1970. At that time it was the world's largest bicycle manufacturing facility.

- Shozaburo Shimano established the Shimano Iron Works in 1921 to produce bicycle freewheels.

- The Shimano 333 freewheel, "the product of Shozaburo's dreams and enthusiasm" was released in 1922.

Shimano

The revolutionary Japanese component manufacturers emerged as a serious challenger to Campagnolo in the 1970s and went on to threaten the Italian company's domination of the component market over the next two decades.

In 1973, at the world road race championships, when Shimano was on the brink of its first success, the Italian cycle component manufacturer, Campagnolo, allegedly "stitched" up its Japanese rival. By the early 1970s, Campagnolo had established a virtual stranglehold on the professional cycling scene by offering a complete "groupset," or *gruppo*, that performed well and was reliable.

Competitors such as Stronglight and Universal had fallen away, beaten by the excellence of the innovative Vicenza company's wares. Poised to establish complete dominance,

Campagnolo was confronted by a new opponent that, although unused to the Europe-centred world of professional road racing, had a long tradition of making high-quality cycle parts. Indeed, Shimano, the apparent upstart, had a longer company history than Campagnolo, having been founded in 1921—almost a decade before the Italian concern.

The first Shimano product was a single freewheel, manufactured to a very high standard. The firm prospered and, by 1931, was able to export its design. A three-speed hub gear eventually followed, but was preceded by the

first Shimano derailleur gear shift mechanism, which appeared in 1956. Pressing on, Shimano adopted cold-forging for aluminium parts in 1960 and laid the foundations for the development of the component group that would first challenge and then depose the mighty Campagnolo. Named Dura-Ace, it made its cycle show debut in 1972. The standard of manufacture was impressive, good enough to persuade the Belgian Flandria team to sign with Shimano for the 1973 season. This was the first time that an Asian manufacturer's components had been seen in a European race.

In truth, the equipment was by no means the equal of Campagnolo's Nuovo and Super Record *gruppos*: it was relatively untried and needed constant attention; the Crane rear derailleur mechanism in particular proved hard to keep in tune. The only item in the group not to wear the Dura-Ace name, the Crane mech was, despite its shortfalls, a technological step ahead of the Campagnolo derailleur thanks to its offset parallelogram design and sprung upper pivot, both copied from Japanese rival SunTour.

The results came, however, with stage wins for Walter Godefroot in the Ruta del Sol and

- The first Dura-Ace components emerged in 1973 and were used by the Flandria team.

- Shimano's three-speed hub gear was popular until its first derailleur gear shift mechanism began selling in 1956.

"Oh God, not him. He rides with Shimano equipment. At all costs Shimano must not be allowed to win on Sunday."

TULLIO CAMPAGNOLO

Tour de France, and a Tour stage for Wilfried David. By the time the best riders in the world turned up in Barcelona for the world road race championships, Shimano's top-flight groupset was looking a real threat to Italian hegemony.

According to some, on the eve of the professional road race, a car containing Tullio Campagnolo pulled alongside the Belgian team on its pre-race ride. Campagnolo is said to have asked Walter Godefroot who was going to win the following day and, on being told that it would be young Flandria rider Freddy Maertens, he is alleged to have exclaimed: "Oh God, not him. He rides with Shimano equipment. At all costs Shimano must not be allowed to win on Sunday."

The finale was fought out by four of the greatest riders of the era—Maertens, Eddy Merckx, Luis Ocana, and Felice Gimondi—who escaped the bunch close to the finish. Maertens was detailed to lead out Merckx, who found himself unable to follow the younger rider's wheel and finished fourth. Maertens maintained that, had he known earlier that Merckx was empty, he would have won; his second place finish behind Gimondi, despite having to make a late second surge, suggests he had a point. Maertens thought that the finale was a stitch-up by the three Campagnolo-equipped riders, and explained in his biography, *Fall from Grace*: "If the rainbow jersey had ended up on my back it would have been me, thanks to Shimano, who would have become a millionaire in one go." In any event, the outcome provided the Belgian press with rich pickings and Shimano with invaluable publicity, although it was not enough to persuade Flandria to stick with Dura-Ace.

For a decade Shimano's top-level componentry remained very much the poor

---

1921	1956	1960	1972
Shimano is founded and its first component is a single freewheel. Within a decade, the Japanese firm is exporting its design.	The first derailleur gear shift mechanism is produced, which is a big step up from the three-speed hub gears that Shimano had been making.	Shimano begins cold-forging aluminium components, which leads directly to the development of its flagship groupset: Dura-Ace.	Dura-Ace makes its cycle show debut and inroads into professional racing when, the following season, Belgium's Flandria team uses the groupset.

relation. This is despite a series of influential innovations, including the first Shimano freehub in 1978, the aerodynamically styled AX version of Dura-Ace, ridden by Alexi Grewal to victory in the 1984 Olympic road race, and the tiny Pac Man–shaped Parapull brakes, which pre-dated Campagnolo's Delta design and were later adopted for time trials by Lance Armstrong.

Even the arrival of the seminal 7400 group in 1984 failed to knock Campagnolo from top spot. Yet 7400, with its slightly stark, angular styling, was the group that paved the way for Shimano's eventual dominance of the professional road race scene, and by the time of its replacement it had been raced successfully at the highest level by teams such as 7-Eleven, Panasonic, Lotto, and Mapei. It underwent constant development over the twelve years of its model life, starting with a selection of components unremarkable except for Shimano Index System, which removed the tiresome and inconvenient need to feather a friction-only shift lever after each shift to ensure smooth running, and ending with gear shifts effected at the handlebars.

By 1988, when Andy Hampsten won the Giro d'Italia for 7-Eleven, 7400 Dura-Ace was

1978	1990	1999	2004
The first freehub is introduced and six years later is ridden to victory in the Olympic road race by Alexi Grewal.	Shimano Total Integration (STI) revolutionizes brakes and gears by combining them in one lever, an innovation inspired by mountain biking.	Shimano wins its first Tour de France thanks to Lance Armstrong, heralding a period of dominance for the American—and also for Shimano.	Shimano introduces a tenth sprocket to the new Dura-Ace 7800 groupset.

clearly in the ascendant against opposition that, while a visual delight, was falling behind in the functionality stakes. The point was hammered home by the introduction in 1990 of Shimano Total Integration (STI), arguably the most important innovation of the post-war era since the derailleur; certainly Eddy Merckx has said it is the one technology post-dating his career with which he would have liked to have raced.

Inspired by the Rapidfire handlebar-mounted shifters they had only a year previously introduced for mountain biking, Shimano engineers looked for a way to combine gear shifting and braking functions, and eventually plumped for a design that located the shift mechanism on the brake lever itself. By using the lever to pull the shifting cable one way and a second paddle behind it to release the cable's tension, STI design provided a slick, precise, and ergonomic action.

It achieved this at the cost of an external cable route from levers to frame. The weight of the shift mechanism would also become something of a drawback, because its inertia would make the levers "clack" when riding over rough surfaces. Nevertheless, the eight-speed version of STI that made its debut in 1990 was a truly revolutionary development that obliged Campagnolo and the few remaining players in the road components market, such as Modolo, to come up with their own dual-control gear shift-cum-brake levers.

None of them were a real match for STI, which borrowed from the small-scale, high-precision technology that Shimano had developed in fishing reel manufacturing. Only Campagnolo's Ergopower system offered a credible alternative, and in eight-speed guise it was significantly harder work to operate. At least Ergopower carried the gear cables under the handlebar tape, thus providing a ready reference for road race fans, who could use the cable route to distinguish between Shimano- and Campagnolo-sponsored riders.

BRAKE AND SHIFT LEVER EVOLUTION

BL-7400

The 1984 Dura-Ace brake levers featured anatomically designed hoods with right- and left-hand grips.

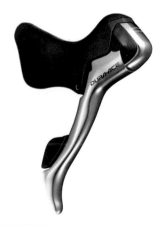

ST-7800

Weighing 14.7 ounces (417 g), the 7800 was the first use of a ten-speed cassette for Shimano.

ST-7900

The 7900 lever is constructed from carbon fibre and the gear cables are concealed beneath the handlebar tape.

ST-7970

STI levers feature two carbon fibre shifter blades for push-button gear changes. It was released in 2009.

The 1996 ST-7700
provides smooth gear
shifting and braking
performance.

■ On a bike equipped with Dura-Ace 7400, Andy Hampsten takes food from Shelley Verses, the 7-Eleven team's female *soigneur*, during the 1988 Giro d'Italia.

Super SLR braking was introduced in 1989. Although it was less exciting than STI, Super SLR was another significant step forward for cycle components and greatly improved braking power, control, and feel. The SLR part of the system was an existing technology developed from an invention of stunning simplicity by rival Japanese firm Dia Compe. All that was required was to place a return spring in the brake lever and to reduce accordingly the strength of the spring in the caliper. Since the resistance to movement of a Bowden control cable depends on the friction coefficient between casing and inner wire and, therefore, on the tension applied to the inner wire, which pulls it against the casing, a reduction in the strength of the caliper spring also reduces the pull that must be applied to the wire and, therefore, internal cable friction.

Super SLR added to this simple concept the dual pivot caliper, which ensured consistent deceleration as braking effort increased; throw in the PD7410 SPD pedal to represent "clipless" pedalling and the truly modern road cycling groupset had arrived.

The next step, of course, was to improve it. However, while Shimano had been busy innovating, so too had other, often smaller companies. In the early 1990s, the Magic Motorcycle Company introduced a crankset that was more advanced than anything else on the market. CNC-machined in 7075 aluminium, the design employed two important features: external bottom bracket bearings and hollow crank arms. The design, bought by Cannondale and marketed under the CODA Magic label, was groundbreaking, and its influence was seen in the next two versions of Dura-Ace.

The first of them, numbered according to custom 7700, was as much a derivation of state-of-the-art mountain bike technology as of the road tradition. In 1996, the top-flight XTR off-road groupset received its first makeover and acquired a grey surface finish, a gearing cassette with eight sprockets, and, importantly, hollow crank arms attached to a splined, large-diameter bottom bracket axle that resembled Magic Motorcycle innovation. The following year, 7700 applied the same thinking to the road and added a ninth sprocket and a sleek new design.

It was fitting that this most elegant of cycle component assemblies should be the basis of the Shimano Dura-Ace twenty-fifth anniversary groupset. Everything about 7700, the nine-speed Dura-Ace group, represented a step forwards from its predecessor, especially the chainset. Manufactured using a complex process that involved welding a sheet of aluminium to the back of a forged U-shaped channel to create a hollow structure, the cranks were notably light given their stiffness. They were attached to a large-diameter hollow steel bottom bracket axle via eight splines that ensured excellent power transfer between the crank and the chainwheels. Compared to the archaic square-taper axle and solid forged cranks still favoured by Campagnolo for the contemporary Record *gruppo*, Dura-Ace was clearly in a different era.

Over the next eight years, the prestige of Shimano's flagship road group grew, helped by the efforts of Lance Armstrong. With his Tour de France win in 1999, the Texan gave Shimano the elusive first victory in the greatest bike race. The Tour hegemony that he established over the following six years also gave Shimano the sort of stranglehold over top-flight bike racing once enjoyed by Campagnolo; something had to give.

The Italian firm, never short of faithful followers, struck back in 2000 with a tenth rear sprocket to back up the increasing sophistication of the Record *gruppo*, which now boasted carbon fibre brake levers of pleasing appearance. Almost inevitably, Shimano too introduced a

CRANKSET EVOLUTION

FC-7400

The FC-7400 was first released in 1984, and built with solid, cold-forged aluminium crankarms.

FC-7703

The 7703 triple crankset was released in 2002 and is made from nickel-plated duraluminum for durability.

FC-7800

Shimano introduced externally housed bottom bracket bearings and a radical change in aesthetics.

FC-7900

An innovative hollow outer chainring boosted stiffness for vastly improved front shifting performance.

tenth sprocket. It arrived in 2004 as part of a completely new version of Dura-Ace, numbered 7800, that represented an even greater leap in performance than its predecessor.

It also challenged conventional thinking on the aesthetics of road bike components with a chainset of stunning originality. As the evident centrepiece of the group, the new design discarded the traditional visual reference of a centre bolt in the right-hand crank, and instead offered a smooth, uninterrupted, and wonderfully lustrous surface sweeping from pedal to chainring spider. The chainrings, too, were styled in order to provide an impression of strength. While the brake calipers, arching over their tyres, caught the mood of the chainset perfectly, matching the STI levers to such a statement was always going to be problematic. Although the 7800 levers looked a little bulbous, they made up for their appearance with the finest shifting performance Shimano had yet achieved and, when 7800's replacement arrived in 2009, remained the reference for light, slick, sensitive shifting.

The 7900 came on the scene in a bit of a hurry. The young firm SRAM, born in response to the perceived complexity of Shimano's mountain bike gear-shifting technology, appeared on the road racing scene with a new, simple, and effective dual-control shift mechanism that ran the gear cables under the handlebar tape. With little beyond a retrograde restyle to differentiate most of its component parts from the 7800, the new group offered as its talking point a complete re-engineering of the STI concept that, after almost two decades, gave Shimano Dura-Ace owners their own clear, cable-free view of the front wheel.

With further competition from Campagnolo in the shape of the new Super Record *gruppo*'s eleventh rear sprocket, Shimano's response was swift. Dura-Ace Di2, introduced as an addition to the 7900, was the first electronic shift system of the Dura-Ace series and one of the first to succeed in the harsh world of professional bike racing. Dura-Ace will not give up lightly its hard-earned position at the summit of the sport and of the industry. *RH*

DERAILLEUR EVOLUTION

CRANE

The Crane D-501, released in 1971, was the first offset parallelogram derailleur to be made from aluminium.

RD-7400

The 1984 Dura-Ace rear derailleur RD-7400 started out as six speed and grew to eight speed.

RD-7800

A 2004 ten-speed derailleur weighing 6.3 ounces (192 g). The pulley is made from DuPont Zytel.

RD-7900

The 2008 RD-7900 has carbon fibre pulley cage sideplates and is Shimano's lightest derailleur.

Lance Armstrong
(centre) leads the US
Postal Service team
through the Pyrenees
on stage sixteen of the
1999 Tour de France.
His win using Dura-Ace
gave Shimano its first
Tour victory.

The Dura-Ace Hollowtech II crankset has a thin-walled aluminium crank and hollow outer chainring; it is also available in a compact version.

Shimano's Dura-Ace cassette has aluminium carriers and comes with eight cassette combinations to appeal to a range of cyclists.

The rear derailleur features a carbon fibre pulley cage to reduce weight.

In 2009 Shimano improved its front derailleur design by making it wider, which eliminated chain rub.

The STI dual-control levers— Shimano finally moved the shift cables under the handlebar tape in 2009.

For the 7900 brake, Shimano revamped the brake caliper geometry in 2009 to improve stopping power and control.

DURA-ACE 7900

The lightweight 7900 series was a wholesale redesign from the 7800 range, and very few components were compatible between the two. There was a huge leap in front shifting performance and the brakes were improved enormously, too. It was the first time Shimano hid the gear cables beneath the handlebar tape.

The Dura-Ace Di2 rear derailleur has a precision stepper motor tucked inside the main housing.

The Di2 lithium battery takes ninety minutes to charge and can last for 1,000 miles (1,609 km) of riding

The Dura-Ace Di2 front derailleur is attached to the computer, the automatic micro-trim adjustments keep the cage from rubbing on the chain.

The time trial brake levers have electronic shifting buttons positioned to allow for fast gear changing without the rider needing to alter their hand position.

The carbon Di2 shifters utilize SEIS (Shimano Electronic Intelligent System) to provide responsive gear changing.

Time trial bikes fitted with Di2 satellite shifters have electronic buttons for gear changing that allow the rider to keep their aerodynamic position during gear shifting.

DURA-ACE Di2

Presented at the Formula One race circuit in Suzuka City, Japan, in 2008, Shimano's Dura-Ace Di2 electronically controlled shifting system was one of the seminal developments in component manufacturing. Professional road teams and keen cycling enthusiasts see this technology as the current pinnacle of gear shifting.

Acqua e Sapone's Mario Cipollini wins the first stage of the Giro d'Italia in Germany in 2002.

1974

Sinyard founds Specialized with the message: "To offer everyone the best bicycle of their lives."

1975

Sales quadruple in the brand's first year. Sinyard makes Specialized's first catalogue by hand.

1981

The Stumpjumper is introduced. It is the first mountain bike made and sold to the general public.

1983

Specialized creates the first professional mountain biking team.

In fact, those initial reservations proved to be justified; sales were slow until mountain biking finally took off in the mid-1980s. When it did, Specialized quickly captured a sizeable chunk of the market. The Stumpjumper remains, for many, the iconic mountain bike.

The company that had started off with a founder who had next to no funds, no car, not even a second set of clean clothes, now had an operation with more than one hundred employees. However, the good times did not last for long, and Specialized was close to bankruptcy within a few years. As Sinyard struggled to get to grips with the growth he had created, he brought in three executives charged with leading the company onwards.

One of their initiatives saw the launch of the Full Force range in 1995. The sub-brand was aimed at the lower end of the market and was distributed in Costco. The launch angered a number of Specialized's long-standing dealers, and it has been reported that Sinyard lost up to 30 percent of his client base. A year later Full Force was pulled.

Over time the company regained its footing in the market but the episode had a huge effect on both Sinyard and the brand. On the advice of a new executive—the previous three left—he wrote a small document detailing Specialized's mission: its DNA when it came to ideas and manufacturing. It became synonymous with the company's heritage and future development as it moved from strength to strength. At the time, the company was producing just one road bike, the Allez, but lacked a presence in the elite peloton. Moreover, Cannondale, Giant, and Trek had moved into the arena and were sponsoring a number of professional outfits.

This changed in 2000 when Specialized signed a deal with the Festina team. It was two years after a Tour de France doping scandal and the team was almost unrecognizable from the squad that was ejected from the 1998 Tour. However, unlike Trek's alliance with Lance Armstrong's US Postal Service team or Giant's relationship with Laurent Jalabert and ONCE, Festina lacked a rider of true star quality.

"We had a placing with professional teams before," said Specialized's former marketing manager Nic Sims. "We'd been there in the past with helmets but we realized that we needed to get back in there and legitimize ourselves with bikes. The deal with Festina was just us dipping our toes in the water there, a far cry from the amount of time we spent with teams after that on developing our technology."

In 2002 Specialized signed a breakthrough contract with the Italian team Acqua e Sapone, who although small in terms of budget had managed to sign one of the sport's biggest names—Mario Cippolini. The flamboyant sprinter had helped Cannondale break into the market in the late 1990s when riding for Saeco, but 2002 proved to be the pinnacle of his career, with a Milan–San Remo win and a world title in Zolder, both of which were ridden on an S-Works E5 frame with a zebra paint job. It mattered little that the deal was struck after the Italian's agent contacted the company because he had seen Festina riders use them at the 2001 Tour de France.

Cipollini's signing earned the brand far more kudos than the years with Festina could ever muster, and the Italian's proactive nature in providing valuable feedback became pivotal in the bike's development. "Mario Cipollini was

"Mario Cipollini was one who was really critical and gave us a lot of fantastic feedback."

MIKE SINYARD

2001

Specialized sign a multi-year deal with the Festina team. It marks Specialized's first venture into sponsoring a major European road team.

2002

Mario Cipollini has his most successful season, riding his Specialized to victories in Milan–San Remo, Ghent–Wevelgem, six stages at the Giro d'Italia, and the Worlds.

2011

Mark Cavendish wins the Worlds in Copenhagen on a Specialized bike. Matt Goss finishes second, also on a Specialized.

2012

Tom Boonen caps a perfect spring for his Omega-Pharma Quick Step team, sealing a second Tour of Flanders and Paris–Roubaix double.

Mark Cavendish (centre) powers through to win stage five of the 2011 Tour de France in Cap Fréhel.

one who was really critical and gave us a lot of fantastic feedback," Sinyard says.

More teams lined up over the coming seasons, including Gerolsteiner, Quick Step, Astana, Saxo Bank, and—most recently—HTC-Highroad. The wins flowed, too. Quick Step provided wins in Paris–Roubaix in 2008, 2009, and 2012 while Alberto Contador claimed the Tour de France in 2010 to give Sinyard his first win in the world's greatest bike race. However, a month after Contador pulled on the yellow jersey in Paris, his world came crashing down when it was announced that he had tested positive for the drug Clenbuterol during the final week of the race. Suddenly, what should have been one of the company's finest moments in terms of sales and public relations became a nightmare.

In many ways the relationship between Specialized and HTC has overshadowed the Contador affair, mainly because Mark Cavendish has racked up win after win. His feedback, stemming from a dedication to perfection on the bike, has helped Sinyard's top engineers to push the boundaries with their top of the range road bikes, culminating in the Venge, which was unveiled at the start of the 2011 Giro d'Italia. "The sprinters are good because they put really intense stresses on the bike. For us balance and handling are also so important, though—it's not just about lightness and stiffness," says Sinyard.

Specialized flew a team of bike engineers to Cavendish's European base, to talk to the rider as he rode and watch his every move as he sprinted. Specialized's attention to detail was a perfect match for Cavendish's desire for the ultimate weapon to guide him to sprinting success. It is a well-known fact how hard Cavendish trains on the bike, but he is also one of the most meticulous riders when it comes to bike position and frame stiffness.

At a press event towards the end of 2011, Cavendish was asked in an open forum what he

would miss from his old team HTC-Highroad. His first answer was Specialized bikes, but while the crowd was consumed with laughter at such a cute response, Cavendish's face remained stony. He was not joking.

Such is Specialized's impact on product development that its reach can influence where professional cyclists sign contracts for future years. Specialized's deal for 2012 with Omega Pharma-Quick Step allowed Tony Martin, the 2011 world time trial champion, to keep his SHIV time trial bike. Like the Venge, the SHIV is another of Specialized's flagship models.

"We've learnt a lot about aerodynamics but what we've learnt with the SHIV blew away what we knew about its predecessor, the Transition. We knew about aerodynamics when riding into the wind, but it's about making a shape that's efficient in a more real world situation with cross winds. That was a big moment for us," says former marketing manager Nic Sims.

Always learning, always developing, and always moving forward, Specialized is now recognized as one of the most powerful manufacturers on the bike scene: a far cry from those days when Sinyard started out—almost broke but extremely ambitious—and a long way from those artisan Italians who inspired him. "In Italy, you get that mystique more than anywhere in the world. Cinelli, De Rosa... their way of working was inspirational to me," Sinyard says.

"We wanted to emulate them—keep it special and bespoke but on a larger scale. I think that's what we've achieved. We made our first road bikes in 1975 and 1976, the LA and the Sequoia, and we've tried to stay true to the same principles all along. I'm very passionate about that artistic element. If you ask me whether there's a point where Specialized could become too big, I'd say it's the point at which we start to neglect that and do things poorly. As long as we're serving riders and helping to make them better, I'm happy for us to carry on growing." **DB**

> *"In Italy, you get that mystique more than anywhere in the world. Cinelli, De Rosa... their way of working was inspirational to me."*
>
> MIKE SINYARD

■ Alberto Contador won the 2010 Tour de France, but lost the title in 2012 because of doping.

■ This Specliazed SHIV features, from top to bottom, a carbon frame with aero position handlebars, Dura-Ace components, bladed seatpost, and S-Works crankset.

MARK CAVENDISH'S SPECIALIZED VENGE

On the eve of the 2011 Milan–San Remo, former winner Mark Cavendish was presented with a new road bike. It was a highly anticipated moment as his supplier, Specialized, in collaboration with McLaren of Formula One fame, had spent nine months designing and moulding a frame and set-up for the fastest sprinter in the world. Just twenty-four hours before the race started, and with Cavendish looking for his second win in La Classica di Primavera, the Venge was unveiled.

One eye-catching feature of the bike was simply how much of its specification was geared towards Cavendish's unique style of sprinting—flat and tucked in on the drops, his power generated through a low profile position with his body thrown forward, nose almost over the front wheel.

Given Cavendish's unusual weight distribution, the designers made sure that the frame was strengthened at the front, adding extra stiffness while still incorporating McLaren-style aerodynamic curves and sleekness along the top tube.

Despite a promising start Cavendish faltered in the race, caught behind a crash and later dropped, but he went on to use the bike to great effect at both the 2011 Tour de France and then at the world championships in Copenhagen, where he became the first British rider to win the race in forty-six years.

The futuristic Venge may have weighed in at a slightly heavy 16.86 pounds (7.65 kg), but it was—and still is—one of the most eye-catching and impressive bikes in the modern peloton.

The Venge was finished with the best modern equipment, including a fi'zi:k Arione CX saddle with braided carbon rails, and a Venge seatpost, with a integrated Shimano Di2 battery.

Cavendish's wheels were handbuilt with Dura-Ace hubs and differential-depth Zipp carbon tubular rims.

A tapered head tube and steerer: ideal for a powerful sprinter such as Mark Cavendish.

Cavendish's Venge incorporated a Shimano-armed SRM power meter as part of the drivetrain.

DESIGN DETAILS

HANDLEBARS

Mark Cavendish's handlebar set-up involves his shifters high on the bars, and the brake lever reach has been reduced to offset the angle. The bars are PRO's Vibe Sprint, which are known for their stiffness.

CHAINRINGS

The Venge incorporated a Shimano-armed SRM power meter as part of the drivetrain, as well as Shimano's super-stiff fifty-three-tooth Dura-Ace 7900 hollow outer chainring. For climbing, Cavendish used the standard 7900 thirty-nine-tooth inner ring.

■ The Grip Shift system was released in 1988 and quickly became a success for SRAM.

■ The carbon fibre Red Crankset Limited Tour Edition was released in 2010 as a tribute to Tour de France racers.

■

SRAM

The upstarts of racing bicycle componentry, SRAM has achieved something remarkable by taking on and breaking the virtual duopoly of the big two, Campagnolo and Shimano. These days, it is likely that the Tour is won on a SRAM-equipped bike.

SRAM has grown to become one of the big three when it comes to road cycling components, joining Japanese giant Shimano and Italian artisans Campagnolo at the top of the tree. This is quite an achievement for a relatively new player on the market, which only came to fruition in Chicago in 1987 when Stan Day, his engineer friend Sam Patterson, and Day's younger brother, Frederick, set out with the goal of creating "the absolute best shifting system" on the market.

The first product, the DB-1 shifter, found little success in the road world, although it did get a foothold in the triathlon market. The trio had planned to sell 100,000 units in their first year—and sold only 800. However, pursuing the mountain bike and hybrid markets with a similar product—the Grip Shift—paid dividends when big-name bike companies such as Cannondale, Specialized, and Trek began to use the new gear-shifting system.

Since then, the company has grown exponentially, but the elevated position it enjoys today has been reached as a result of a combination of closely following market trends and expertly finding solutions, as well as through canny business acquisitions and smart risk-taking.

Still based primarily in Chicago, SRAM today has more than 2,500 employees, with a European headquarters in Nijkerk, the Netherlands, and the Asian headquarters in Taiwan.

In 1997, SRAM acquired German hub-gear manufacturers Sachs, thus increasing its presence in the hybrid market—and the spending spree continued as it subsequently acquired RockShox suspension forks, Avid brakes, and Truvativ bars, stems, and cranksets. This put SRAM into a position where it could provide virtually every mechanical component imaginable.

In 2007, SRAM acquired Zipp—a huge player in the wheel market. As with the other companies that it had acquired previously, rather than just badge everything with the SRAM name, the Zipp name was retained and the company's profile boosted even further thanks to the additional income. Quarq power meters were

the most recent acquisition in 2011, which reflected consumer demand for high-end, do-it-yourself training technology.

By taking advantage of its acquired companies' production facilities, and also the new know-how and experience at its disposal, SRAM has always been in a position to develop new products, and this has included SRAM-branded components to add to its burgeoning arsenal. In time for the 2006 season, SRAM was ready to hit the market with a full road groupset, and it was at this point that things really shifted up a gear for the US company. With its two new DoubleTap groupsets—Force and Rival—SRAM made serious advances into the road market. While consumers had enjoyed the luxury of new frame materials, such as titanium and then carbon fibre in the 1990s and 2000s, the DoubleTap system was something different in a market that had seen very little in the way of

■ Schleck, Contador, and Armstrong on the 2009 Tour de France podium. Each racer used SRAM.

□ Alberto Contador's win in the 2009 Tour de France did a lot to raise the company's profile.

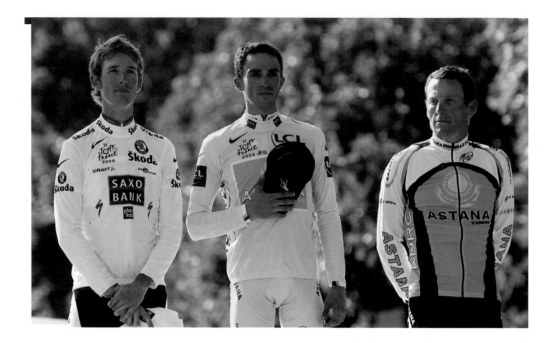

innovation in gear shifting since the introduction of combined brake and gear levers with Shimano Total Integration in 1990 and Campagnolo's similar Ergopower system in 1992.

SRAM's simple, innovative system—a single paddle behind the brake lever for both up and down gear shifts—was very well received. It was fast, lightweight, and modern, and was improved yet further for the 2008 season with the introduction of a new top of the line groupset, the SRAM Red. As the first complete groupset to dip under the 125-ounce (2,000-g) mark, it was designed to compete with, and be just as desirable as, Shimano and Campagnolo's flagship groupsets—Dura-Ace and Super Record, respectively—and there was no real time lag between development and success for the newest DoubleTap groupset.

SRAM became the new equipment sponsor for the Kazakh Astana squad, whose team leader, Alberto Contador, rode SRAM Red to its maiden Grand Tour victory at the 2008 Giro d'Italia. In a sport that was dominated by Campagnolo and Shimano, it was a giant coup for the new kid on the block. However, although he was the defending champion and had ridden for a different team (Discovery Channel) the previous year, Contador and his Astana outfit were not invited to the 2008 Tour de France because Alexander Vinokourov had tested positive for drugs at the 2007 event.

Instead, Contador had to focus on his home race, the Vuelta a España, two months later, where he once again rode a magnificent race, definitively delivering SRAM Red its second three-week Grand Tour victory in only its debut

1987	1988	1990	1991
The company is established in Chicago by brothers Stan and Frederick Day and their friend Sam Patterson.	After an inauspicious start with its ill-fated DB-1 shifter, SRAM finds success with the release of its Grip Shift system.	SRAM sues Shimano for unfair business practice and wins an estimated US $3 million out of court settlement and the right to compete with its components.	Trek and Specialized bikes are released with SRAM Grip Shift fitted as standard. A plant is opened in Taiwan the same year.

season. Britain's Nicole Cooke then rounded out the year with a Red victory at the road race world championships in Varese, Italy.

In 2009 came the big one: Contador won the Tour de France, but what was even more remarkable was that the other two podium places were also filled by SRAM Red riders in Saxo Bank's Andy Schleck and Contador's new Astana teammate, Lance Armstrong. Contador and Armstrong may not have seen eye to eye at that 2009 race, but SRAM's already rapid rise could not have been done any harm when Armstrong decided to invest a considerable amount of money into SRAM at the end of 2008, and also became a technical adviser to help develop new products. His shift to the US brand in 2009 in time for his comeback season was another major coup for the company—especially when he had previously won all seven of his Tours de France on Shimano-equipped bikes.

Since then, SRAM has truly become part of the furniture when it comes to international road racing. The success has kept coming, with all the major races steadily being checked off the "big win" list: Fabian Cancellara's time trial world championship victory in 2009, Cancellara's success on the punishing cobbles of Paris–Roubaix in 2010, Thor Hushovd's men's road race world title in Melbourne at the end of the season, and another Contador victory at the 2011 Giro d'Italia.

Evidence of SRAM's spectacular rise can also be seen when looking at the spread of the big three component manufacturers' provision of equipment to the eighteen Union Cycliste Internationale's ProTeams for the 2011 season. For the first time, SRAM had the biggest share at eight teams—up from five in 2010. Shimano

2000	2002	2003	2005
Branching out into new territories, the company employs 1,000 people at its facilities in Taiwan, China, the Netherlands, Portugal, Germany, Ireland, and Mexico.	SRAM acquires RockShox's range of mountain bike suspension products for US $5.6 million.	SRAM goes from strength to strength and successfully enters the road bike market with cassettes and chains. Sales for the year are estimated at US $150 million.	Non-profit organization World Bicycle Relief is created to supply bikes in response to the Indian Ocean tsunami.

Riding a SRAM-equipped bike, Fabian Cancellara crosses the finish line at the men's time trial world championships at Mendrisio in 2009.

dropped just one team from 2010 to six teams in 2011, whereas Campagnolo parted company with two teams, to supply only four. However, SRAM still lags some way behind when it comes to the true gauge of road success: Tour de France wins. Campagnolo is still a long way ahead there, with twenty-nine victories, whereas Shimano has ten. SRAM, through Contador, has only one win—for now.

Success in the mountain bike world has gone hand in hand with the on-road growth. Off-road, SRAM has a market share of around 50 percent with Shimano, although SRAM's latest development—its XX twenty-speed groupset—has threatened to put it in pole position ahead of the Japanese manufacturer. Shimano responded by introducing a double-chainring option for its top of the line mountain bike groupset, the XTR.

Pressurizing the more established bigger boys into following its lead has enabled SRAM to end what was almost a duopoly within component manufacturing and left it in an enviable position as the young, forward-thinking upstart. However, with such great success comes responsibility, and SRAM has also taken its elevated position within

the industry seriously. While doing everything to ensure that riders such as Contador, Hushovd, and others have benefited from top-notch components, the company has also shown itself to be committed to more worthy projects, doing its bit to promote the bicycle as a practical solution to some very real problems in parts of the world that have been blighted by poverty or ravaged by natural disasters.

At the heart of this commitment is World Bicycle Relief. The non-profit organization was set up in 2005, following the Indian Ocean tsunami at the end of 2004, by the younger of the SRAM-founding Day brothers, Frederick, (whose older brother Stan still runs the SRAM business proper as chief executive.) Initially, more than 24,000 bikes were distributed in Sri Lanka to help its people rebuild their lives following the tragedy. They provided transport to schools and work places, facilitated the delivery of medical supplies and treatment, and were also used to transport food and water.

Next, Zambia, in Africa, benefited from 23,000 bicycles, which allowed volunteer healthcare workers to visit patients and their families who were suffering from the effects of HIV and AIDS. Moreover, the bike programme has continued to spread through the poorer African nations, where there are now nearly 100,000 bikes being put to good use, maintained by almost 1,000 trained mechanics—with access to tools and spare parts—to help keep them running smoothly.

In addition, the company set up the SRAM Cycling Fund in 2008 to help improve cycling infrastructure in Europe and North America. It provides grants to organizations that are looking to improve road safety for cyclists, and also funds campaigns that promote cycling to school and work as a viable, healthy alternative to motor vehicles. With a thriving business and two projects to help health and humanity, it is safe to say that SRAM has come a long way in a short time. **EB**

SRAM WHEELS

S30 AL SPRINT FR
Mid-depth aero rim made from 6061-aluminium with eighteen SAPIM CX Sprint spokes. The S30 AL Sprint weighs 23.98 ounces (680 g).

S30 AL SPRINT RR1
The front wheel weighs 24.86 ounces (705 g) and has eighteen spokes; the rear wheel weighs 29.10 ounces (825 g) and has twenty spokes.

2010 S40 FRONT
The handmade, 26.80-ounce (760-g) 2010 S40 features a structural woven carbon rim and an aluminium tyre bed and breaking surface.

2010 S80 REAR
The 39.85-ounce (1,130-g) rear 2010 S80 is another woven carbon rim model that, like the S40, features hybrid-toroidal shape.

SRAM uses a cold-forging process to manufacture its Apex cranksets—the result is a lightweight, stiff alloy crank.

The exact actuation Apex rear derailleur is compatible with a very wide-ratio cassette.

The front derailleur has an aluminium body and steel cage, and is compatible with standard and compact chainrings.

Apex shifters use a single lever to change to both easier and hard gear ratios.

Just like its RED brake range, SRAM's Apex brakes use a dual pivot design; the Apex comes with alloy calipers.

APEX

Apex may be SRAM's entry-level groupset, but it still combines the brand's commitment to fast, reliable, and lightweight components. The Apex group also offers a wide enough gear range to avoid using a triple chainring.

The SRAM RED LTE groupset was used by professionals during the 2010 Tour de France and was made commercially available later that year.

The SRAM RED LTE (Limited Tour Edition) rear derailleur featured a yellow custom paint job to coincide with the 2010 Tour de France.

The front derailleur features a titanium cage .

The R2C (Return to Centre) bar-end shift levers are designed specifically for time trial bikes—after each gear shift, the levers automatically return to centre.

The SRAM RED brakes have a dual pivot design that improves braking power.

SRAM carbon brake levers weigh in at just 3.1 ounces (90 g).

The levers are carbon fibre and are distinctive because of the yellow SRAM logo.

RED LTE

To celebrate the fact that three previous winners of the Tour de France—Contador, Sastre, and Armstrong—began the 2010 edition of the race using SRAM RED, the Chicago-based company designed a smart update to its leading groupset and gave the RED components yellow livery to match the race's *maillot jaune*.

■ Time 50.1 pedals
are still sold online,
although it is hard to
find compatible shoes.

■ Time iClic2 Titan
carbon pedals have a
hollow titanium axle
and weigh 6.1 ounces
(175 g) per pair.

Time

This French company introduced "floating" clipless pedals to the peloton in
the 1980s, before turning to the production of carbon fibre frames in the 1990s—
in which it remains an industry leader.

The stories behind some brands are told as much
through the exploits of riders as the company's
contribution to the technological development of
the bicycle or its parts. However, Time is a little
different. In order to appreciate the story of Time,
it is necessary to dwell on the actual machinery
because Time is a company that was founded on
technical innovation.

It is fair to say that one of the most significant
developments of the modern bicycle has been
the introduction of the clipless pedal. Although it
was not seen in the professional peloton until the
1980s, there were a number of prototypes and
designs that went all the way back to 1895. None,
however, threatened to usurp the traditional
chrome steel clip and leather strap. The challenge
was to produce a mechanism that secured the

rider's foot to their pedal yet allowed ease of
release when stopping—or automatically in the
case of an accident.

Cino Cinelli created the M71 pedal in the
early 1970s, but although it provided a very
secure locking mechanism, it was perhaps its
awkward, not to mention temperamental, release
mechanism that condemned it to a relatively small
number of converts; in the main, its use was
restricted to time trials.

A few years later, in 1984, the ski binding
innovator Look introduced the first safe and
efficient clipless pedal system, which gained rapid
acceptance thanks to Bernard Hinault and Greg
LeMond, who rode their pedals to first and
second place in the Tour de France two years
in a row, in 1985 and 1986. (Hinault was first,

LeMond second in 1985; they swapped steps on
the podium the following year.) Yet, although the
Look pedal was a great step forwards, the design
was by no means perfect.

In the normal pedalling motion, most cyclists
experience a small, and in some cases more
pronounced, rotary motion of the foot: the
movement is not dissimilar to stubbing out a
cigarette butt with a shoe. The original design of
the Look pedal, by Jean Beyl, did not allow for
any lateral movement; instead, the fixed cleat
held the rider's foot rigidly in place. Several early
adopters of the pedal complained of knee pains
and other niggles.

When this became known to Beyl he
immediately began to work on a solution. He
returned to his original design and began tinkering.
However, after the substantial effort and money
that had gone into the original pedal, his bosses
were reluctant to fund a Look Mk II model.
Frustrated at Look, in 1987 Beyl turned to Roland
Cattin, an entrepreneur who would become
the founder of a rival company. Time Sport

International was the new French company's
name. And, under the Time banner, Beyl set
about developing the revolutionary Time Racing
50.1 pedal.

This pedal reduced the space between the
pedal axle and the foot, which made it more
efficient, it was said. However, the critical
innovation was lateral movement: the foot was
no longer fixed in place; instead, it "floated,"
thus allowing the rider's leg to follow its natural
(non-linear) path during the pedal stroke. Another
difference was in the cleats, which were very
different to Look's three-bolt triangular model.
In other words, the two clipless pedals were
incompatible. This led to the outbreak of a
"format war," which was cycling's equivalent to
the VHS versus Betamax debacle.

Time upped the ante again when it launched
a dedicated shoe, in its distinctive—and back
then highly unusual—white and red colours. The
advantage of the dedicated shoe was in the sole:
it was very slim and took the rider's foot even
closer to the axle, but it was extremely rigid, too.

1987	1988	1993	1995
Roland Cattin establishes Time, manufacturing and distributing a clipless pedal system.	Pedro Delgado (Reynolds) becomes the first rider to win the Tour de France using Time pedals. Delgado beats Steven Rooks and Fabio Parra to the top step of the podium.	The company begins to diversify with carbon composite frames, forks, stems, and seatposts using resin transfer moulding technology.	Miguel Indurain (Banesto) wins the last of his five Tours. His winning run—stretching back to 1991— was accomplished using Time pedals throughout.

For non-Time shoes, an adaptor was available, but it was clunky and it increased the distance between foot and axle. Later revisions to the design made Time cleats compatible with other brands of shoe, but the launch of such easily identifiable shoes was a stroke of marketing genius. Many of the riders in the pro peloton switched to Time—and also to their shoes. How else would fans have known which of the two brands of clipless pedal—Look or Time—they were using?

Early adopters of Time pedals included Laurent Fignon, who after his two Tour de France wins in 1983 and 1984, suffered terribly with injuries. It could be a coincidence, but he returned to something like his old form when he switched to Time. LeMond was another who moved from Look to Time. But a year before Fignon and LeMond fought out the closest Tour in history, the company's first Tour victory came thanks to Pedro Delgado, the 1988 winner.

The original pedal and cleats weighed in a little heavier than their Look equivalent, but this was rectified when a magnesium-bodied version followed the original 50.1 model. A titanium axled pedal appeared not long after. The association with top riders continued and enhanced Time's credibility. Delgado's teammate Miguel Indurain also used them to each of his then-record run of five consecutive Tour wins.

In recent years, new versions of Time pedals have come and gone, with each subsequent design aiming to reduce weight, but never with reduced ergonomics. The concepts of Beyl's original design have stood the test of time—no pun intended—with each new model a refinement of the original 1987 pedal.

Time has not restricted itself to pedals. In fact, the success of its revolutionary pedal system spurred the company on to investigate the world of composite bicycle frame manufacture and apply its thorough and exacting approach to this side of product development. As a relatively young company in "old Europe," Time has perhaps not been as burdened by tradition as other companies. Thus it was quick to invest heavily in carbon fibre manufacturing technologies in 1993, at the outset of the "carbon revolution."

It did not take the cheap option of heading straight for the Far East in search of a quick fix; rather, Time preferred to keep as much production in-house as feasibly possible. Today, its designers work as closely with the manufacturers of the carbon fibre filament they use to make their frames as they do with the professional racers they sponsor, which should help to ensure that product development is swift but well informed.

The decision to weave its own carbon fibre on the premises—from the highest-quality suppliers such as Toray in Japan—gives this French company, housed in a fairly austere-looking complex not far from Lyons airport, the ability to control quality of product far easier than many of its competitors. It also means that Time has a deep understanding of manufacturing difficulties and is well placed to change practices quickly if necessary.

In this respect, it stands a little apart from other frame manufacturers. Early carbon fibre frame design tended to use fairly conventional tubular sections bonded to aluminium castings at each junction. Time very quickly worked out that the reliability of these types of frame was going to boil down to the integrity of these junctions;

■ Thomas Voeckler wears the yellow jersey for Time during stage thirteen of the 2004 Tour de France.

2004

The Athens Olympic Games sees Paolo Bettini win the men's road race on a Time bike. The Italian is considered one of the finest one-day riders of his generation.

2005

Tom Boonen wins the world road race championships in Madrid, on a Time bicycle. During the same year he wins Paris–Roubaix and the Tour of Flanders.

2006

Time builds a new frame, the VXS, for Boonen to compete on in the spring Classics. He retains his title at the Tour of Flanders, but finishes second in Paris–Roubaix.

2011

Stéphane Heulot's Saur-Sojasun team rides Time bikes and makes its Tour de France debut in 2011.

"A pro team is a source of inspiration, because they are always pushing us to be better, to be lighter, but also to be stronger."

ROLAND CATTIN

■ Resin transfer moulding (RTM) technology allows for complete freedom in form design.

■ Time claims to be the only manufacturer that has mastered the RTM fabrication process.

its subsequent efforts to develop composite lugs overcame many of the concerns regarding previous bonding practices.

As Time's founder and president, Roland Cattin, has said: "The bicycle is a tough business, because you need to have the lightest product but you also need to be secure and have the safest product. If you have a carbon tennis racket crack, it's not a big issue. But you cannot break a frame, it's too dangerous."

Moulding techniques continue to advance, thanks in no small part to Time's research and development. As Cattin suggested, the ultimate goal is a frame that is both as light and as durable as possible. That is what the design team is focused on, not wanting to compromise on strength for the sake of saving weight.

Time also advocates the resin transfer moulding method of production over the more conventional inflated bladder system. The use of solid internal formers made from wax, which is melted out after the moulding process is complete, results in an internal finish that is extremely good. This might not be apparent to the naked eye, but the interiors of its frames have the same flawlessly smooth finish as the outer surfaces. Naturally, the point of this is not aesthetics—again, it is all about durability. The resin transfer moulding technique means that individual fibre compression is more consistent; the tube density more controlled; the likelihood of failure reduced.

Riders who have enjoyed success on Time frames include Tom Boonen and Paolo Bettini, with three world road race titles (2005–07) and numerous Classics between them. Conscious of their French roots, the country's two top riders of recent years, Thomas Voeckler and Sylvain Chavanel, have both graced Time frames.

The company continues to push the boundaries of innovation, in particular with its pedals and frames. Time—you could say—does not stand still. **RD**

■ Trek pioneer Richard "Dick" Burke founded the company in 1976 in Wisconsin.

■ The 850 was Trek's first mountain bike, the frame mimicking a Trek road-touring model.

■ Lance Armstrong in 1999 on the Futuroscope TT, on the way to his first Tour de France victory.

Trek

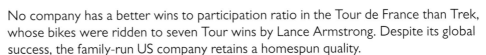

No company has a better wins to participation ratio in the Tour de France than Trek, whose bikes were ridden to seven Tour wins by Lance Armstrong. Despite its global success, the family-run US company retains a homespun quality.

The goal of any manufacturer—no matter what the industry—is to grow and turn a profit. Give a company the opportunity of massive worldwide exposure and it will jump at the chance. When it comes to Trek Bicycle Corporation, no one could have foreseen just how big a brand it would become when, in 1998, it began to provide a US professional rider, who at the time was only well known in cycling circles, with bikes. Lance Armstrong went on to win seven straight Tours de France astride a Trek road bike. In tandem, two legends were born.

Trek's success may have come at the highest level of cycle sport, but despite this it remains the "little big company" that wants nothing more than to get people on bikes. It is not a money-motivated business model because Trek has a genuine passion for bicycles and surrounds itself with people who are possessed of that same enthusiasm, drive, and love of riding.

The story of how Trek became the global player it is today begins in 1976—and continues to the present day—in Waterloo, Wisconsin. Its steel touring frames were the brainchild of Dick

Burke and Bevel Hogg, but by 1980 Trek was building complete bicycles and, in 1982, started manufacturing its own racing bikes. When mountain biking really began to take off in the late 1980s and early 1990s, Trek was more than ready for the boom, having built its first mountain bike model—the 850—as far back as 1983.

The first half of the 1990s saw the US company become one of the leading lights in mountain bike design. Along with Specialized, "Made in America" cool kept Trek comfortably at the top end of customers' wish lists across the world, while its factory team ensured multiple world titles and exposure to a public hungry for the new cycling discipline.

One of the early adopters of carbon fibre as a bicycle frame material, Trek established its special OCLV composites division in 1992. The company's now widely recognized OCLV acronym stands for Optimum Compaction, Low Void, which more simply stands for Trek's own carbon fibre manufacturing process. This involves building frames and components through "optimum compaction"—compressing multi-directional layers of carbon fibre together to eliminate gaps, or voids, in the material (low void). This creates the strength for which properly manufactured carbon fibre frames and parts are renowned.

Trek pushed things forward yet again in 1996 with the establishment of its Advanced Concepts Group. This is the semi-secret division at Trek where team members have the enviable job of dreaming up the next design capable of keeping Trek-supported athletes at the top of their game. Testing prototypes on the surrounding trails or using wind tunnel technology to test the latest theory on frame aerodynamics is the name of the game here, and the Advanced Concepts Group remains a small, elite outfit, busying itself with the future by manufacturing new ideas in small, testable quantities. These days, under the rules of cycling's world governing body, the Union

Cycliste Internationale, all bike designs have to be commercially available, so only when the Advanced Concepts Group has given its stamp of approval to the new products do they get the green light for large-scale production and find their way into the athletes' hands.

The Armstrong chapter of Trek's story—and it is a large, integral chunk—begins with the rider's return to the sport having overcome testicular cancer. Armstrong signed for the 1998 season with the Trek-riding US Postal Service team—still a small, US pro outfit, albeit one in

cycling's top division, which had been handed its first tentative Tour de France ride in 1997.

Having passed over riding the Tour in his comeback year, Armstrong went instead to the end of season Vuelta a España, where he finished fourth overall. He then took that form on to the road world championships in Valkenburg, the Netherlands, finishing fourth in the road race and in the time trial. Armstrong was back to full health and clearly meant business, but no one could have foreseen his overall victory in the following summer's Tour de France.

Storming the opening 4.3-mile (7-km) time trial to take US Postal Service's first-ever Tour stage win, Armstrong went on to claim three more stages of the 1999 edition, finishing in Paris in the famed yellow jersey with a hefty seven-minute thirty-seven-second advantage over the Swiss rider Alex Zülle. The win rocketed the Trek name into the stratosphere as a consequence. What had already at that point been a relatively large and successful bike company suddenly became the company producing the bike that everyone wanted.

And that was just the beginning. Armstrong repeated his win—again and again and again. In all, seven straight Tour wins made him the most successful Tour rider of all time. And Trek was along for the ride every time. Most importantly from a commercial point of view, Trek's new test pilot was in an excellent position to help it develop new designs throughout his tenure as Tour champion, too.

In 2003, the Madone 5.9 road frame made its first appearance, designed for Armstrong and his US Postal Service teammates, and named after the climb in the South of France where Armstrong would regularly put his legs through

1976	1983	1990	1997
Richard Burke, a former accountant, and Bevel Hogg, a bike shop owner, set up business with a US $100,000 investment and a renovated barn in Waterloo, Wisconsin.	Trek sales manager Harry Spehar tests a prototype of the 850 mountain bike on the Whiskeytown Downhill in Redden, California.	Although the company expands into making aluminium bikes, producing more mountain bike frames than road ones, it also begins testing with early carbon machines.	The US Postal Service team rides its first Tour de France using Trek as its bike supplier.

Lance Armstrong in 1999, during stage twenty of the Tour de France.

Armstrong's Trek OCLV frame bears his team name, United States Postal Service. This was one of the lightest carbon fibre bicycles in the world.

a workout in training. It may have gone through a few different incarnations over the years, but today the Madone is still Trek's flagship model, and it remains a true example of handbuilt workmanship of the highest level.

Production time for a Madone can stretch to twelve hours, with a team of more than forty engineers and craftsmen overseeing each frame's production at the Wisconsin facility. The Madone series of bikes are much sought-after machines, and US $8,800 will get you the same Madone 6.9 SSL—the top of the range model—as ridden by the Schleck brothers, Fränk and Andy, and their RadioShack squad.

In 2005, in time to propel Armstrong to his seventh—and last—Tour de France victory, Trek's Advanced Concepts Group set to work on a new time trial frame: the TTX. The goal

was to make the quickest frame possible, both through aerodynamics and by concentrating on keeping weight to an absolute minimum. Such an ambitious project doubled up to help top triathlete Chris Lieto of the Trek/K-Swiss tri team stay ahead of the competition. The fact that Trek did not see fit to update the TTX until 2009, when the Speed Concept TT frame saw the light of day in time for the Tour de France, says a lot about Trek's designers. The introduction of the Speed Concept happened to coincide with Armstrong's memorable comeback to the sport, too.

The Texan rider's return in 2009 (or "Comeback 2.0" as he called it, acknowledging his first return) gave Trek another boost. While Armstrong fans might have stayed faithful to Trek following his retirement in 2005, in the interim

1999	2009	2010	2011
Fully recovered from cancer, Lance Armstrong wins his first Tour de France. He goes on to win seven straight editions of the race.	In the Tour, Alberto Contador and Lance Armstrong both ride for Astana and both on Treks, but there is no love lost as the Spaniard wins the race with Armstrong finishing third.	Greg LeMond and Trek settle a long-standing legal battle out of court.	Lance Armstrong announces his retirement from professional cycling but Trek remains, sponsoring two of the world's top professional teams.

Trek's 2012 Speed
Concept 9.9 has a
Kamm tail virtual airfoil,
integrated handlebars,
brakes, and cables, as
well as Bontrager aero
skewers and speed
management.

years the company found a new road rider to fly the flag in the guise of Spaniard Alberto Contador.

Contador picked up pretty much where Armstrong had left off. He joined Discovery Channel—the team Armstrong had retired with in 2005—for the 2007 season, and helped Trek to retain its reputation at the top of the tree, just as Armstrong had helped it grow eight years previously.

The Spanish rider won the 2007 Tour—an eighth for Trek—but when Discovery Channel ended its involvement in the sport at the close of the season, Contador moved to the Astana squad, which found itself barred from the 2008 Tour because its rider, Alexandre Vinokourov, had failed a drugs test the year before. Instead, Contador settled for victory in both the Giro d'Italia and the Vuelta a España: two more Grand Tour prizes for Trek, who provided Astana with bikes for the 2008 and 2009 seasons.

The relationship between Contador and Trek was far more harmonious than the relationship between Contador and Armstrong. Although Contador won his second Tour in 2009, with the returning Armstrong finishing third, the teammates spent much of the race feuding. At the end of the season, Armstrong and Contador parted company, and Armstrong established his own, new Trek-riding team: RadioShack. But Contador's dominance could not be shaken: he won his third Tour in 2010 (but was stripped of this title in February 2012 after he was found guilty of doping), this time aboard a Specialized, while Armstrong and his Trek spent much of the race on the tarmac.

Images of Armstrong on the ground after one of his many crashes provided a neat metaphor. By the 2010 Tour, which coincided with a federal investigation into allegations of doping against him (which was finally dismissed by the US authorities in February 2012), Armstrong's name seemed to be taking as much of a battering as his body. So closely did Armstrong and Trek seem to be

aligned in the public consciousness, it is possible that the bad publicity may have affected the bike manufacturer, too.

Another controversy also dogged the company, when Armstrong and Trek were involved in a long-running battle with the United States' other Tour de France winner, Greg LeMond. Trek had been in partnership with LeMond's own bike company, but when Armstrong fell out with LeMond—after LeMond publicly questioned Armstrong's performances—so too did Trek. A legal case gained momentum until the two parties finally agreed to settle out of court in 2010, with Trek making an undisclosed donation to a charity of LeMond's choice.

The Armstrong era finally ended in January 2011, the same year that Trek became a co-sponsor of a road team for the first time when it joined Andy and Fränk Schleck's Leopard-Trek outfit. It meant that there were two top-end pro teams on Treks that season, although the latest twist in the tale was the return to focusing on supplying just one superteam for the 2012 season. It was RadioShack who became the new sponsor of Leopard-Trek to create RadioShack-Nissan-Trek.

Rather than rest on its laurels—nine Tour de France victories—and concentrate only on top-level carbon superbikes, Trek ensures that its philosophy remains all about the bike, from racing bikes to real-world utility and commuter bicycles, and every type of bike imaginable in between.

It practises what it preaches, too, by encouraging employees to ride their bikes to work with incentives—and disincentives for driving. The car park right next to the Trek headquarters is reserved for those commuters who car pool. Those going it alone have a much longer walk from their car to the office. But if car pooling is considered good, cycling is even better: there is a free breakfast for every employee who rides 12 miles (19.3 km) or more to work. For those who have ever had the luck to try a full

American breakfast after an early morning ride, this is quite an incentive.

The Trek headquarters in Waterloo has had to expand in accordance with the company's growth, but it remains a proud, US frame-builder, albeit with international renown. Founder Dick Burke died in 2008, and today his son, John, is president of the company. He has maintained his father's commitment to philanthropic and environmental initiatives. Trek helped to establish non-profit organization DreamBikes in Madison and Milwaukee, both in Trek's Wisconsin home state, providing local people with affordable, used bikes. It also offers young people a place of work in the shape of the shops themselves, from where the bikes are sold and repaired and where unusable bikes are stripped down to recycle the steel and aluminium components.

As carbon becomes ever more ubiquitous, many of the bigger name bike brands, such as Trek and Specialized, are ensuring that in the future a programme is in place for the recycling of carbon fibre, too. Trek subsidiary Bontrager now uses 100 percent recyclable card mounts for its accessories, while US Trek dealers will send customers' old inner tubes to partner Alchemy Goods, who will recycle them to create Bontrager bags and panniers.

Today, Trek may be one of the most recognizable names in cycling, thanks in no small part to Lance Armstrong, but as a company it stays true to its roots. Indeed, this is the incongruity at the heart of the Trek empire: its global renown coupled with the homely, family atmosphere of its headquarters in Waterloo, Wisconsin. The company's original goal was simply to build the best bikes in the world. Tour de France titles would persuade most that this has been achieved, but the company is not prepared to stop there. Trek simply sees bikes as a solution: to promote fitness, to reduce traffic congestion, and to help save the environment. As the company motto states: "We believe in bikes." **EB**

■ Alberto Contador proved his dominance at the 2009 Tour de France with a win in the Annecy time trial.

LANCE ARMSTRONG'S TREK OCLV

Lance Armstrong had not raced since the 2005 season, when, at the age of thirty-three, he hung up his bike after winning his seventh straight Tour de France. His return to competition in the 2009 Tour was dominated by a bitter feud with Spanish team-mate Alberto Contador, a broken collarbone sustained in a crash at the Vuelta Castilla y León in Spain, and continued allegations of doping.

Yet among the most interesting and original elements of Armstrong's return were the seven personalized bikes that the Texan rode during the year. He handpicked seven of his favourite artists, and asked each one to design a coat of splendid decoration for his Trek Madone road and time trial bikes. At the end of the year, each frame was auctioned off at Sotheby's, New York, raising a total of US $1.25 million for Armstrong's LiveStrong Foundation.

The most eye-catching design came from British artist Damien Hirst, whose beautiful "Butterfly" frame with matching Bontrager deep "V" rims was used by Armstrong during the final stage of the Tour de France in Paris. Hirst had originally been approached by U2's Bono, a longtime friend of Armstrong, and—typically for Hirst—he used real butterflies in the design because of the way they shimmered in the light. The finished piece generated an enormous amount of interest (and indeed criticism from animal rights activists) at the Tour because it epitomized the concept that it really was all about the bike.

Armstrong and Trek pioneered a number of new technologies but one constant, throughout Armstrong's career, was his use of Selle San Marco saddles. In this image, however, the bike is fitted with a Bontrager model.

Each of Armstrong's 2009 race bikes was labelled with the number 1274. It signified the number of days that he spent in retirement after hanging up his wheels in 2005.

Handbuilt in the United States, the Trek Madone has become a legendary bike, winning multiple Tours de France and one-day Classics. Armstrong's bike, decorated by Damien Hirst, was used in the 2009 Tour.

Lance Armstrong rode with the SRAM Red DoubleTap levers high on his signature Variable Radius-bend Bontrager handlebars.

Damien Hirst decorated Armstrong's Trek with real butterflies, positioning them on the frame as well the Bontrager rimmed wheels.

DESIGN DETAILS

FORKS

The Trek Madone is the company's flagship model, designed to be both stiff and compliant. The finished bike uses an asymmetric steerer, designed to improve the transition between the front fork and the frame.

CRANKSET

Armstrong's pre-2005 Treks used Shimano components, but upon his comeback in 2009 he shifted to SRAM RED. In 2008 Armstrong invested millions of dollars into the SRAM brand.

■ Greg LeMond (left) and
Bernard Hinault on the
Alpe d'Huez during the
1986 Tour de France.

■ Pedro Delgado in blue
astride a TVT 92 takes
on LeMond in the 1991
Tour de France.

TVT

As early pioneers of precision carbon fibre bike manufacturing, TVT made frames that
were ridden to Tour victory by some of cycling's legendary racers of the 1980s. Despite
its success, TVT remains relatively unknown for the contribution it has made to the sport.

Composites specialist TVT—"Technique du Verre
Tisse"—is something of an enigma in bicycle
manufacturing history. Based in Saint-Genix
Guiers, in the foothills of the French Alps, and no
longer producing bike frames, this little-known
company, founded in 1975, played a major role
in revolutionizing the way bicycles are built.

During the 1980s and into the early 1990s,
steel was still the most commonly used material in
frame construction. Companies such as Reynolds
and Columbus had developed cunning weight
reduction techniques using butting, but ultimately
steel frames were relatively heavy and prone to
corrosion, especially if brutalized by the rigours
of chrome plating.

Aluminium was starting to be used by frame-
builders because it offered a lighter alternative,
but these frames had to be built to the same
external dimensions as steel ones—in order to

ensure compatibility with commercially available
components—so results were variable. Even if
they were lighter, many early aluminium frames
felt more flexible than steel ones. In one pedal
stroke, that inefficiency effectively nullified any
weight gains. Stiffer steel still ruled.

However, bike frames were evolving rapidly
and the steel hegemony could not last forever.
TVT was one of the first manufacturers to exploit
the benefits of carbon fibre and apply them to
bicycle design. The company decided that it was
the lamination and fibre orientation that was
critical in developing a suitable alternative to the
high-end steel frames. Its engineers understood
the demands that a rider puts on a frame and
set about creating a set of tubes that would be
strong, lightweight, and able to absorb impacts
and dissipate vibrations. The end result was the
TVT 92 frameset.

In 1986 this frame, adorned with the Look badge, attracted attention when Greg LeMond and Bernard Hinault, of the all-conquering La Vie Claire team, rode them to first and second place in the Tour de France. Not only was LeMond the first native English-speaking winner of the Tour, he was also the first to ride to victory on a bike made of carbon fibre. Yet it was Look, rather than TVT, who took the credit. The team was sponsored by Look, who had developed the equally groundbreaking clipless pedals used by both riders. Only a close inspection revealed the truth behind the decals: the frames were constructed by TVT.

This was the start of a trend. Other leading riders switched to carbon, and to TVT, in the following years, even if the stickers on their frames suggested otherwise. Pedro Delgado won the 1988 Tour on a bike that looked like a Pinarello, all the way down to the small Columbus tubing stickers that were applied in an attempt to conceal the frame's true origins. In fact, Delgado was riding one of the original TVT 92s. LeMond then rode to his 1989 Tour win and world road race title using bikes with TVT tubing, while other leading riders to use the frames included Gert Jan Theunisse, Gilles Delion, and Steve Bauer. Some of Miguel Indurain's Tour-winning bikes, especially those he used in mountain stages, also featured TVT tubes. The average cycling fan would not have been aware of TVT's contribution to these successes, which suggests that TVT is comfortable being a company that is shy and reserved. Given TVT's low profile, this is a fair assumption. **RD**

Vitus

This French frame manufacturer is behind some of the sport's myths and legends, including many of Sean Kelly's greatest triumphs. Although the company suffered a few setbacks in the 1990s, new innovations and designs have brought Vitus back to the top.

■ The Vitesse has a uni-directional carbon fibre frame weighing 33.5 ounces (950 g), fitted with the Dura-Ace 7900 groupset.

■ The Sean Kelly Signature Edition features, from top to bottom, Dura-Ace shifters with a 3T Rotundo Pro handlebar set-up, Dura-Ace crankset, bladed full UD carbon front forks, and a high modulus UD carbon frame.

Vitus is the bike brand that took Sean Kelly, one of cycling's finest riders, to many of his 188 professional victories. Today, the Irishman is an ambassador for the new incarnation of the well-known marque, which is only appropriate. It was on a Vitus that Kelly rode to so many of his Classics wins, not that you would necessarily realize that from studying the photographs, for the simple reason that any brand badge would be hard to discern beneath the liberal coating of mud covering both rider and machine—Flandrian road grime is a great leveller.

The French tubing company branched out from supplying major bike manufacturers into producing its own frames in the 1970s, and its

Vitus 979 was set to become an instant classic. Aluminium tubes, little used by frame-builders of the era, were lugged and bonded, which made for a striking appearance and seemed to put the nail in the coffin of steel as a material for the professional peloton.

The subject of Vitus bonded frames and breakage has attracted much attention and debate, with no conclusive evidence either way. It is fair to say that it was a revolutionary design and, therefore, was likely to have teething problems, but there are plenty of 979s still being ridden today, which suggests that longevity was not an issue. Moreover, rust was certainly a thing of the past.

One of the issues that is commonly raised involves flex, and the general consensus is that big riders were—and are—best off avoiding the 979. Sean Kelly acknowledges the "flex" but prefers to dwell on the bike's main strength: "It was a really light bike, that was the thing that struck me first off. We were all riding steel up to that point. I must have been riding Vitus for six years before I went to PDM [in 1989]. Most of my wins were on their bikes."

Kelly was quick to see the advantage of the 979 Duralinox over the heavier steel frames ridden by most of the peloton. The Irishman won Paris–Nice an astonishing seven times in succession, starting in 1982 with one of the greatest finishes to the "Race to the Sun."

"I was made a special bike by [Sem team manager] Jean De Gribaldy for the time trial at Col d'Eze," says Kelly of his attempt to beat Peugeot's Gilbert Duclos-Lassalle on the final stage when he was four seconds adrift of the leader. It seemed inevitable that the mountain test would go to the Frenchman, but it did not work out that way. Kelly won by fourteen seconds, with Duclos-Lassalle a further thirty seconds in arrears. Kelly the sprinter was now Kelly the general classification contender.

He is happy to acknowledge the part that the specially designed Vitus played in the first of his seven victories, but was surprised to find that things had not moved on by the following century. "I remember talking to the mechanics when Andreas Klöden won the time trial at Paris–Nice in 2000," says Kelly. "It was probably the last time the TT decided the race [until the 2012 edition, won by Britain's Bradley Wiggins], and Klöden's bike wasn't as light as mine in 1982, which was amazing to me."

For some, the issue of flex remains contentious. For a sprinter like Kelly, stiffness was always going to be an issue. "They did used to flex pretty quickly," Kelly confirms. "That sort of tubing didn't break—people had the impression

"It was a really light bike—that was the thing that struck me first off. We were all riding steel up to that point."

SEAN KELLY

■ Kelly suffered considerable wear and tear in the 1992 Paris–Roubaix.

■ Sean Kelly (KAS) edges out Eric Vanderaerden (Panasonic) in the sprint for second place in the 1987 Tour of Flanders in Belgium.

"That sort of tubing didn't break—people had the impression we were getting a lot of breakage, but we had very few problems."

SEAN KELLY

we were getting a lot of breakage, but we had very few problems. But they did get flexy after a while compared to the steel frames, so I used to change them regularly."

Changing frames regularly is not a realistic option for non-professionals, so anyone considering buying a vintage 979 should expect it to give a little. However, it remains a classic bike and rightly so. Italian company Alan and its handsome Super Record frameset—not to mention the ubiquitous cyclo-cross version— preceded Vitus by a year or two, but the French company had captured a solid share of the market and aluminium had made an impression as a serious option.

The 979 was revolutionary, but the St Etienne–based company did not rest on its laurels and brought out the 992 (utilizing ovoid—egg-shaped—tubes in a bid to tackle the flex issue),

followed by the 979 Carbone in 1982. The lugged, seven-tube carbon fibre frame was another trendsetter. Competitors such as Look and Trek admired the example set by Vitus and soon moved into carbon production themselves. "The carbon version had problems with the lugs and the resin—there were difficulties there," Kelly confirms, and seemingly Vitus was not the only company to have trouble in that department. The notion of narrow carbon tubes and lugs fell by the wayside and the age of fat bottom brackets and increasingly wide diameter tubes took hold. Vitus weighed in with its own carbon monocoque, the ZX1, in 1991, but that was as good as it got for the French company.

The Americans led the way in the 1990s, feeding off the advances made by the automotive and aerospace industries. Sports equipment underwent rapid change: tennis, boating, archery,

1931	1982	1986	1988
Ateliers de la Rive, a French company, begins making tubing. In the post-war years the company evolves and begins developing Vitus tubes, the first of which is the Vitus 171.	Following the success of the Vitus 979, the company launches the Carbone. It is one of the first lugged and bonded composite frames to be used in professional cycling.	Irish cycling legend Sean Kelly wins his second and final Paris–Roubaix on a Vitus frame.	While riding for the Kas-Canal 10 cycling team, Sean Kelly wins the Vuelta a España, becoming the first Irish winner of the race.

skiing, golf, and fishing all benefited from the new composite materials. Cycling was no different, but it seems that some companies were quicker to adapt (and put in the serious research and development costs) than others. Vitus began to struggle and by the late 1990s was barely surviving. However, the downturn did not last, and today the Vitus name is back, helped on its way once again by Kelly: "I think they had been making low-cost, basic bikes in France for a fair few years before Vitus came to me and started talking about doing some higher-end models," he explains. "I did some testing in Majorca, especially on the downhills—the handling has to be spot on. The ride is my major concern. It has to be right."

Reservations have been raised about the appearance of the bikes, however. The cool, understated look of the 1980s has gone and the designers have opted for flashy graphics and a chunky typeface—a style that has met with mixed feedback. Kelly is quick to point out that this is not his department and rightfully so: there is only so much that one man can do, even if he is one of the greatest living cyclists. Thankfully, Vitus has listened to the feedback, and toned-down models that are more in keeping with the brand's heritage—but with a modern twist—will be seen on the roads before long.

Furthermore, the brand ambassador has provided the exact dimensions of his own bike for the Sean Kelly Signature replica, so a 21 ¼-inch (54-cm) bike will be exactly the same as the one ridden by the man himself. The cycling world sincerely hopes that the new model is a success. It is always sad to see a bike brand suffer, but the Vitus name deserves to live on more than most. After all, it always seemed odd to see Sean Kelly on anything other than a Vitus. *IC*

1989	1995	2011	2012
Lotto, the Belgian professional cycling team, signs Vitus as its bike supplier. The bikes are used by Dirk Demol and Hendrik Redant, but the relationship ends after one season.	The relationship with the Lotto team is resurrected and lasts five more seasons, but with mixed results as the team struggles to register major wins.	Chain Reaction Cycles buys the Vitus name and begins producing a new range of bikes.	Vitus launches its Sean Kelly model, a top of the range road bike fitted with Shimano's Dura-Ace.

Wilier Triestina

This century-old Italian firm was established on the banks of the river Brenta and its bikes, affectionately known as "copper-coloured jewels," have been raced by many of the country's greats, from the 1930s to the modern era.

The name "Wilier" is often thought to be German in origin, but Wilier is in fact an Italian brand steeped in tradition, and even its name, while sounding Germanic, derives from an acronym. This distinguishes Wilier from many of its manufacturing rivals, especially in Italy, where a bicycle company's identity is usually synonymous with the founding frame-builder The company name originates from the phrase "l'Italia liberata e redenta," and the "W" at the beginning is an abbreviation of "Viva." Wilier, therefore, means "Long live Italy, liberated and redeemed."

However, the company was originally known as Ciclomeccanica Dal Molin and was founded in 1906 by Pietro Dal Molin, a businessman and cycling enthusiast from northern Italy. It was

located in Bassano del Grappa, a town previously known as Bassano Veneto that was renamed in 1928 as a mark of respect to the thousands of soldiers who lost their lives on the slopes of the nearby Monte Grappa during World War I.

After the war, one of Pietro's sons, Mario, took over Wilier and, thanks to his creative use of plating techniques, produced the distinctive copper finish that became a trademark aesthetic of Wilier bicycles. Mario decided to compete in the 1946 Giro d'Italia and put together a professional cycling team. His star rider was Giordano Cottur, who hailed from Trieste and was strong enough to give two of Italy's cycling greats—Fausto Coppi and Gino Bartali—a run for their money. Cottur, who passed away in 2006 at

■ Giordano Cottur
(centre, standing) in
1946 as part of the
Wilier Triestina team.

■ During his time with
Wilier (1945–49),
Cottur (centre) won
four stages in the Giro
d'Italia.

the age of ninety-one, racked up several victories during a career that spanned the years 1938 to 1950. He finished on the podium of the Giro on three occasions: 1940, 1948, and 1949—in third place each time.

It is the Cottur connection that partially explains the second part of the company name. Back in 1946, Cottur's home town of Trieste was owned neither by Italy nor the recently formed Yugoslavia. It stood as an independent town, but Mario felt so strongly that Trieste belonged to Italy that he added Triestina to the team's name and went into the Giro d'Italia making both a marketing and political statement. That year Trieste hosted a stage finish and in difficult conditions Cottur broke away to win alone. To commemorate this victory the name Wilier Triestina was retained.

Despite the efforts of Mario, the strong economic growth during the post-war years saw a nation turn its back on the bicycle as scooters and motorbikes became affordable and objects

of desire. Pietro's company was not able to cope with the dramatic downturn in business and the doors to his factory closed in 1952.

Seventeen years later, the company was bought by Giovanni Gastaldello and his two sons. The Gastaldellos took what they could use from the original factory and then set up shop a few kilometres away in their home town of Rossano Veneto, roughly halfway between Verona and Venice. They reintroduced the trademark copper-finished bikes and set about growing the company into the small but tightly knit and passionate outfit that is still run by the Gastaldello family today.

Wilier Triestina remains active in the professional peloton and has embraced modern methods and materials to build bikes that rival those of its bigger competitors. In fact, most Italian stars of the modern era— Alessandro Petacchi, Damiano Cunego, Davide Rebellin, Stefano Garzelli, and Marco Pantani, and others— have ridden to victory, at some stage of their career, on a Wilier. **RD**

■ Marco Pantani riding a Wilier Triestina on Alpe d'Huez during the 1997 Tour de France.

■ The Wilier Twinfoil is designed to reduce air turbulence and rider resistance.

Appendices

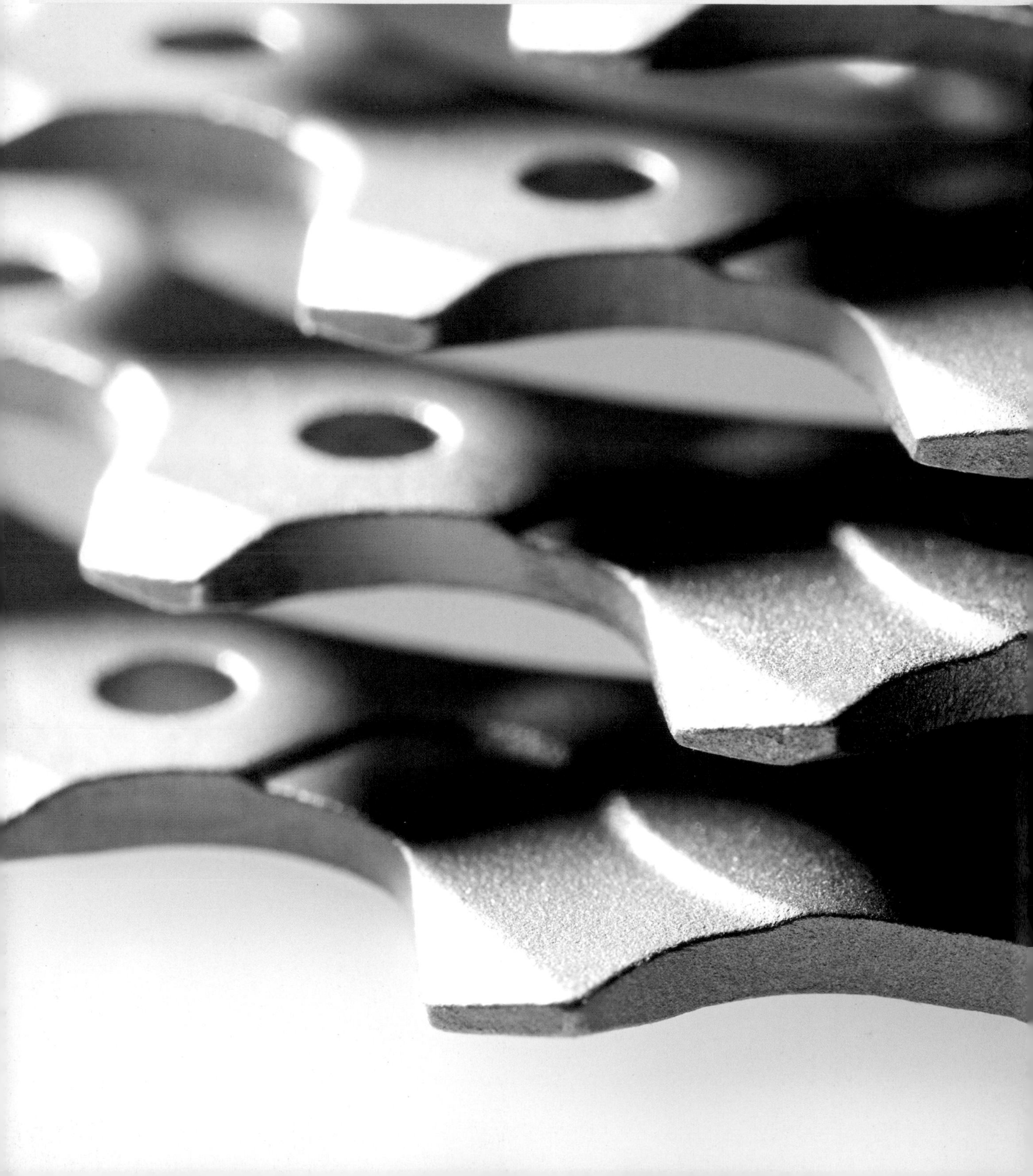

Tour de France winners

YEAR		WINNER	TEAM	FRAME	COMPONENTS
1903	▮▮	Maurice Garin	La Française	La Française	Not applicable
1904	▮▮	Henri Cornet	Cycles JC	Cycles JC	
1905	▮▮	Louis Trousselier	Peugeot	Peugeot	
1906	▮▮	René Pottier	Peugeot	Peugeot	
1907	▮▮	Lucien Petit-Breton	Peugeot	Peugeot	
1908	▮▮	Lucien Petit-Breton	Peugeot	Peugeot	
1909	▬	François Faber	Alcyon	Alcyon	
1910	▮▮	Octave Lapize	Alcyon	Alcyon	
1911	▮▮	Gustave Garrigou	Alcyon	Alcyon	
1912	▮▮	Odile Defraye	Alcyon	Alcyon	
1913	▮▮	Philippe Thys	Peugeot	Peugeot	
1914	▮▮	Philippe Thys	Peugeot	Peugeot	
1919	▮▮	Firmin Lambot	La Sportive	Not known	
1920	▮▮	Philippe Thys	La Sportive	Not known	
1921	▮▮	Léon Scieur	La Sportive	Not known	
1922	▮▮	Firmin Lambot	Peugeot	Peugeot	
1923	▮▮	Henri Pélissier	Automoto	Automoto	
1924	▮▮	Ottavio Bottecchia	Automoto	Automoto	
1925	▮▮	Ottavio Bottecchia	Automoto	Automoto	
1926	▮▮	Lucien Buysse	Automoto	Automoto	
1927	▬	Nicolas Frantz	Alcyon	Alcyon	
1928	▬	Nicolas Frantz	Alcyon	Alcyon	
1929	▮▮	Maurice De Waele	Alcyon	Alcyon	
1930	▮▮	André Leducq	France	Not applicable*	
1931	▮▮	Antonin Magne	France		
1932	▮▮	André Leducq	France		
1933	▮▮	Georges Speicher	France		
1934	▮▮	Antonin Magne	France		
1935	▮▮	Romain Maes	Belgium		
1936	▮▮	Sylvère Maes	Belgium		
1937	▮▮	Roger Lapébie	France		Super Champion
1938	▮▮	Gino Bartali	Italy		Vittoria Marghetta
1939	▮▮	Sylvère Maes	Belgium		Super Champion

*From 1930 to 1939 the Tour supplied all riders with standard bicycles.

YEAR	WINNER	TEAM	FRAME	COMPONENTS
1947	Jean Robic	Ouest	Lucifer	Simplex
1948	Gino Bartali	Italy	Legnano	Campagnolo
1949	Fausto Coppi	Italy	Bianchi	Simplex
1950	Ferdinand Kübler	Switzerland	Fréjus	Simplex
1951	Hugo Koblet	Switzerland	La Perle	Campagnolo
1952	Fausto Coppi	Italy	Bianchi	Huret
1953	Louison Bobet	France	Stella	Huret
1954	Louison Bobet	France	Stella	Huret
1955	Louison Bobet	France	Bobet	Campagnolo
1956	Roger Walkowiak	Nord-Est-Centre	Geminiani	Simplex
1957	Jacques Anquetil	France	Helyett	Simplex
1958	Charly Gaul	Holland-Luxembourg	Learco Guerra	Campagnolo
1959	Federico Bahamontes	Spain	Coppi	Campagnolo
1960	Gastone Nencini	Italy	Unbranded	Campagnolo
1961	Jacques Anquetil	France	Helyett	Simplex
1962	Jacques Anquetil	St-Raphael	Helyett	Simplex
1963	Jacques Anquetil	St-Raphael	Gitane	Campagnolo
1964	Jacques Anquetil	St-Raphael	Gitane	Campagnolo
1965	Felice Gimondi	Salvarini	Magni	Campagnolo
1966	Lucien Aimar	Ford	Geminiani	Campagnolo
1967	Roger Pingeon	France	Peugeot	Simplex
1968	Jan Janssen	Holland	Lejeune	Campagnolo
1969	Eddy Merckx	Faema	Merckx	Campagnolo
1970	Eddy Merckx	Faemino	Merckx	Campagnolo
1971	Eddy Merckx	Molteni	Merckx*	Campagnolo
1972	Eddy Merckx	Molteni	Merckx*	Campagnolo
1973	Luis Ocaña	Bic	Motobecane	Campagnolo
1974	Eddy Merckx	Molteni	Merckx/De Rosa	Campagnolo
1975	Bernard Thévenet	Peugeot	Peugeot	Simplex
1976	Lucien Van Impe	Gitane	Gitane	Campagnolo
1977	Bernard Thévenet	Peugeot	Peugeot	Simplex
1978	Bernard Hinault	Renualt	Gitane	Campagnolo
1979	Bernard Hinault	Renault	Gitane	Campagnolo

*In 1971 and 1972 a Colnago frame was possibly also used.

Tour de France winners

YEAR	WINNER	TEAM	FRAME	COMPONENTS
1980	Joop Zoetemelk	TI-Raleigh	Raleigh	Campagnolo
1981	Bernard Hinault	Renault	Gitane	Campagnolo
1982	Bernard Hinault	Renault	Gitane	Campagnolo
1983	Laurent Fignon	Renault	Gitane	Simplex
1984	Laurent Fignon	Renault	Gitane	Campagnolo
1985	Bernard Hinault	La Vie Claire	Hinault	Campagnolo
1986	Greg LeMond	La Vie Claire	Look	Campagnolo
1987	Stephen Roche	Carrera	Battaglin	Campagnolo
1988	Pedro Delgado	Reynolds	Concorde	Campagnolo
1989	Greg LeMond	ADR	Bottecchia	Mavic
1990	Greg LeMond	Z	LeMond/TVT	Campagnolo
1991	Miguel Indurain	Banesto	Pinarello	Campagnolo
1992	Miguel Indurain	Banesto	Pinarello	Campagnolo
1993	Miguel Indurain	Banesto	Pinarello	Campagnolo
1994	Miguel Indurain	Banesto	Pinarello	Campagnolo
1995	Miguel Indurain	Banesto	Pinarello	Campagnolo
1996	Bjarne Riis	Deutsche Telekom	Pinarello	Campagnolo
1997	Jan Ullrich	Telekom	Pinarello	Campagnolo
1998	Marco Pantani	Mercatone Uno	Bianchi	Campagnolo
1999	Lance Armstrong	US Postal	Trek	Shimano
2000	Lance Armstrong	US Postal	Trek	Shimano
2001	Lance Armstrong	US Postal	Trek	Shimano
2002	Lance Armstrong	US Postal	Trek	Shimano
2003	Lance Armstrong	US Postal	Trek	Shimano
2004	Lance Armstrong	US Postal	Trek	Shimano
2005	Lance Armstrong	Discovery Channel	Trek	Shimano
2006	Óscar Pereiro	Caisse d'Epargne	Pinarello	Campagnolo
2007	Alberto Contador	Discovery Channel	Trek	Shimano
2008	Carlos Sastre	Team CSC-Saxo Bank	Cervélo	Shimano
2009	Alberto Contador	Astana	Trek	SRAM
2010	Andy Schleck	Team Saxo Bank	Specialized	SRAM
2011	Cadel Evans	BMC	BMC	Shimano

WINNING RIDERS

7	🇺🇸	Lance Armstrong	1999, 2000, 2001, 2002, 2003, 2004, 2005
5	🇫🇷	Jacques Anquetil	1957, 1961, 1962, 1963, 1964
	🇧🇪	Eddy Merckx	1969, 1970, 1971, 1972, 1974
	🇫🇷	Bernard Hinault	1978, 1979, 1981, 1982, 1985
	🇪🇸	Miguel Indurain	1991, 1992, 1993, 1994, 1995
3	🇧🇪	Philippe Thys	1913, 1914, 1920
	🇫🇷	Louison Bobet	1953, 1954, 1955
	🇺🇸	Greg LeMond	1986, 1989, 1990
2	🇫🇷	Lucien Petit-Breton	1907, 1908
	🇧🇪	Firmin Lambot	1919, 1922
	🇮🇹	Ottavio Bottecchia	1924, 1925
		Nicolas Frantz	1927, 1928
	🇫🇷	André Leducq	1930, 1932
	🇫🇷	Antonin Magne	1931, 1934
	🇧🇪	Sylvère Maes	1936, 1939
	🇮🇹	Gino Bartali	1938, 1948
	🇮🇹	Fausto Coppi	1949, 1952
	🇫🇷	Bernard Thévenet	1975, 1977
	🇫🇷	Laurent Fignon	1983, 1984
	🇪🇸	Alberto Contador	2007, 2009

COMPONENT WINS

38	🇮🇹	Campagnolo
11	🇫🇷	Simplex
9	🇯🇵	Shimano
3	🇫🇷	Huret
2	🇫🇷	Osgear/Super Champion
2	🇺🇸	SRAM
1	🇮🇹	Vittoria Margherita
1	🇫🇷	Mavic

MANUFACTURER WINS

10	🇫🇷	Peugeot	1905, 1906, 1907, 1908, 1913, 1914, 1922, 1967, 1975, 1977
9	🇫🇷	Gitane	1963, 1964, 1976, 1978, 1979, 1981, 1982, 1983, 1984
	🇺🇸	Trek	1999, 2000, 2001, 2002, 2003, 2004, 2005, 2007, 2009
8	🇮🇹	Pinarello	1991, 1992, 1993, 1994, 1995, 1996, 1997, 2006
7	🇫🇷	Alcyon	1909, 1910, 1911, 1912, 1927, 1928, 1929
4	🇫🇷	Automoto	1923, 1924, 1925, 1926
	🇧🇪	Merckx	1969, 1970, 1971, 1972
3	🇮🇹	Bianchi	1949, 1952, 1998
	🇫🇷	Helyett	1957, 1961, 1962
2	🇮🇹	Legnano	1938, 1948
	🇫🇷	Stella	1953, 1954
	🇫🇷	Geminiani	1956, 1966

WINS BY COUNTRY

36	🇫🇷	France
18	🇧🇪	Belgium
12	🇪🇸	Spain
10	🇺🇸	United States
9	🇮🇹	Italy
4		Luxembourg
2	🇨🇭	Switzerland
2		Netherlands
1	🇮🇪	Ireland
1	🇩🇰	Denmark
1		Germany
1	🇦🇺	Australia

Manufacturer details and useful links

ATALA
Via della Guerrina 108
20052 Monza (MB)
Numero REA MB-1857109
Italy
www.atala.it

BATAVUS
Industrieweg 4 8444 AR Heerenveen
The Netherlands
www.batavus.nl

BH
1829 West Drake Drive
Suite 104
Tempe, AZ 85283
USA
www.bhbikes-us.com

BIANCHI
Via delle Battaglie, 5
24047 Treviglio (BG)
Italy
www.bianchi.com

BILLATO
Viale Austria 6 Z.A. Roncajette
I-35020 Ponte San Nicolò (PD)
Italy
www.billato.com

BOTTECCHIA
Viale Enzo, Ferrari 15/17
30014
Cavarzere VE
Italy
www.bottecchia.com

CAMPAGNOLO
Via della Chimica 4
36100 Vicenza VI
Italy
www.campagnolo.com

CANNONDALE
172 Friendship Road
Bedford, PA 15522
USA
www.cannondale.com

CANYON
Karl-Tesche-Straße 12
56073 Koblenz
Germany
www.canyon.com

CERVÉLO
171 East Liberty Street
Toronto
Canada
www.cervelo.com

CINELLI
Via G. Di Vittorio, 21
20090 Caleppio di Settala (MI)
Italy
www.cinelli.it

COLNAGO
Viale Brianza, 9
20040 Cambiago (Mi)
Italy
www.colnago.com

COLUMBUS
Via G.Di Vittorio 21
20090 Caleppio di Settala
Italy
www.columbustubi.com

CONCORDE
Via Guglielmo Marconi, 56
Curno
Bergamo
Italy
www.ciocc.it

DACCORDI
Via Ilaria Alpi, 26/28
56028 San Miniato Basso
Italy
www.daccordicicli.com

DE ROSA
Via Bellini, 24
20095 Cusano Milanino
Milan
Italy
www.derosanews.com

EDDY MERCKX
Frans Schachtstraat 29
B-1731 Zellik
Belgium
www.eddymerckx.be

FLANDRIA
Unit 33a, Progress Business Park
Kirkham, PR4 2TZ
United Kingdom
www.flandriabikes.com

FOCUS
Siemensstraße 1–3
D - 49661 Cloppenburg
Germany
www.focus-bikes.com

GAZELLE
Koninklijke Gazelle N.V.
Wilhelminaweg 8
6951 BP Dieren
The Netherlands
www.gazelle.nl

GIANT
3587 Old Conejo Road
Newbury Park, CA 91320
USA
www.giant-bicycles.com

GIOS
Fasco International LTD.
Unit 03-05, 25/F,
Trendy Centre
682-684 Castle Peak Road
Lai Chi Kok, Kowloon, Hong Kong
www.gios.it

GITANE
161, rue Gabriel Péri - B.P 108 - 10104
Romilly-sur-Seine Cedex
France
www.gitane.com

GUERCIOTTI
Srl Via Petrocchi, 10 - 20127 Milan
Italy
www.guerciotti.it

LeMOND
15540 Woodinville-Redmond Rd NE
Bldg A-800
Woodinville, WA 98072
USA
www.lemondfitness.com

LITESPEED
PO Box 22666
Chattanooga, TN 37422
USA
www.litespeed.com

LOOK
27, rue du Dr Léveillé BP13
58028 NEVERS Cedex
France
www.lookcycle.com

MASI
1230 Avenida Chelsea
Vista, CA 92081
USA
www.masibikes.com

MAVIC
Les Croiselets
74370
Metz-Tessy
France
www.mavic.com

MERCIAN
7 Shardlow Road, Alvaston, Derby
Derbyshire DE24 0JG
United Kingdom
www.merciancycles.co.uk

MERCIER
Postbus 435, 8440 AK
Industrieweg 4, 8444 AR
Heerenveen, The Nederlands
www.cyclesmercier.com

OLMO
Via Poggi, 22
17015 Celle Ligure (SV)
Italy
www.olmo.it

ORBEA
Polígono Industrial Goitondo s/n
48269, Mallabia (Bizkaia)
Spain
www.orbea.com

PEGORETTI
Via dei Golden, 3
38052 Caldonazzo (TN)
Italy
www.pegoretticicli.com

SPECIALIZED
15130 Concord Circle
Morgan Hill, CA 95037
USA
www.specialized.com

SRAM
1333 N. Kingsbury,
4th Floor
Chicago, IL 60622
USA
www.sram.com

TIME
2 rue Blaise Pascal
38090 Vaulx Milieu
France
www.time-sport.com

TREK
801 W Madison Street
Waterloo, WI 53594
USA
www.trekbikes.com

VITUS
St. Etienne
France
www.vitusbikes.com

WILIER TRIESTINA
Wilier Triestina S.p.A.
Via Fratel Venzo 11
36028 Rossano Veneto (VI)
Italy
www.wilier.it

USEFUL LINKS

INTERNATIONAL CYCLING UNION
www.uci.ch

TOUR DE FRANCE
www.letour.fr

GIRO D'ITALIA
www.gazzetta.it

VUELTA A ESPAÑA
www.lavuelta.com

NATIONAL CYCLISTS' ORGANISATION
www.ctc.org.uk

USA CYCLING
www.usacycling.org

AMERICAN CYCLING INC.
www.americancycling.com

LEAGUE OF AMERICAN BICYCLISTS
www.bikeleague.org

CYCLING AUSTRALIA
www.cycling.org.au

AUSTRALIAN CYCLING CONFERENCE
www.australiancyclingconference.org

JOURNALS

www.cyclingnews.com
www.rouleur.cc
www.cycling.magazine.co.uk
www.australiancyclist.com.au
bicyclingaustralia.com.au
www.ridemedia.com.au
www.bicycling.com
www.cyclesportmag.com
americancyclemag.com
www.bikemag.com
velonews.competitor.com

Glossary

ABANDON
Term for a rider who quits a race before the finish.

AERO
Abbreviated version of aerodynamic, which is used to describe efficiency against wind resistance.

ATTACK
A jump, quick acceleration, to ride away from a group of riders.

BIDON
Drinking bottle.

BOTTLE CAGE
Holds a water bottle to a bicycle frame.

BOTTOM BRACKET
Holds the cranks inside the frame (bottom bracket shell) with a system of cups and ball bearings.

BREAKAWAY
Attack that distances one or more riders from the chase pack or peloton.

BUNCH SPRINT
The mass dash for the line at the end of a race when the whole peloton is still together.

CADENCE
The speed of the cranks as they revolve.

CASQUETTE
French for "cap." Traditionally made from cotton and designed to keep the sun's rays at bay.

CASSETTE
The rear cog cluster.

CHAIN
Set of links that connect the cogs on the rear wheel with the front chainring.

CHAINRING
These help to provide the motion to power the chain, which transfers power to the rear wheel. They have teeth on the outside, where the chain sits.

CHAMPS-ELYSÉES
Parisian street on which the Tour de France finishes.

CLASSIC
The major one-day races, including Milan-San Remo, Tour of Flanders, Paris–Roubaix, Liège–Bastogne–Liège, and Tour of Lombardy.

CLEAT
Metal or plastic base on a shoe. The cleat attaches the shoe to a pedal on a bicycle.

CLIMBER
A rider who specializes in racing uphill.

CRANK
The two cranks, one on each side, connect the pedals to the bottom bracket. They can vary in length, with build materials including aluminium alloy, titanium, carbon fibre, and chromoly steel.

CRANKSET/CHAINSET
The system comprising cranks and chainrings.

CRITERIUM
A multiple-lap race held on closed roads.

DECALS
Abbreviation of decalcomania, the adhesive transfers that are applied to bicycles to give them their unique style of branding and personalization.

DERAILLEUR
The gear-changing mechanism; the rear derailleur shifts the chain between sprockets on the rear wheel; the front derailleur shifts the chain between the chainrings on the chainset.

DIRECTEUR SPORTIF
Loosely translated as "team manager."

DOMESTIQUE
A rider who works solely to support his or her team leader in a race.

DOPING
The use of performance enhancing drugs or blood doping.

DOUBLE BUTTED
Higher thickness bicycle tubing.

DRAFT
Efficient way of riders saving energy as they sit in the slipstream of the rider in front, therefore reducing their own wind resistance.

DURA-ACE
Shimano's flagship groupset.

ECHELON
French term for a group or line of riders aiming to gain the maximum amount of wind shelter. Echelons are typically formed in cross winds.

EPO
Erythropoietin: a blood booster that improves athletic performance.

ERGOPOWER
Campagnolo's integrated braking and gearing system.

ESPOIR
French term for a rider aged between nineteen and twenty-two years of age.

FLAME ROUGE
A red flag shown above the road with 0.62 miles (1 km) to go in a race.

FORKS
Hold the front wheel in place.

GENERAL CLASSIFICATION
The overall standings in a stage race.

GIRO D'ITALIA
Tour of Italy, an annual road cycling race.

GRUPPETTO/AUTOBUS
A group of struggling riders, typically non-climbing specialists, whose sole intention is to ride together and survive difficult mountain stages.

GROUPSET/GRUPPO
Full set of bike components.

HEADSET
The bearing system at the front end that connects forks to head tube and handlebar stem.

HORS CATEGORIE
French for "beyond category," relating to the most difficult of climbs.

KING OF THE MOUNTAINS
A title and jersey given to the best climber.

LANTERNE ROUGE
French term for the last rider in the race.

LEAD OUT
Technique used to deliver sprinters to the finish line of a race in the perfect position from which to open their final sprint.

MAGLIA ROSA
Pink jersey of the Giro leader.

MAILLOT JAUNE
Yellow jersey of the Tour de France leader.

NEO-PRO
A first year professional rider.

PALMARÈS
French term meaning list of achievements. Relates to the races a rider has won in their career.

PAVÉ
Stoned roads.

PELOTON
French term for the main group in a road race.

PROLOGUE
Short individual time trial held at the start of a stage race.

RAINBOW JERSEY
White jersey with rainbow bands awarded to the world champion.

RIM
Outer section of the wheel, on which the tyre is fitted.

ROULEUR
A rider who is typically suited to flat or rolling terrain.

SEAT STAYS AND CHAIN STAYS
Two pairs of thin tubes at the back end of the bike, which hold the rear wheel in place.

SEAT TUBE
Runs from saddle to bottom bracket shell.

SIX-DAY RACING
Mainly winter sport held in mainland Europe, with riders competing in daily sessions on a velodrome.

SOIGNEUR
Non-riding assistant to a professional rider. Offers post-race massage, transportation, and food.

STEM
Component that attaches the handlebars to the frame (headset).

STI
Shimano Total Integration, integrated braking and gearing system.

SUPER RECORD
Campagnolo's flagship groupset.

TEAM PURSUIT
Four-man (or three-women) teams race to catch each other on a velodrome or track.

TEAM TIME TRIAL
Riders race as teams over a set distance with the winning time set by the first team to complete a set course.

TEMPO
"Riding tempo" means setting the pace for the peloton or for another rider, usually at a high but not excessive level.

TIFOSI
A word used to describe Italian cycling fans.

TIME LIMIT
Riders in each day's stage must finish with a certain percentage of the winner's time or they are eliminated from the race.

TOP TUBE
The top tube connects the top of the head tube to the top of the seat tube.

TRI-BARS
Aerodynamic handlebar extensions first used by triathletes and popularized by Greg LeMond in the 1989 Tour de France.

TRIPLE CROWN
Term for a rider who wins the Giro d'Italia, Tour de France, and Worlds in a single season.

UCI
Acronym for Union Cycliste Internationale, the sport's governing body, based in Switzerland.

VELODROME
A cycling track for racing.

VUELTA A ESPAÑA
Tour of Spain, an annual, three-week road cycling race.

WORLDS
Term for the UCI's world championships. Each cycling discipline has its own championships on a yearly basis.

WORLDTOUR
The UCI's premier list of races and status for the elite eighteen teams in professional cycling.

Index

Index

Contributor biographies

ELLIS BACON has spent a decade covering professional cycling as a journalist. Formerly the deputy editor of *Procycling* magazine, he now freewheels as a freelancer and recently has translated Saxo Bank team manager Bjarne Riis's autobiography from Danish into English, while also remaining a regular contributor to *Cycle Sport* magazine. He lives in south-west London and wishes he had more time to go riding in Richmond Park.

DANIEL BENSON is the managing editor of Cyclingnews.com, the world's leading cycling news-based website. He has reported on four Tours de France and the Spring Classics. Born in Ireland, he now lives in Oxfordshire.

IAN CLEVERLY has been racing bikes intermittently for thirty-five years, tackling practically every discipline of the sport with spectacularly average results every time. A mid-life career crisis saw him retrain as a journalist and, after a year at *Cycling Weekly*, he joined *Rouleur* magazine and is now the managing editor.

SARAH CONNOLLY came into her obsessive love of cycling through watching track in 2007 and has not been able to escape yet. She blogs, mainly about women's cycling, on www.podiumcafe.com, and has been a contributor to Cyclingnews.com.

PETER COSSINS has been writing about all aspects of cycling for the past twenty years, during which time he has been the editor of *Procycling* and *The Official Guide to the Tour de France*. He has recently collaborated with Tour de France winner Stephen Roche for a book about his life and career, due for publication in May 2012.

SAM DANSIE writes for *Procycling* magazine in the United Kingdom. After training as a news reporter and starting out on a busy regional daily newspaper, he spent three years living in South Africa where he began writing for cycling magazines. Upon returning to the United Kingdom, he took up the post at *Procycling*.

ROHAN DUBASH has worked in the cycle industry for more than thirty years and in that time has earned himself a reputation as an obsessive Italophile. He currently runs his own specialist bicycle servicing business (www.doctord.co.uk) and is also a regular contributor to *Rouleur* magazine.

RICHARD HALLETT is a cycling enthusiast of the old school and has written for titles including *Winning*, *Procycling*, and *Cycling Plus*. Formerly technical editor of *Cycling Weekly* and *Cycle Sport*, Richard was more recently editor of online cycling magazine roadcyclinguk. com. He is now editor of cycletechreview.com.

PETER HYMAS is an editor for Cyclingnews.com, who calls North Carolina home. He has turned wheels in anger for more than thirty years on the road and prior to that sought out big air on BMX bikes.

FEARGAL McKAY is is a Dublin-based freelance writer and cycling fan.

RICHARD MOORE is a journalist and author. His first book, *In Search of Robert Millar*, won Best Biography at the 2008 British Sports Book Awards. His second book, *Heroes, Villains & Velodromes*, was long-listed for the 2008 William Hill Sports Book of the Year. He is also a former racing cyclist who represented Scotland at the 1998 Commonwealth Games and Great Britain at the 1998 Tour de Langkawi. He is also the author of *Slaying the Badger: LeMond, Hinault and the Greatest Tour de France*, and *Sky's the Limit*.

JOHN STEVENSON followed the classic cycling path from young mountain biker to forty-something roadie, with a career that includes *Mountain Biking UK* magazine, *Australian Mountain Bike*, Cyclingnews. com, and BikeRadar.com. John was most recently editor-in-chief of cycling at Future Publishing; he is now a freelance writer and editor, and loves getting out on his bike in the lanes around Bath.

SAM TREMAYNE was a relatively late convert to cycling, having preferred the motorized version of events throughout childhood. Lance Armstrong put cycling into the mainstream and aroused his curiosity, however, and Sam has slowly become more and more hooked on what is one of the most brutal, punishing, and glorious of sporting endeavours.

Picture credits

9 Getty Images 10 Miroir Archives / PhotoSport Int 11 Bianchi 12 Trek 14 Pegoretti 16 © The Art Archive / Alamy 19 Miroir Archives / PhotoSport Int 20 BH 21 BH 22 BH 23 Getty Images 24 BH 25 BH 26 Bianchi 26 Bianchi 27 Bianchi 28 Bianchi 28 Bianchi 29 Bianchi 29 Bianchi 30 AP/Press Association Images 31 Miroir Archives / PhotoSport Int 32 Archivio Campagnolo 33 Bianchi 34 © Ray Dobbins 35 Getty Images 36 Bianchi 37 Bianchi 38-39 Bianchi 40 Billato 41 Billato. Photography by Pete Goding, The Frame Builder's Guide 42 Bottecchia 43 Bottecchia 44 Getty Images 45 © Ray Dobbins 46 © Willy Miticagraziella 47 Getty Images 48 Bottecchia 49 Miroir Archives / PhotoSport Int 50 Bottecchia 51 Bottecchia 52 Campagnolo 53 Campagnolo 54 © Paulo Rubin 56 Campagnolo 56 Campagnolo 57 © Ray Dobbins 58 Campagnolo 60 (top) Campagnolo 60 (bottom left) Campagnolo 60 (bottom right) © Paulo Rubin 61 (bottom left) © Bicycle Club Magazine, Tokyo 61 (bottom middle) Campagnolo 61 (bottom right) Campagnolo 62 (far left) © Hulton-Deutsch Collection / Corbis 62 (middle left) © Universal / TempSport / Corbis 62 (middle right) Campagnolo 62 (far right) Campagnolo 63 Campagnolo 64 Campagnolo 65 Campagnolo 66 Campagnolo 67 Campagnolo 68 Cannondale 69 Cannondale 70 Getty Images 71 Cannondale 72-73 AFP / Getty Images 74-75 Cannondale 76 Canyon Bicycles GmbH 77 Canyon Bicycles GmbH 78-79 Canyon Bicycles GmbH 80 Cervélo 81 (top) © Richard Wareham Fotografie (Nieuws) / Alamy 81 (bottom) © Richard Wareham Fotografie (Nieuws) / Alamy 82 Cervélo 83 AFP / Getty Images 84 © NICOLAS BOUVY / epa / Corbis 85 Getty Images 86-87 Cervélo 88 Cinelli Archive 89 Cinelli Archive 90 (top) Cinelli Archive 90 (bottom) Cinelli Archive 91 © Ray Dobbins 92 Cinelli Archive 93 © Tim De Waele/Corbis 94-95 Cinelli Laser by Keith Haring. Courtesy Cinelli Archive. 97 Getty Images 99 Popperfoto / Getty Images 100 Colnago 101 Colnago 102 Colnago 103 Colnago 104 (far left) AFP / Getty Images 104 (middle left) Sirotti 104 (middle right) Miroir Archives / PhotoSport Int 104 (far right) Sirotti 105 © Ray Dobbins 106 Colnago 107 © Jerome Prevost / TempSport / Corbis 108-109 Colnago 110 Columbus 111 Columbus 112 Columbus 113 Columbus 114 Miroir Archives / PhotoSport Int 115 Columbus 117 Miroir Archives / PhotoSport Int 118 Daccordi 118 Daccordi 119 © Ray Dobbins 120 De Rosa 121 De Rosa 122 © Universal / TempSport / Corbis 123 De Rosa 125 Getty Images 126 © Ray Dobbins 127 De Rosa 128-129 De Rosa 130 © Pierre Vauthey / Sygma / Corbis 131 Popperfoto / Getty Images 132 Miroir Archives / PhotoSport Int 134 © Ray Dobbins 135 © Pierre Vauthey / Sygma / Corbis 136-137 Eddy Merckx 138 STEEN HERDEL FILMPRODUKTION / THE KOBAL COLLECTION 139 Flandria 140 Miroir Archives / PhotoSport Int 142 Flandria 143 Flandria 144 AFP / Getty Images 145 Focus 146 Miroir Archives / PhotoSport Int 147 Gazelle 148 Giant 149 AFP / Getty Images 150 Getty Images 151 Giant 152 Giant 153 Getty Images 154-155 Phil O'Connor 157 Gios 158 Gios 159 Miroir Archives / PhotoSport Int 161 Gios 162 www.GitaneUSA.com 163 www.GitaneUSA.com 164 Miroir Archives / PhotoSport Int 166-167 Miroir Archives / PhotoSport Int 168 Guerciotti 169 © Ray Dobbins 170 © Thierry Prat / Sygma / Corbis 171 © Jean-Yves Ruszniewski / TempSport/Corbis 172 LeMond 173 LeMond 174 Miroir Archives / PhotoSport Int 175 LeMond 177 AFP/Getty Images 178 AFP / Getty Images 179 Litespeed 180 Litespeed 181 Litespeed 183 Gamma-Keystone via Getty Images 184 Look 185 Look 186-187 Look 188 © Tim de Waele / Corbis 189 Look 190-191 Look 193 AFP/Getty Images 194 Miroir Archives / PhotoSport Int 195 © Ray Dobbins 196 Mavic 197 Mavic 199 Mavic 200 Mavic 201 Mavic 202 AFP/Getty Images 203 Getty Images 204 Mavic 205 Mavic 206-207 SSPL via Getty Images 209 Mercian 210 Mercian 211 Matt Assenmacher www.assenmachers.com 212 Miroir Archives / PhotoSport Int 213 Miroir Archives / PhotoSport Int 214 Miroir Archives / PhotoSport Int 217 Miroir Archives / PhotoSport Int 218 (top) © Universal / TempSport / Corbis 218 (bottom) Olmo 219 Olmo 220 AFP / Getty Images 221 Orbea 222 Pegoretti 223 Pegoretti 224-225 Pegoretti 226 Peugeot 227 Matt Assenmacher www.assenmachers.com 228 Miroir Archives / PhotoSport Int 229 Miroir Archives / PhotoSport Int 233 © Bettmann / Corbis 234-235 © Franck Seguin / TempSport / Corbis 236 Miroir Archives / PhotoSport Int 238 Miroir Archives / PhotoSport Int 239 Pinarello 240-241 Pinarello 242 (top) Popperfoto / Getty Images 242 (bottom) Raleigh 243 Collection of Andrew Ritchie 244 Raleigh 245 © Hulton-Deutsch Collection/Corbis 246 Sturmey Archer 249 Miroir Archives / PhotoSport Int 250 Miroir Archives / PhotoSport Int 252 Reynolds Technology Ltd. 253 Reynolds Technology Ltd.

254 Reynolds Technology Ltd. 255 Reynolds Technology Ltd. 256 Miroir Archives / PhotoSport Int 258-259 Phil O'Connor 260 First Flight Bicycles 261 © Ray Dobbins 262 Schwinn / Paramount 263 The Bicycle Museum of America 264 Mike Cotty 265 First Flight Bicycles 266 Scott 267 Miroir Archives / PhotoSport Int 268 AFP / Getty Images 269 Scott 270 (top) Getty Images 270 (bottom) AFP / Getty Images 271 Scott 272 Scott 273 Scott 274 Serotta 275 Getty Images 276 SHIMANO INC 277 SHIMANO INC 278 SHIMANO INC 279 SHIMANO INC 280 SHIMANO INC 281 SHIMANO INC 283 SHIMANO INC 284 SHIMANO INC 286 SHIMANO INC 287 SHIMANO INC 288 Specialized 289 Specialized 290 AP / Press Association Images 292-293 Miroir Archives / PhotoSport Int 294 Specialized 295 Specialized 296-297 Specialized 298 SRAM 299 SRAM 300 Miroir Archives / PhotoSport Int 301 Miroir Archives / PhotoSport Int 302 AFP / Getty Images 303 SRAM 304-305 SRAM 307 Time 308 © Tim de Waele /Corbis 309 Time 310 Time 312 Trek 313 Miroir Archives / PhotoSport Int 314 Getty Images Europe 315 Trek 317 Trek 318-319 AFP / Getty Images 320-321 Trek 322 AFP / Getty Images 323 Miroir Archives / PhotoSport Int 324 Vitus 325 Vitus 326 Miroir Archives / PhotoSport Int 327 Vitus 328 Wilier Triestina 329 Wilier Triestina 330 Miroir Archives / PhotoSport Int 331 Wilier Triestina

ACKNOWLEDGEMENTS

Thanks to Ray Dobbins (www.raydobbins.com), Daniel Friebe, John Pierce, Fotoreporter Sirotti (www.sirotti.it), James Huang, and all the manufacturers who were kind enough to supply images and expertise.